What I Saw at the Fair

Ann Birstein

WELCOME RAIN

What I Saw at the Fair
Copyright © 2003 by Ann Birstein
All rights reserved.

Library of Congress CIP data available from the publisher.

Direct any inquiries to
Welcome Rain Publishers LLC

ISBN 1-56649-267-X

Printed in the United States of America by
HAMILTON PRINTING COMPANY

Interior design and composition by
MULBERRY TREE PRESS, INC.
(www.mulberrytreepress.com)

First Edition: February 2003
1 3 5 7 9 10 8 6 4 2

For Bel Kaufman
and her grandfather
Sholom Aleichem

Acknowledgment

THE AUTHOR WISHES TO THANK the Virginia Center for the Creative Arts for invaluable residencies during the writing of this book.

"You head for a fair full of hope.
You have no idea what you will find
and what you will accomplish. . . .
But on the way back you know."

—*From the Fair*,
the autobiography of Sholom Aleichem

Birstein

Introduction

I AM A PRINCESS. I am an adopted child, stolen from gypsies. My father is my real father. My real mother is definitely not the one I have been saddled with and who hates me but loves my sister, Julia.

None of the above is strictly true. Except the part about my father being my father. For one thing, even I realize that I am the only child to be stolen *from* the gypsies, not *by* them—which doesn't sound right. For another everybody's got a mother somewhere, and the one I've got says positively that mothers love all their children the same, evidence to the contrary notwithstanding. Also, I look like her. Everybody always said so, most notably at her funeral.

There is a place, however, that for a long time fed into my fantasies of noble origin—a town in Germany called Birstein, in the province of Hesse, not far from Frankfurt. In fact, my father came from Brest-Litovsk, a city on the Russian-Polish border, as did his immediate forebears. But Birstein, as a name, is so odd that I am now the only Birstein in the Manhattan telephone directory, and anyone with this name anywhere is bound to be a relative. Obviously I'm often told that I must

9

have got the spelling wrong, and at one point contemplated marrying a Bernstein, Boorstin, Burstyn, Brustein, et cetera, just to get the whole thing over with. But there was always that town, spelled exactly like us. I looked it up. It had a saw mill, a river, a Furst, which is equivalent to a Prince, and a castle attached to him. Clearly the place of my family origin, no matter when we were kicked out. (Not to boast, could it have been as early as the Middle Ages?) I kept wondering what would happen if an actual Birstein returned to Birstein, and in my wilder dreams, based on old musical comedies, saw myself arriving in the open back of a train, arms filled with ermine muff and flowers, while beribboned villagers danced around me.

Last year I finally made it, not in an open train but in an ordinary car driven by a bewildered German driver who could not understand why every road sign elicited cries of stupefaction. Birstein 7 kilometers? Birstein 2 kilometers? But *I* am Birstein! (By now, thanks to correspondence back and forth I had also acquired a zip code.) I tried to concentrate on the countryside, wondering if it looked subliminally familiar. It was certainly beautiful, rolling and agricultural, with cattle and little red roofed houses nestling in clusters, narrow winding roads. If there was some ancient family gene that recognized all this, however, I couldn't get through to it. Never mind, my subconscious had failed me before. Anyway, it was raining, which probably misted over everything, including memory. I had been told that it always rained in Germany this time of year, in late autumn. The important thing, the amazing thing was that we were actually on our way to the Birstein castle. I had written to the Furst, explaining the strange nature of my visit, the peculiarity of my name, et cetera, though omitting any suspicions that his schloss might actually belong to me. In return I had received a surprising invitation from his wife to a reception in the castle that morning, November eighth. What reception meant in this connection I had no idea, probably just coffee and cake, but even that was far more than I had expected. We had arrived in Birstein itself now, a little wet town that I would investigate later, and drove up a not very steep hill, across a cobblestoned courtyard to the heavy castle door. The driver opened it for me, took one look inside, and beat it.

In fact, what awaited me *was* a reception, one astonishingly close to my fantasies. The castle foyer was crowded with smiling faced, expectant functionaries, reporters. A major domo welcomed me formally. I signed a huge ancient guestbook, which was open on a table. Flashbulbs popped. Then I was led upstairs, bags still hanging from each arm, to a formal and lovely salon where stood the Furst and the Furstin and the Furstin Mutter, to whom I was gravely introduced. The three of them were straight out of central casting. The Furstin was a tall slim woman with grayish brown hair, pale green eyes, probably in her early fifties. I was grudgingly grateful that my sister had talked (harangued) me into a new suit, nothing I would usually wear, a tweed Chanel ripoff, but clearly expensive. Like me the Furstin was also wearing a suit, slate blue wool with a bit of a silk scarf at the neck, no designer copy, but we were kind of in the same league. Unlike me, however, the Furstin had perfect posture as well as perfect manners. She was also impeccably cordial, if a bit chilly. The Furst, too, looked exactly as he should. Tall, burly, rosy complexioned, wearing a tweed jacket. Best of all was the Furstin Mutter. A bit stout, her gray hair marcelled just so, with a triple strand of pearls at her neck, large pearls at her ears, she was graciousness and charm personified. A White Russian, from St. Petersburg, maiden name Irina Tolstoya, yes, from *that* family.

The functionaries and reporters had crowded in. Champagne and hors d'oeuvres were circulated. The Lord Mayor began to read a long, heavy German speech of greeting, with consequential verbs weighing down the ends of sentences. The local minister, equally sober faced, translated paragraph by paragraph into English. Did I know German? No, I knew Yiddish. Everybody nodded gravely, no longer smiling, the subject was serious—flashbulbs popped again. The Lord Mayor presented me with gifts. A beautiful framed old aquatint of the schloss and environs of Birstein. I held it up appreciatively, wrong side presented to the world, and to the photographers. "Turn it around," the Furstin said. More gifts, beautiful books, a map of Birstein, even the postal zip codes with Birstein underlined. Each accompanied by more speeches, more nods, smiles now, more flashbulbs popping. I gave a short formal response of my own, babbling about having come full circle, and had to be reminded to stop so *I* too could be translated. What impressed me and everybody else most was that I was the only Birstein in Birstein. In fact, according to the castle archives, there had never been a Birstein in Birstein. We went off to lunch at a local restaurant, some of the functionaries, a couple of reporters, and I, the Furstin soon to follow. We left the Furst seated in a wing chair with two dogs at his feet.

After lunch and more photographs came a tour of Birstein and the surrounding area, which, like the functionaries and the nobility, looked exactly as they should. The little village had narrow curving streets, pretty houses crisscrossed with timber. The countryside, as it had been on my way in, was still infinitely rolling, green and beautiful, dotted with red roofs, grazing cattle, but still remote, like the landcape in the aquatint I had just been presented with. We also went to the old Jewish cemetery, which the Furstin had told me was very placid, like a park. Which, if it hadn't started to rain again, it probably was. Anyway, there were no family names on the tombstones that I could recognize, not even first names. Also, since the last grave was dated 1933, they were the lucky ones, a remark I made aloud but that seemed to fall on deaf ears.

The next day, the Furstin showed me around the castle personally, first handing me clippings about my visit, which had been immediately written up in all the local papers and even in the prestigious *Frankfurter Zeitung*. There was a picture of me à deux with the Furstin Mutter, smiling upon each other. The fake Chanel suit looked good. As the little tour proceeded, the Furstin showed me many treasures: old guns—for diversion, she and her husband went on shooting parties—an old sleigh, a suit of armor, mooseheads, paintings of relatives such as Catherine the Great, a display case with the exquisite satin dress and shoes of a young princess who had attended a Congress of Vienna ball thus attired, in an attempt to influence Metternich. We went into grander and grander salons and reception rooms, including one, pale and lovely, where musical evenings were held. The view of the countryside I had driven through was exquisitely presented through the windows. The Princess confessed to me that when she was first married, before the children came, she had felt rather lonely in the castle. It was so large, the rooms went on and on. She explained that she herself had been brought up in a much smaller castle. Ah. Encouraged, by this domestic revelation and also by the fact that we had both put little mops over our shoes to glide across the polished floor of one beautiful salon, I asked how they heated the place—wood, it seemed they owned a lot of local forests—and how much domestic help—only two regulars, one of whom cooked. Outside the castle windows the omnipresent rain was coming down harder, making everything slick and slippery. The winding roads looked forlorn. Suddenly, they did seem subliminally familiar. I wondered what it was like to be a Jew fleeing down them for my life, in the Middle Ages, in the seventeenth century, any time.

Downstairs the Furstin was graciously inditing her good wishes on a folded card with a beautiful picture of the castle, in honor of my visit. I thanked her for that, and for everything, and she said how fortunate they considered themselves that I should be so lovely and charming. She meant it as a compliment, obviously, but now I asked myself if I had merely passed, if they were relieved that I hadn't come with a sewing machine on my back. No, that was paranoid. I had done what I had come to Birstein to do and more that I hadn't dreamed of. I had restored my family name to honor, justified the spelling anyway. I had been feted, received, treated nobly by actual nobility. So why did I keep thinking about the punch line to that old joke, "Yes, but by a *captain* are you a captain?" The driver was waiting for me in the courtyard outside the castle door. Heading toward him, I fell on my face, right there on the cobblestones. My nose was streaming blood. Blood gushed all over me, on my hands, which I had put up to stop it, on my chin, my cheeks, my clothes. Nobody needed to tell me it was November ninth, or what had happened in 1938. Or that by evening, what with my black eyes and encrusted, swollen nose, I looked like a Jew who had been beaten up on Kristallnacht.

Okay, so it's not my my castle. I'm not a German princess, or any kind of a German, and don't want to be. I'm the child of two Russian-Jewish immigrants, and, as it happens, now the mother of another immigrant, which is a story for later. The reality is that I woke up in America and don't know how I got here. In exile from a place I never knew and that my parents hated even the thought of.

Chapter 1

*H*ONEY WAS NOT THE NAME on my birth certificate, though I was called that. Nor did it have anything to do with my long blond hair. (My mother's hair, of course, had once been blonder. Aggravation from me had made her go gray.) My hair wasn't golden anyhow, but kind of silvery, as if it belonged to a little old lady, which was sort of what I looked like at six, dubious expression, dark circles under my eyes and all. But Honey was how the goyim in Hell's Kitchen, where we lived, interpreted my Yiddish name, which was actually Chana, and familiarly Chanie. Goyim had no gift for the guttural. At home I was also often Channele, a diminutive. In school, which I had just started, I became Anna, another person altogether.

This was already a big complication—these days it might even be a prelude to schizophrenia. However, multiple personalities weren't in fashion yet, so nobody gave it a thought. And anyway, all our lives were split in two. We were all different people with different brand names: one for the outside American world, the other for domestic consumption. To start at the top, my father, Rabbi Bernard Birstein, was Beril, but only to relatives and to other rabbis. My big brother, Samuel Joseph, was Yossie at home. Then came my sister

Sarah aka Sookie, and, by a kind of dreary bad luck that plagued her whole life, Malke Leah wound up saddled with Mildred. Somehow my mother remained Clara in any language, and Julia, the child of her heart, remained Julia. I think they had no patience with complex personalities.

We had recently moved from a railroad flat on Forty-seventh Street between Eighth and Ninth Avenues, where my father's synagogue and my dreaded elementary school were located side by side, to Fifty-first Street, also between Eighth and Ninth, which wasn't much of a step up, though this larger apartment had a bathtub in the bathroom instead of in the kitchen and also a telephone. The turmoil inside was pretty much the same. Cooking, crying, laughing, fighting. Food at all times but you had to wait hours after you ate meat to eat dairy. How we all slept would have made a sardine packager proud. Sarah and Julia and I spent the night in a tiny bedroom with two single beds jammed together, the three of us head to toe. Mildred slept on a daybed in the dining room, where all business was conducted when visitors came, whether she was actually asleep or not. Yossie had his own room, tiny though it was, because he was a boy, and Mama and Papa had a small bedroom off the dining room with just enough space for a double bed and a dresser. We must have had closets because we had clothes, Sarah/Sookie especially since Mama said she put her whole salary on her back. But where these closets were I have no idea. In any case, clothes were produced when morning came. And then everybody went off to the outside world. Yossie to study journalism in college as S. Joseph Birstein—he had taken to writing letters to various publications, saying such things as "kudos to *Time*"—very impressive. But then he was the intellectual in our family, as if being the oldest and only boy weren't enough. Mildred went to her day job as an assistant to a dentist near Madison Square Garden, whose chief clientele for obvious reasons was circus performers, cowboys, and prizefighters, then to Hunter College at night. Julia was off to Washington Irving High School to be the same obedient drone she was at home. Sarah, after first depositing a totally unwilling me at PS 17, continued on to her job at the Film Center on Forty-second Street in one of her natty Sookie outfits, maybe a navy blue fitted reefer coat and a hat to match tilted over one eyebrow. She too, like Millie, went to Hunter at night, but in her case it sounded glamorous. Daddy had left before anybody was up to go to shul, conduct services, and direct his other extremely important affairs. Mama stayed home to start another day which, to hear her tell it, began and ended in bitterness and unappreciated toil.

Outside, a totally other world reigned, the strange world of Christians—with dark bars run by retired prizefighters, unkosher restaurants, movie houses, the local Automat, and inevitably PS 17, a huge stone Gothic fortress that smelled of sour milk for the free lunchers, whose parents were on relief. (An almost unmentionable disgrace.) Inside there were long silent lines of silent children waiting for a bell to ring. A heart stopping change from home, where everybody carried on all the time. But this silence was clearly the American way. Silence at desks, hands clasped in front. No speaking unless spoken to. Having to go to the bathroom was an even worse crime, which was another big difference. At home, bodily functions were frequently alluded to, bowel movements a big topic. (When I was very little, my father, a proud Litvak, would discreetly ask me whether I had been a Litvak or a Galitzianer that day.) There were only a few Jewish children in the school on account of it being in Hell's Kitchen. Everybody else was either Irish or Italian, a basically scary situation. But the Italians, though technically Gentiles, were in the same boat as Jews, linguistically speaking, which made them less of a menace. The Irish, it was plain, were the *real* Americans. Not only were they Gentiles, they actually spoke English. At home! It was their native tongue. There couldn't be anything more American than that, especially when they were glibly spewing out their catechism.

Making the situation crystal clear was the fact that PS 17 was a Tammany stronghold, The principal was a Miss Bohan, sister of a judge, and the teachers, all normal school graduates, were also political appointees. Such as Miss Riordan, who hated children, always wore black, had double forearms, and took a grim pleasure in teaching grammar. But they were all named Miss, and they all seemed to hate children, Jewish children especially, though some were ecumenical. There was Miss Bartlett, Miss Yeats, Miss Ward. Sometimes a Mrs. snuck in, which made for a somewhat kindlier atmosphere, but introduced other problems, as with Mrs. O'Connor, who smilingly insisted that we put a period after every title, and that the English assemblage of lawmakers be pronounced Parly-a-ment. She also called me to her desk to explain after I had picked bluestocking from a multiple-choice question as a definition of pedant, that a pedant was something you hung around your neck. Metaphorically this may be true, but I didn't know that until later. It didn't matter that technically she was dead wrong. Teachers were always right, except for Mrs. Sinsheimer in connection with the notorious affair of her bloomers, a matter that I will come to later.

Each school day, trudging home the long four blocks for

lunch, I toyed with the idea of never going back there. But that would have entailed telling my mother I was sick, and then she would clutch her heart, carry on, and call my father at the shul to come home and take my temperature *that* way. My mother couldn't read English, and Yiddish only with difficulty, and she expanded this to numbers as well as letters. It was a much luckier day when I got a quarter for lunch at the local Automat, a vegetable plate because I was kosher, featuring mashed potatoes, peas, and Harvard beets—which I considered terribly Ivy League and still do—eaten at a table that said LADIES ONLY. Everything that wasn't vegetables or dairy was out. Food represented other vast differences between them and us, being kosher only part of it. Social workers were always coming by to give us questionnaires about what we had for breakfast. One of the Jewish kids wrote down "skimbles and bumbles," which translated as skinless and boneless sardines. But I gave myself a lovely American breakfast of cereal, milk, toast, and scrambled eggs. This was my first real fictional creation, since my actual breakfast was a bagel and coffee, and I wouldn't have had it any other way. Yossie said this wasn't right, considering my age—he started saying it when I was six—but Mama said I was stubborn and what could she do?

All the seasons at PS 17 were terrible, in fact, all days there were terrible, but Christmas was right up there in terms of terribleness if you were Jewish. "Jesus" and "Christ" were constantly being said in hallowed tones, which was absurd, since it was perfectly clear to us that he wasn't the Messiah. (The *virgin* birth also gave us all a big laugh. It seemed that goyim would believe anything.) There was fake snow and tinsel, crèches all over the place, and worst of all the singing of Christmas carols in class and in assembly. It wasn't that we weren't allowed to sing them, it was that we weren't allowed to sing *all* of them. When we came to the *C* and *J* words, we three Jewish kids in the class would zipper our mouths shut and give each other meaningful looks. It was the looks more than the not-singing that enraged the Irish teachers and they were always threatening to do something about it, besides making us generally miserable. Actually, after careful consultation with my father, I *was* allowed to sing *Adeste Fideles,* first because it was in Latin, a language my father felt every cultivated person should study, including his own children, and also because, really, Dominum could mean anybody.

Sometimes Christmas coincided with Chanukah, which didn't alleviate matters since Chanukah was such a zero holiday we had to go to school through all of it. The few compensations were that Mama, who was handy, made little wax tea sets out of the melted orange menorah candles, and also a little muslin bag on a string, which I wore on my neck when I went around trying to cadge pennies from my relatives. Easter was also a killer. Often it coincided with Passover, but Passover I liked, the first two and the last two days, anyhow, when I wasn't allowed to go to school. Before that I would go down to the Lower East Side on a shopping expedition with Daddy, and Mama too, of course, into tiny dim stores crammed to the rafters with decaying books and tchochkes and presided over by old guys with beards. Some of the things we brought back were wondrous. Carved olive-wood pen holders with a bead through which, if you squinted you could see the Wailing Wall, miniature torahs with shiny rayon covers that could be slipped off so the paper scrolls could be unrolled, usually once too often, kosher Pesach wine from Palestine, not the Manischewitz stuff—but Tokay, Malaga, Muscatel, straight from the

Rothschild vineyards, matzohs, matzohs and more matzohs, Pesadiche honey cake, tagelach, mandel brot, and candy—little squares of red, yellow, and green marmalade, and, the real wonder of wonders—a marzipan salami! This salami could have fooled anyone.

Mama naturally carried on to the bitter end about the huge preparations and changing all the dishes, right up to the final search for *chometz*, little packets of bread crumbs rolled in newspaper which she herself had planted, when I followed around my father with a candle and a little feather. At the seders, Daddy was a vision in his white robe and white yarmulke, pillows propped behind him, and I not only got to ask the Four Questions, because I was the youngest, translating from Hebrew into Yiddish, but always got a prize for finding the afikomen too, Julia's protests notwithstanding. But when we went back outside to everyday life, all of us from S. J. Birstein on down carrying matzohs and hardboiled eggs in a brown paper bag for lunch, the Gentile world impinged again, with a vengeance. By the end of the week, matzohs were crunching away in my stomach. Easter baskets, Easter eggs, fluffy marshmallow stuff were featured in all the store windows. Even an authentic looking marzipan salami, which didn't taste that great anyhow, couldn't compete with the cheapest chocolate bunny in the five-and-ten. I had always hated macaroons, and matzoh and coffee for breakfast wasn't the same as coffee and a bagel. Worst of all, especially by the last day, was the lure of the caramel apples in the window of the Penny Arcade. Put there by Satan, who was a Catholic anyway. The minute the sun went down on that eighth day, I made Sookie take me over to buy one, and it tasted just as good as it looked, though Mama always warned against hoping or, in fact, even trying, so that you wouldn't be disappointed. The worm in this particular apple was that it brought back PS 17 the next day, and yet another struggle to exist in the Christian world.

Besides the holidays, the other big injustice was that after school, the Jewish kids had to go learn Hebrew. But the Catholics lucked out again, this time with their catechism and their confirmations. I didn't envy them their catechism—none of the questions and answers they were always throwing at each other made sense to me. They could have been in Hebrew, which I could read but not understand, except that this thought was sacrilege. But confirmation, here was the rub! In my circles only the boys were bar mitzvahed, and who cared anyhow, they were all so mean and stupid, and my poor father had to listen to them practice in cracked voices so often he finally made a demonstration Haftorah record at the Penny Arcade on Broadway that sold the caramel apples. But confirmations were different. The Catholic girls got to have mock weddings—there were little brides all over the streets. It didn't seem fair. My father was always marrying people and as a matter of course I used to dress up my dolls in veils and such and marry them too. Therefore I was dying for a little girl's bridal outfit of my own. Of course, I was dying for a nun's outfit too, which I didn't mention to anyone except Julia, who told Mama. But where could be the harm in dressing up as a bride? "Channele, do you know who they think they're marrying? Where are the little grooms?" my father asked. It wasn't the point. I didn't want to get married, ever. It was the outfit I was after.

Meanwhile, back in the child-hating hell of PS 17, the boys took shop and the girls took sewing and cooking. We made our own gym bloomers, cooking aprons, and long "day" dresses of flowered dimity—what you were supposed to wear for tea, I think, which in my house was drunk out of a glass, sugar cube held between the teeth. The Italian girls cheated by making their inside seams on a sewing machine at home and hand sewing the outer one. The Italians all had sewing machines at home. But the Irish sewing teacher, on the watch for anybody trying to make life easier, poked around and made them rip it all out. Cooking and Home Economics we studied with a Mrs. Sinsheimer. That the Jewish kids didn't have to eat what they made because it wasn't kosher and the Gentile kids hated us because they did—sometimes our slop too—went without saying. But there was no Halachic law that got us Jewish girls out of the how to do laundry part.

Which finally touches on the notorious affair of Mrs. Sinsheimer's bloomers. I have left this for last because, however obliquely, it introduces my father's real position and power on the street and in the neighborhood. He might have been the rabbi of a very tiny synagogue next door to the huge fortress of PS 17, but he was a force just as great as it. The English name of the synagogue, along with Congregation Ezrath Israel, and also The West Side Hebrew Relief Association, was the "Actors Temple," which my father had appended to the stationery when he first came in 1925 and realized that the shul was just a block away from Broadway. Thanks to his efforts, big "famous celebrities" as we called them, now appeared among us regularly for services. Show biz types like Eddie Cantor, Milton Berle, Henny Youngman, Oscar Levant, sports figures like Hank Danning, the catcher for the New York Giants, Barney Ross, middleweight champion, and two of the Three Stooges, who were Jewish. Almost every week would find one of them in the shul to say Kaddish, though their big joint appearance was on the High Holy Days, when we even got *police* protection. It was, I must confess, a sweet kind of revenge to pass PS 17 all dressed up in my new *yomtov* clothes, new shoes killing me, while the hoi polloi, hating us more than ever had to go to school. Then I would march upstairs to the Ladies Balcony where my mother, my three sisters, and I took our seats near Sophie Tucker, who was weeping copiously—a copious person altogether—for what reason I never knew, though my mother was running her a close second. Down below, my father in his long white tallis with the silver brocade collar, and tall white yarmulke, hands upraised, talked to God directly. Except when he glared up at us and slapped a huge tome to get the women to stop talking.

Even on ordinary days, however, and with the rest of the congregation a set of very dubious Orthodox Jews who looked askance at the flashy show business types popping up among them now and then, the shul was my father's kingdom. Naturally, my father, having concocted his volatile mixture, was always having to keep it from combusting, his heart being with the actors, whom he really loved, and who returned the compliment. He was in fact, if I can say so without disrespect, perfect for the part. Tiny but dapper, handsome, beardless. He had a widow's peak and was graying at the temples, like many leading men of the day. And every afternoon when I left PS 17 at three o'clock and went next door to visit, I turned from a prisoner into a princess. "The rabbi's Channele." A lot of the diehards, of course, said my father didn't look like a rabbi. They also said, because I had blond hair, that I didn't look Jewish, much less like a rabbi's daughter. All of which was kind of thrilling. My mother, whose hair as she never got tired of informing me, had been blonder and her cheeks rosy, had often been told, she said proudly, that she looked like a Polish shiksa. But nobody meant it. It wasn't serious. It would have been unthinkable for my father not to have been a rabbi, for us not to be Jews. Even the thought was terrifying. No, Daddy belonged in shul, talking to God from the bimah, delivering thundering sermons which when I was little were in Yiddish, then became thundering sermons in not always so hot English (he had a lot of trouble with such words as *sinews,* to which he tacked on an extra *s*), answering housewives' questions about whether a chicken had accidentally become unkosher, presiding over the Hebrew school, conducting bar mitzvahs, marrying people, burying people. The one who was always called Rabbi, even in the outside world.

Everybody for blocks around knew him, from the fruit men on Ninth Avenue to the sleazy ex-pugs on Eighth, from the denizens of Tammany Hall and our own congressman Michael J. Kennedy, all the way over to the ticket takers, and theater owners and vaudevillians on Broadway. The man had connections with and for everything. There wasn't a movie we couldn't get passes for, a pair of house seats he couldn't lay his hands on, a play we couldn't go to if we wanted—except that he refused to let me see *Tobacco Road*, no matter how hard I pleaded. "Don't worry, Channele," he said, "it will still be playing when you grow up." He also had circus connections, since at least one giant, Dave, who stood outside movie theaters in the off season with an advertising billboard, and an occasional midget, were Jewish. Yes, he knew everybody, famous and not so famous, though when we asked him, "Daddy, do you know so and so?" he would say importantly,

"He knows me," and once even gave me that answer when I asked about President Roosevelt.

These powerful affiliations, and the fact that the regular shul members were not only congregants but also constituents, had begun to pay off early, when Sookie and Millie, who had also gone to PS 17 but long before my time, reported that in the home economics course they had found themselves washing Mrs. Sinsheimer's bloomers. My father took the matter seriously. Laundry was okay as a school subject, you didn't eat it, it didn't even require kosher soap like dishes. But no daughters of his were going to wash a teacher's bloomers, especially bloomers the size of Mrs. Sinsheimer's. What kind of a name was Sinsheimer anyway? Not Jewish, thank God. And not Irish—under the circumstances, thank God for that too. German, probably, which explained a lot. There were serious negotiations with Congressman Michael J. Kennedy, who passed the word to the principal, Miss Bohan, who laid down the law to Mrs. Sinsheimer. It was so well adjucated that by the time graduation came around all was a picture of harmony. The invocation and benediction were delivered by a priest from St. Malachy's, Congressman Kennedy heartily wished the seniors a grand future in high school, where some but not all were headed, and my father, as was the custom, gave out the medal for journalism. Nobody even thought of asking a rabbi to bless an auditorium full of Roman Catholics, never mind that they were terrible anti-Semites to begin with.

The night that my father did get to bless a mixed audience was at the Actors Temple Annual Theater Benefit. Held in December, it was the big secular event of our year. For months my father had prepared for it, walking what had now become his beat, lining up acts, coaxing a free theater out of the Shuberts, riffling blocs of tickets, which he sold to a general audience as well as to his congregation of dubious believers, arranging to have Broadway columnists put items in the papers, producing unlikely charitable impulses in the Stagehands Union. Finally the big night came. Daddy, resplendent in a tuxedo, went to the backstage of the Imperial or the Alvin or whatever big musical comedy house had been donated. We his family were installed in a box. As the years went on, the acts changed or reassorted themselves, but the format was always more or less the same, a dream vaudeville bill with top acts all the way. First a big name band, such as Cab Calloway or Duke Ellington or Sammy Kaye, maybe acrobats or a dog act, but they had to be very good, singers like Ted Lewis or Belle Baker or our own Sophie Tucker singing "My Yiddishe Mama," Harry Richman, dancers like the Nicholas Brothers, even Bill Robinson, impersonators who were always doing James Cagney and Bette Davis, then the comedians, which was what everybody was really waiting for—Jack Benny doing a duet on his violin with Phil Baker on his accordian, Willie Howard giving a French lesson, Jimmy Savo doing a hopeless card act in pantomime, Red Buttons with a hand to his ear, singing in Yiddish, Milton Berle telling stolen jokes about stealing jokes, Henny Youngman playing an even lousier violin than Jack Benny, the Ritz Brothers, Jimmy Durante breaking up a prop piano.

Most of their material we knew by heart, but that was the whole point. We weren't looking for new stuff, but old stuff that was familiar and we could laugh at year after year. Where else would we have heard it? Radio wasn't the same. And just one of the performers alone would have headlined the bill at the Palace. Then, just as I was transfixed by whatever was happening in the spotlight, Daddy would materialize in the box and in darkness and with a finger to his lips take me backstage. Me. Not Julia, not Sookie, not Millie, not Yossie. It was a little like the Haggadah. Me, and no other.

Backstage, I was allowed to watch from the wings, which was scary. In the strange darkness all the magic evaporated. It wasn't only that the acts were eating donated kosher cold cuts and drinking booze waiting to go on, or after they came off. It was the look of them, the aura they emanated. Daddy always said how good it was of them to work for nothing on Sunday night, their one night off, that an actor would spend his last dollar to rent a tuxedo to play a benefit. No doubt this was true—lots of the acts donating their services to the shul weren't even Jewish. But they didn't *seem* generous, or kind, or nice. They looked cold as ice, darkly unhappy, as they glanced unseeing at everyone else, or stared out through the wings. Then there would be some kind of intro or drumroll, and they would do their little half run onto the stage, be hit by the spotlight, brighten up, be all full of color and joy. Applause, then they would do a half-run return, all smiling until the minute they hit the wings, and became dark and cold as ice again in the backstage shadows.

Eventually, again without warning, Daddy would lead me back again through secret corridors to the box. I would pretend I had just had the thrill of my life, mostly to give Julia aggravation, but it wasn't easy to get lost again, not to remember that the laughing funny comedian actually had plastered pots of makeup on some very tough features. Then, at the very end, when the whole show was over, came my father, not wearing makeup, but in a nifty little tuxedo, walking not running to the center of the stage accompanied by the pit orchestra, playing something sedate like "A Pretty Girl Is Like a Melody." The orchestra stopped. He would thank everyone, and raise his hands and bless us and keep us, and those of us in the family box who had already compared him favorably to Ronald Coleman began to mention Clark Gable.

Obviously, such a father could be produced anywhere anytime with impunity and pride—though he was a potential source of guilt in PS 17, as in, "Anna, would your father like to hear that you behaved this way?" My mother, who made one of her few official public appearances anywhere on Open School Night was quite another matter. She would stick a black pot of a hat on her head to go with her dumb black dress, and sit in the back row of the classroom, mute and smiling foolishly, until the time to leave, when she sadly told the teacher I was smart, as if it were a burden they both shared. She was hopeless in other ways too. The woman didn't even vote, though she was an American citizen—"On Papa's papers!" she countered desperately. But I kept taunting her about it, making her life miserable straight through registration, which I dragged her to, even helping her to write the letters of her name in proper sequence. And then on election day she staggered out of the voting booth in PS 17, and said not to tell Papa, but she thought she'd voted for Landon. Probably the only vote in the whole country not for Roosevelt, except in Maine and Vermont.

She was embarrassing in other ways too. Not only was she very plump but also incredibly short. She was four feet, nine and a half, my father was five four, but she said she had always wanted to marry a tall man and thought she had. Her hair, which, again, had turned gray because of aggravation from me, was cut by a man's barber named George, with three spit curls for decoration, one in the middle of her forehead and one on each cheek, and the two of them had the nerve to call it a "personality bob." Once upon a time, I admit, there had been a certain rapport between us. When we still lived in the railroad flat on Forty-seventh Street, and I was about four, and everybody else was off at work or school, she would cut a pumpernickel across her chest in one long spiral, tear off two pieces, rub them with garlic, and we would sit at the kitchen table, eating and talking about life, mostly hers and how terrible it was. But in time this rapport had faded. There was her obvious predilection for Julia for one thing, and somewhere along the line I had discovered she was only nine and a half inches taller than a midget. Still, I was doomed to go shopping with her, being schlepped around from the fish store, where the guy whacked live fish over the head with a mallet, to the vegetable store, where she haggled over what she called *zuppen greens,* to the kosher butcher ghoulishly eviscerating chickens. (Though I never caught him with a thumb on the scale, where Daddy said he always had it.) Usually my mother spoke Yiddish, sometimes English, or a mixture of both. She really didn't know where one language ended and another began. Some words she used I didn't realize were actually English pronounced *her* way until years later. Not only "zuppen greens," but such phrases as "cahmin gattrections," which referred to movie previews. She also was tight with money—the five-and-ten was full of toys she took pleasure in saying we couldn't afford—unlike my father who was known as a real sport.

The joke was that this same woman had a marvelous younger sister named Sarah, Big Sarah to distinguish her from *my* sister, aka Little Sarah. Big Sarah was Mama's complete opposite, and also nemesis, the one I wished Daddy had married.

She had red hair, a wide snub nose, gummy white teeth, and a ready laugh, especially at Mama, who tended to worry anyway when people laughed. Mama looked like a butterball, but this lady was pear shaped, with an ample, beckoning bosom complete with cleavage, pretty legs, and little feet. She smelled of scented face powder and Evening in Paris perfume. She lived far away in Brooklyn at the end of an interminable subway ride. But at the end when we finally emerged of a Sunday, it was to the amazing fact that people actually lived in a Jewish neighborhood and that the delicatessens had kosher signs in English and Hebrew in the window. On the way to Big Sarah's apartment house was Dubrow's cafeteria, which Mama viewed with suspicion as the place, she muttered under her breath, where Big Sarah drank coffee in the *mornings* when she should have been cleaning her house, and bantered with strange men. The other wonderful thing was that inside the apartment the living room furniture, a sofa and two upholstered chairs all *matched*, as did the dresser and double bed in the bedroom. These sets were called suites, which was surely the height of elegance. Not only that, but the light in the bedroom was dim and rose colored, and on the bed sat a sofa doll in an old-fashioned pink crinoline, with her legs splayed. Big Sarah had two boys, the younger one a smart alec, like me, Mama said dourly, though he made *his* mother laugh, and an older one kind of stupid but rather pretty who Big Sarah boasted, had long eyelashes, just like a girl's. The big treat was a lunch of hot dogs and french fries from a kosher delicatessen just down the block—a situation unknown in Hell's Kitchen, and then Daddy and Big Sarah's husband Harry, a cutter in the garment district, settled down to play pinochle while Mama complained and Big Sarah laughed.

Sometimes other relatives drifted in, not always to my father's delight, though we saw enough of them in our house too. The fact was that except for Mama herself, her side of the family, the Gordons, was Americanized and assimilated in perhaps what wasn't quite the way to be. There was Uncle Max, the house painter, who also did stippling work at the BMT and yearned to be a "boss painter." Unfortunately, he was also a Communist and marched in the May Day Parade where he boasted of being spat on, so that when he came to borrow money from my father he wasn't always allowed in the house, except for the years when Stalin was fighting Hitler. Then there was Uncle Alex, also a Communist, though with the sly soul of a capitalist, who was a clerk in a grocery store. And the youngest of the litter, who was the same age as my brother, Uncle Hymie aka Jack, who sporadically worked in the garment business, chewed on toothpicks, wore a cigarette behind his ear, and played the horses. He married a very skinny girl named Goldie who had platinum hair, huge exposed teeth like those of the horses he was so fond of, and called herself an "exotic dancer." She even had studio photographs of herself in scanty costumes to prove it. There were also a couple of brothers down in Norfolk, Virginia, whose children sometimes came up to visit, under the impression that we would all stay up late and go to nightclubs. Except for Big Sarah, Daddy viewed all of them with varying degrees of disdain. In fact, there was another sister, Fanny, who couldn't be mentioned at all, at least not in Daddy's hearing, since she had run off and married a man whispered about as "The Italianer."

For a while, Zayde, their father, was part of the family picture. Having no home of his own, he drifted from one of his children to another, spending a week or two in each place. In our house he used to sit under a large framed photograph of himself, a rather distinguished man—oddly he looked something like Mama with a little gray goatee—and boast of being able to crack nuts with his own teeth. Sometimes Zayde and I played casino with a deck that had been rigged by my father in my favor. Mama complained about this but not seriously. Zayde had been a bad father to all of them. Now Zayde was no longer with us, and all Mama's relatives—with the exception of Fanny—came to sit shiva in our house. (This might have been when I realized that the famous "Italianer" was a Greek.) They talked about life, about *parnosseh,* making a living, and the fact that in the Depression it was impossible, they were always being laid off. But as to the cost of Zayde's funeral, Uncle Max kept saying, "Money is no objection," to which Uncle Alex heartily concurred. My father lifted an eyebrow in the direction of my mother, who turned away haughtily, not wishing to acknowledge that her brothers were being Communists at my father's expense, since he was footing the bill. Not that Daddy had any money, either, he just gave that impression and family was family, even alas, his in-laws. In fact, the name Morris Plan was mentioned so often I thought Mr. Plan was a close personal friend of Daddy's until Yossie told me it was a loan company, and even then I didn't realize you had to pay it back.

Mama's family, raunchy and proletarian, was Ukrainian, from a little shtetl called Shpikov, which Daddy said laughingly was six miles even from the railroad station that had the train that went to Odessa. Daddy's side, on the other hand, was from Brest-Litovsk, a real, big-time city on the Russian-Polish border. No blonds or redheads or exotic dancers in this bunch. They were all Litvaks, dark haired, by implication brainier, somehow more elevated. Daddy's older brother, Uncle Cathrael, was everybody's favorite. Cathrael lived in Norfolk, Virginia—my parents had met and married there through arrangement—and when Cathrael came up north it was a bigger holiday than Rosh Hashonah. He was a squarer, stockier version of Daddy, but enough alike in his jokes and charm to make it seem we were getting two for the price of one. He brought us figs from his garden. Imagine living in a place where figs grew on trees! By profession he was a furniture maker and in his house was a large carved chest he had bought at the Jamestown Exposition in 1906. Furthermore, his children all had Southern accents! All this and because they lived in what we considered a small town made them seem more part of the real American world than we were. Especially Cousin Easy (born Israel), who was almost as much of a favorite as his father, and who said "Ma'am" and called stockings *hose*. Cathrael was less lucky in other members of his family. His wife Freydel, was a virago, with a bony face and a mouth that turned down at the corners. She spoke *Yiddish* with a Southern accent, which didn't count. Oscar Brandeis, aka Ooshie, another son, was dark and glowering and suspicious of everything. Big Joe, the oldest, to distinguish him from my brother, was on the other hand rather unnervingly cheerful and drew little smiling faces on his many notes and letters. Up north, in Brooklyn, Daddy had another older brother, Herschel/Harry, who was kind of gray in the face and extraordinarily spare of speech for a Jew, both conditions ascribed by my father to Harry's having been hit in the head with a shovel when he was a conscript in the czar's army. Harry's wife, Goldie, however, was very much a sparkler, from her red hair—even redder, and much more spurious than Big

Sarah's—to her gold front tooth. *Her* American dream was to own a black cloth coat with a silver fox collar, giving my father to understand she would never rest until she got it from one of his wholesale furrier connections.

But behind all these relatives, their accents and aspirations, their ways of trying to fit in, there was always a sense of loss. No wedding, no bar mitzvah was complete without everybody bursting into tears. They were always singing and crying over places, like Belz, *"mein shtetele Belz,"* where they had never even been. *"Vos is gvayn is gvayn is mer nisht du,"* they also sang. What used to be, used to be, but is no more. Not that they wanted to go back there. Pooh! They didn't even want to talk about it. But what made the sense of loss more real and scary was the specter of Hitler in the background. When I was very little I had sat in front of the radio and heard Haile Selassie pleading with the League of Nations to save Ethiopia from Mussolini. Now we would hear Hitler ranting, ranting, ranting. Letters from Europe weren't coming so often.

After Zayde, who had died with his own teeth, death began to spring up all over the place. Julia said it was like going to sleep and never waking up, which created instant insomnia. It wasn't like the European relatives, who were merely missing, since to me they had never existed. The shammes died. Somebody's kid brother died of pneumonia, then somebody's older sister of something else. My father would be awakened in the middle of the night, throw his trousers over his pajama pants, give instructions to the funeral parlor, which sounded horribly like "put him on ice," and be off. Most notably, Millie's employer, the circus dentist, who was also president of the synagogue, died. His mother tried to throw herself into the grave. People throwing themselves into graves was the style. Actually, men didn't do it, the women did. It was the ultimate act of the Jewish mother. In fact, the mothers didn't do it, either. They weren't that spry. They *tried* to throw themselves into graves, but were handily prevented. They got full points anyway. But then again we viewed nothing as too extreme. Children and adults were smelly, cockeyed, kinky haired, hunchbacked, stuttering, and we referred to them by these attributes as a matter of course. Except for Miss Bohan, who was an albino, but there wasn't much to call her except Whitey, which didn't do for a principal and didn't take into account the pink eyes.

Summers were a respite from PS 17, worth all the heat and boredom, and endless days of playing potsy on the sidewalk, and Mama throwing down a wrapped sandwich from the fifth-floor window, plus a nickel for a popsicle. Daddy, the sport, sometimes came by on his way back to shul and gave me a *dime*. Otherwise, when I wasn't playing potsy I was jumping rope—failing utterly at Double Dutch. Other summer fun included being taken to Brighton Beach, either by my friend Peppy's mother, who hauled us into prison-like concrete lockers, then out to an enormous, densely populated pool where she yelled at me for not letting go of the edge, or worse, by the parents of one of Julia's friends—the father was a laundry man and had a car—where the sand burned up the soles of your feet long before you finished dodging people to get to the water where you didn't want to go anyway and which was full of people too, and the mother made us eat cold hamburger sandwiches. Either way, nightfall meant white strap marks and fiery red skin slathered all over with Noxema.

But the worst respite from summer on the city streets was

two weeks in the country. These were spent at a *cochalein* in the Catskills, which I could certainly have lived without. A *cochalein* was a farmhouse complete with farmer, and a huge communal kitchen where mothers quarreled over whose turn it was to use the stoves, and the children quarreled outside. The fresh fruits and vegetables were supposed to be good for you, but they tasted awful, like everything else my mother cooked. The fresh air was supposed to be good for you too, but it didn't do a thing for me, either. Nor did the landscape, which was nothing more interesting than parched fields and trees. In the evenings mothers and children walked along dark country roads, again smelling the fresh air. One night the farmer took us for a hayride in a horse-drawn wagon, but it was extremely scratchy. On the weekends, the fathers came up, including my father, who was, as always, himself, utterly urbane, even when reclining in a hammock. But then he left, abandoning me to the haystacks. I cried. Still, when we came back to Fifty-first Street, our apartment looked peculiarly small, a series of little boxes, and I cried again.

To cheer me up, my father *said*, and also expose me to some more fresh air, he began to take me to baseball games on Friday afternoons, which were Ladies Days. This meant that for a quarter in federal tax for me and another tax quarter for him—after he had stood on the Press Line with the other priests and rabbis—we would be entitled to grandstand seats in Yankee Stadium, or the Polo Grounds, depending on whether the Yankees or the Giants were at home. Personally, I preferred the Polo Grounds. It was more sociable, since Section 33 was a famous Broadway hangout. There, to welcoming cries of "Hi, Rab," we would join Ted Lewis, and Johnny Broderick, the famous detective whose gun and holster were

fascinatingly apparent, and comedy teams like Block and
Sully, or half a comedy team such as Sam Dody, formerly of
Lewis and Dody, who vainly tried to teach me some of his
songs and routines. ("Hello, hello, hello. Hello, hello, hello.
Fish don't perspire. Hello . . ." et cetera.) Obviously, I could-
n't have the unkosher hot dogs being hawked, which smelled
tantalizingly delicious, better than the "specials" at Big
Sarah's. But my father, always the sport, was free with peanuts
in the shell, and sodas. Our baseball schedule worked out fine
during the long summer days, when there was still plenty of
time for my father to whisk into the subway and get back to
shul for Friday night services, but in September when sunset
started to come early we would often wind up walking out
backwards before the game was over, ninth-inning tie with
bases loaded or not.

Like Daddy, Sookie also had a foot in the outside world. Both
feet actually. In addition to working all day at her job in the
Film Center and going to Hunter at night, she had taken an
interest in modern dancing and could be seen weekends leaping around the dining room table in a gauze tunic and chamois slippers, an outfit Mama considered very dubious. At one
point Sookie also rented a violin, practicing in the bathroom,
the only room with a door that locked, and putting the music
stand in the tub. But in our house the bathroom door couldn't
stay locked for very long and then Mama got diarrhea and
Sookie had to give the violin back. Along with everything else,
Sookie also managed to take care of me. She was the one who
rocked me to sleep and cut my toenails when I was little. She
was the one who combed the nits out of my hair when I
picked them up at PS 17. She was the one I had to wait for to

come home from work when I got my period at eleven and a half, and Mama said I couldn't go to school because I was sick and she didn't know what to do about it. In the old country they had used rags which they burned up in the oven. In the old country mothers slapped their daughters across the face at such a moment to drive the devil out of them. Even Mama understood that in this country it wouldn't do, and it was a long boring day waiting for Sookie, who knew what did.

But then, Sookie knew about so many things, including some French. *"Lafayette, je suis ici!"* she often exclaimed, a phrase, I believe, she got out of some movie. Her whole life was like the movies, anyhow. She went out on dates, boys took her to eat in restaurants, to dance in hotels, for drives in the country in an open convertible, ice skating at Rockefeller Center. And her clothes! The ones that Mama said cost her whole salary to put on her back. Outfits for every occasion. Among them, a smart little red wool suit for winter, a navy blue linen suit for summer, a wine silk paisley princess dress with tiny buttons up the front, a salmon-colored chiffon evening gown, a fitted reefer coat, adorable fedoras that tilted rakishly over one eye, black velvet pillbox hats with veils, shoes of every description but mostly high-heeled pumps to wear with silk stockings. (I would watch her go out, as usual poking back the cotton lisle undershirt that was leaking out of my puffed sleeves.) Besides where they took her, Sookie's boyfriends were in themselves a source of wonder. There was Walter, the florist, who gave her a real gardenia plant on which real gardenias grew, though they looked unnervingly strange—we had never seen them outside of a corsage. There was also Ace, so called because he wore a short leather jacket and a white scarf swirled around his neck. I'm not sure even

Sookie knew whether he had ever been up in a plane. But Sookie herself had now transmogrified into Dixie, based on the fact that she had been born in Georgia, even though she had left there at about the age of two. The chief feature of her new Southern accent was that she drawled all affirmatives as the word *Yuh-ass*. "Oy, what kind of a language is this?" Mama cried.

The sister next to Sookie, Millie, sometimes went along with Sookie's schemes, including a later one when they would be called Sookie and Mookie and dress as twins, in schoolgirl jumpers and Breton hats. However, though Sookie was glamorous and slender with a tiny waist and a zest for life, Millie was chunky and reticent, with curly black hair and a space between her front teeth. What she really wanted to be was an artist, and in her two daytime years at Hunter before she had to start working and go at night, she majored in art, and sketched half-naked people in charcoal—another matter futilely explained to Mama, who went running to Papa, who calmed her down. Sookie did rope Millie into the interpretive dancing, though. And once, me. I didn't have a tunic or chamois slippers. So I wore a pair of flowered midriff pajamas and ran around the dance studio in bare feet, complaining bitterly, when they schlepped me home, of splinters.

My brother, Yossie, the oldest, fifteen years older than I and only twenty years younger than our father, didn't need to *want* to be anything. He *was* everything. He knew everything. For example, he was a painter *and* a sculptor *and* a writer, and when I was little spent his time working on a novel called *Boris Borscht,* which was clearly going to be a masterpiece, the "great American Novel," as he put it. His best friend was a handsome easygoing blond guy named Dave Fisher and the two of them palled around so much Mama laughingly called Dave "Yossie's wife." But like the potential schizophrenia, this carried no heavy psychic weight, and after a while we all called Dave Yossie's wife, including Dave.

At this time Julia was still toiling away at something boring in high school. She was very fat, and therefore especially dear to Mama, who for Julia's thirteenth birthday had bought her a corset, thereby making them physical as well as spiritual twins. The original reason that Julia was fat was that she had been a premature baby, weighing only two pounds. Daddy had wrapped her in a roll of cotton soaked in warm olive oil and put her on top of a tin box which he had poked holes into and set a candle under. His version of an incubator. Since then, Mama had spent her whole life trying make Julia gain weight. Mama had been successful, feeding Julia like a goose, so that by age five Julia was so round that when she tripped at the top of a hill she rolled down the rest of it. Her shape was better now, at least her shape had a shape, but she was still Mama's girl. Ergo, my sworn enemy, there was nothing more to say about her.

My loyalty was with the three older siblings, Sookie of course most of all, and like them I too had certain artistic aspirations. I had won a Charlie McCarthy doll at a rigged shul bingo game, and this convinced me briefly that I had ventriloquist potential. But I really didn't want to be a mouthpiece for this dummy. More to the point, I was about the same age as Shirley Temple, and so I tapdanced on the street a lot, in between playing potsy. One day, I was discovered by a man who said I was a natural for tap lessons and wanted to sell them to Daddy. Yossie pointed out it was a scam and that Daddy had really important show-business connections, but I saw my brother only as standing in the way of my career. I changed my mind, though I didn't admit it publicly, and so did the teacher when, after two lessons, he gave Daddy his ten-dollar deposit back. "And in a Depression," Yossie said.

That left me with nothing to do but write stories. I assumed that all written stories—as opposed to the interminable ones told by my relatives, which always included the line "To make a long story short"—had surprise endings, and so the first one was about a man who went around all day saying, "This is my unlucky day," until at the end he gets a telegram saying, "Congratulations, you have just won a million dollars, *ect!*" But nobody was surprised at the ending and Sookie and Yossie laughed because I had spelled etc. wrong. Much later on, when I was twelve, I started a mystery novel in a speckled notebook called *Adventuresome Phyllis.* I didn't know how it would end, but by now I was set on great beginnings. So this started with Phyllis riding up Riverside Drive on the top of an open double-decker bus, and a scenic description something about, ". . . to the east were tall apartment buildings, to the west the sun was setting." But Yossie said everybody knew the sun set in the west so there was no point in saying it, and besides, there was no such word as adventuresome. Daddy remarked thoughtfully, "Yossie should have been a rabbi, he talks so much." I don't remember when Sookie threw the speckled notebook out by mistake.

Finally, one summer of the *cochaleins,* Sookie met a doctor at the adult camp, Tamiment, where she and Millie went to catch husbands. She had met the doctor by strolling across the golf course in a two-piece, red satin bathing suit. This was the beginning of the end in every way, since Sookie came home triumphant in September 1939, just as Hitler invaded Poland.

Soon, Yossie went down to Norfolk to work in the Navy Yard and live with Uncle Cathrael's family, and then he enlisted in the army even though the United States wasn't at war. Daddy tried to enlist too. But a rabbi with one deaf ear and five children wasn't exactly what the Army wanted. He had been turned down in World War I also when he already had the deaf ear, but only two children. So I was revising and writing a fair number of benedictions and invocations, which had been Yossie's job. "May the Lord bless you with the fruit of His goodness" was one of my favorites, though Daddy liked the more flowery ones, and also the Rabbi's messages for the Benefit Journal. Daddy's English was good—we weren't talking here about Mama—but he didn't trust it. This ghost writing was half pain, half pride, but I accepted the anonymity of it. Nobody ever admitted I had anything to do with the stuff, partly because Daddy immediately went into denial, and also because I was only twelve. Anyway, I had given up on Shirley Temple and was now on a loftier plane, having discovered that I was also more or less the same age as Princess Elizabeth. Then there was the coincidence that she also had a handsome skinny father who happened to be a king. "Dear children everywhere," I practiced saying in a high-pitched English accent. But I wasn't much interested in children. Mama said proudly I had never been a child.

Sookie's wedding was the stellar event in our lifetimes. Not only was the oldest of four daughters getting married, she was marrying a *doctor*. Personally I hated him on sight. He was nothing like Walter the florist or Ace the aviator, both of whom were tall and had manly five o'clock shadow, but small and sandy colored—he was even called Sandy—and always saying things like, "Shouldn't this kid be in bed by now?" It was none of his business, and it was also easy to see that this guy enjoyed giving enemas. Still, there was Sookie, a real bride with a veil, walking down the shul aisle with Daddy in his white yomtov robe on one side and Mama on the other, in her blue *yomtov* dress with the beading across the front, and all the other females in long dresses too, and a cantor and a choir and Julia and I fighting over who would sit next to Easy. Daddy's connections at the Paramount Hotel near Times Square had donated the reception, and there was a bit of a flurry over a fake lobster that had been set to grace the buffet table and needed to be snatched away. (Unfortunately, the huge wedding cake turned out also to be a fake, but not before I had eaten a large piece of what I took for icing.) There was a band, and liquor and dancing, and I got drunk and flirted and danced with Sookie's husband's young doctor friends who practically had apoplexy when Sandy, always the first to spoil a good time, told them I was thirteen years old.

Other than that, my social life was nil. Being the rabbi's daughter had certain social disadvantages—like being avoided like the plague. By boys especially. I'd like to say I hated them too, but this wasn't true. Not at all, not ever since I had seen *Gone With the Wind* with Peppy and a light went on in my head after Clark Gable carried Vivien Leigh up those red stairs, though what they did when they got there or why she was smiling so merrily the next morning, I had no idea. My friend Peppy could have explained it to me, but I didn't want her to realize that there was anything I didn't know. Besides being stupid about everything but boys and being blind as a bat—she said excuse me to fire hydrants when she bumped into them—Peppy's movie going was rationed, and so there were only a limited number of times we could go to see double features at the Tivoli, or GWTW at the Capitol (we had already seen it three times), or play Monopoly for that matter, or fight over whose turn it was to walk whom home. The same went for Rochelle the Stutterer, who also had a big sister who was getting married, which made for a melancholy connection, though we treated the matter with great bravado and claimed we and our big sisters would be even closer afterward. Rochelle's sister went to CCNY downtown, the only part where girls were admitted, and had a lot of snappy sayings, such as "What has that got to do with the price of tea in China?" Secretly, of course, I did have crushes on boys, though I publicly denounced them as loathsome. And I even developed a kind of platonic friendship with the boy whose mother took us to Brighton Beach and made us eat cold hamburger sandwiches. What kept it platonic was that he had six toes— on one foot—which tended to cool the fires. Besides, his sister Ruthie was friends with my sister Julia, not much of a plus.

When I was little and had to use the children's section at the library I was always taking out a picture book about an unpopular duck whom no one invites anywhere, and then at the end there's a picture of him in a birthday hat at the head of a table. He's very happy because he's finally been asked to a party. In fact the party's in his honor. In real life when asked what I wanted to be I always said an oral hygienist, because everybody was very impressed that I knew such words, unaware that they came from Millie. But if I had a life's ambition then, it was to be that duck.

The last entry in the Riverside Memorial Chapel clergyman's diary, which Daddy had handed over to me and where I kept my secret thoughts, was that I didn't trust Peppy. And then: "Tomorrow is Valentine's Day. But who would send me a Valentine?" The next page is blank. It was a good thing I was going on to high school.

At graduation from PS 17, I wore a long dress of flowered white organdy that had taken me months to make—exclusive of the fake gardenias that ran across the top of my chest in a manner vaguely reminiscent of Ginger Rogers—and whose hem I stepped through on my way up to get my diploma. The hem trailed behind me as I also accepted a bronze medal on a blue ribbon that was inscribed Anna Birstein, Valedictorian, PS 17. Daddy had already given the medal for journalism, and the Catholic priest had blessed us not at all ecumenically. We had also saluted the American flag, sung "The Star-Spangled Banner" as we did at all school assemblies, and finished up as usual with the New York City song:

> "Oh Watchman, of the City Gate,
>   how doth the city fare?
> Does any Foeman lurk and wait
>   to pierce her armor there?
> And Watchman is the wall made strong
>   with Freedom's holy light
> And is it girded roundabout
>   with honor, truth, and Right?"

> CHORUS:
> "Oh, yes, the city wall is strong
>   and dee dum dee dum dee
> Our lives protect New York from harm.
> Our *deeds* defend her fame!"

Afterward Congressman Kennedy, accompanied by two henchmen in square, double-breasted suits, their hands in pockets, came up to me and congratulated me on my medal, and said didn't I look pretty with my long blond hair and white dress, and didn't time fly, here I was graduating already. And how was my father, darling? Was he still in the same business?

Chapter 2

MY THREE SISTERS had gone to an all-girls high school called Washington Irving, so I chose an all-girls high school called Julia Richman. Anything to escape the pattern, though it had to be all girls because the only two coed high schools in Manhattan were famously tough—breeding places for crime and who knew what else. (Actually, we did know what else.) Even if my parents had permitted it, which they never would have, the idea of being in proximity with boys in such places would have frozen my soul. Besides everything else, how would anyone have known I was smart? It took me two buses to get to my new high school, one uptown from Fifty-fourth Street, where we had moved shortly before Sookie's wedding, to Sixty-eighth Street, then another bus across town to Second Avenue. The move to the apartment on Fifty-fourth Street, between Seventh Avenue and Broadway, was as far as we could go and Daddy still be able to walk to shul on shabbos. The reason we had done it was that with Sookie being taken out of the picture—yes, by a doctor!—my mother had persuaded my father that the remaining single daughters needed a decent place to bring potential husbands, and our somewhat shady former residence, despite Sookie's singular stroke of luck, wasn't it. I think Mama meant a decent place for Julia especially, though she wouldn't have minded getting rid of us all in one fell swoop, including me, never mind that I was still only thirteen.

In any case, our new home was in a small elegant building on a small block which in 1940 was very much uptown, and very much in a residential area—an incredible improvement over where we had lived before. There were polished brass trimmings on the outside door, red carpet running up the inside stairs, and a combination doorman–elevator man presiding in a nifty uniform trimmed in red to match. Prestige was written all over this place, though how we could afford it I never thought to ask. (It was understood that Daddy always found money for his children, even if it meant being permanently indentured to the Morris Plan.) Marginal show-business figures also lived there, and our own apartment, it was rumored, had once been occupied by Polly Adler, the famous madame. I don't think it was her workplace because our quarters weren't all that ample. There was one bedroom with two daybeds that opened into four at night and made it into a girls dormitory, a tiny maid's room where Yossie slept and worked on his clay sculpture and his Great American Novel, a little kitchen, a living room where Daddy now had floor to ceiling bookcases built across one wall, and a bedroom for my parents with a bathroom that also opened out into the living room and was accessible to all. Oddly, though I can remember where everyone slept when we were all at home, I can't remember where we ate. Probably in the kitchen, in shifts, as usual— which doesn't take into account Friday nights and seders.

Julia Richman wasn't particularly appealing as a building. From the outside it looked like a huge penitentiary or a mental hospital, with wire grating across the windows and a chiseled motto over the front door that said something frightening; "Knowledge Is Power." Still, the bottom line was that it still wasn't the same high school where my sisters had gone, and it wasn't PS 17, either. No, in Julia Richman girls were expected to act like grown-ups and call each other "Miss," even on the bus, such as in "Miss in the Blue Dress, would you please get off my foot?" Somehow, I also started being called Ann, by a teacher who had misread my name, and that sounded right, though it didn't affect my home life where I was still Chana or Honey. I had managed to finesse a grade and so I started Julia Richman in the January session of 1941. At first the building seemed overwhelmingly vast, but as it turned out I was hardly ever in its higher reaches, certainly not on the sixth floor, where the dreaded swimming pool was located and from which I had gotten excused right off the bat on account of sinus trouble. No, most of my time I spent in very small set of classrooms on the first floor. This was called the Country School, for what reason I never understood, and was the exclusive domain of the smart girls of the school. Mostly smart Jewish girls, as it turned out. Apart from never having seen such a collection of smart Jewish girls in one place—in fact, I was used to being the only one—I had never seen this style of being Jewish at all before.

Since Julia Richman was districted across town, most of the students in the Country School lived on West End Avenue or Riverside Drive or in the fancy blocks in between. Not only that, but everybody in their families spoke *real* English, since the parents had all been born in America or come as infants, too young to have any memories of the old country, much less to cry over it. It was the grandparents who had been the immigrants, and who if present, were smiled at and doted upon as if they were relics of some forgotten age. The fathers were all jewelers or furriers or garment manufacturers, genial men who liked to tell stories about their early days, such as how they were so young and skinny when they first applied for working papers that they had had to put lead in their pants to qualify. The mothers boasted of no such pasts, in fact, they seemed to have no pasts at all. They looked and dressed like Sookie, not like Mama, and played mah-jongg regularly at one another's homes. The whole family went to Temple, not to shul, and these places *were* temples, vast and ornate structures on the Upper West Side, that made our little shul seem another breed altogether. Sometimes I got invited to stay for dinner (not supper) at someone's house, if I was hanging around anyhow. This meal was almost always eaten in the foyer, at a table that opened up, and was served by the maid, who had also cooked it. Two children to a family seemed to be the rule. Each child had a separate bedroom. That I was one of five was cause for astonishment, if not ill-hidden mirth.

Sometimes my schoolmate's sibling was a sister, but older brothers were the rule. How this was managed I don't know. It seemed to be connected with having so much money and speaking English without an accent. Fabulous, mythical older brothers, who went to private schools—one of them was actually in Harvard!—and who strode across the beige wall-to-wall carpeting into the living room to glance at us disdainfully, or make some joshing remark if said brother happened to be in a good mood. I immediately got a crush on every single one of them, without getting so much as a nod in return. No, that wasn't strictly true. Helen Weisgal's brother, Mendy—the one who went to Harvard!—once idly remarked that I looked like Celeste Holm, and this sent Helen and me into a tizzy for days, particularly since we didn't know who Celeste Holm was, and never did find out until *Oklahoma* opened. And then it was a big disappointment. She was hardly what you would call glamorous.

Another impressive household was lived in by Leonora Margaret Pearlstein, on Central Park West. This large apartment was also slathered in pale wall-to-wall carpeting, an invitation to dirt that miraculously never appeared, but in addition boasted a view of the park and a genuine grand piano in the living room. (I tried to banish thoughts of poor Sookie staggering in and out of the bathroom with her violin.) On the wall was a real oil painting of Leonora and her older brother, Byron. "The children when they were small," their mother said, smiling upon it. The father, whose type of business I never did get straight—they didn't talk about it, but I *think* he was a furrier—was condescendingly called Izzy by his children. The mother, a tall American-looking woman in spite of her big nose, who clearly ruled the household, was sometimes referred to as Rose, but in a tone of daring, not condescension. The real wonder in that place, however, far more so than the park view or the grand piano, was big brother Byron, tall and fair, with strong features. He and Leonora, also tall and fair, looked alike. But Leonora wore her blond hair long, held in place with a black velvet hair band, like Alice in Wonderland—she sometimes also wore black velvet dresses with lace collars—the unfortunate effect of which was that when she stood next to Byron she looked like a female impersonator. Byron didn't go to Harvard, but, judging from the family attitude, to an even more prestigious institution, Queens College, which had just opened and where all sorts of academic and intellectual wonders were taking place. I immediately fell in love with Byron, and once even left my fake gold embossed compact behind a cushion, so that I would be able to return and get it and maybe catch Byron at home alone. Mama Rose, however, seemed to have caught on, and handed my compact back to me as soon as I came in the door. It was clear that no one of my social standing could lay claim to her son, compact or no compact. It was enough that I was accepted as a friend of her daughter.

Classes in the Country School were hard, with lots of homework. The teachers were pretty nice and clearly well-educated. Some of them were married and signed themselves impressively with three names: one first name, two last, and no Mrs. before any of them. I had never seen this before and wasn't sure how I felt about it, though I knew instinctively that Mama would disapprove, asking what was the point of being married if you didn't have a Mrs. in front of your name? The unmarried teachers were nice too—including Mlle Gertrude Goldberg, who was an American but taught French. The exception was a nasty, adolescent-hating Miss Christine McCarthy, who pitted us against one another in history class and was a direct heir to the terrible tradition of PS 17. Unfortunately I did very well in school, including in the awful Miss McCarthy's class. This had always been my curse and I kept quiet about it, though sooner or later Leonora Pearlstein or Helen Weisgal, and later on another girl named Maria Shulman would find out and laugh at me. Now it was not just a matter of boys avoiding you, but that being a good student was intellectually beneath contempt. Especially to Maria, who was tiny and had a heart-shaped face, and a little heart-shaped mouth, and whose smile was totally sad. Boys were crazy about her. She went out on millions of dates and loathed them all. But then Maria was extremely sensitive. Once, when I was talking about a recipe that required raw fish she shuddered and turned away. "I can't stand ugliness," she said. Which was odd, because she seemed to see it everywhere. She also said she had a low pain threshold. She was sure I was as sensitive as she was, if I would only let myself admit it. But I just wasn't that delicate in my feelings, and if I openly despised boys, I sure didn't feel that way secretly.

In addition to the Leonoras and the Helens, girls named Anneliese began to appear. They wrote compositions about boots coming up the stairs that scared everybody. I myself had a rocky time of it early on in my English class when I was accused of not having written what I had written. The particular composition that came into question was about a derelict, who had a piece of rope for a belt, and who at the end of a fruitless encounter, ". . . turned, sighed, and shuffled slowly onward." I kind of loved that line. Yossie said to be accused of plagiarism was a compliment, but it was a compliment I could have lived without. Finally, everybody got used to the idea that I had written what I wrote, and at the urging of a married teacher with three names, Marian Bader Green, I submitted a story to the school magazine. I had written it the past boring summer in one of those lulls when I was hanging around the shul and got to use the typewriter. It was called "Carousel," and the plot was about a little boy named David who's sitting on a merry-go-round, hating it, while his doting grandfather is watching him. His wooden horse begins to talk to him, urging him to kick it and get out of there, and fly away on all sorts of adventures. But a funny thing happened with this story. Instead of kicking his horse, as I had intended, David looks at his grandfather wanting him so much to have a good time on the dopey merry-go-round, and lets his foot drop.

The school magazine took this story, and published it with illustrations in the next issue. It even won a prize for best story, a copy of the James Gould Cozzens novel, *Guard of Honor,* which sounded sufficiently Gentile to be impressive. Even more impressive, the school somehow took credit for my story, even though I had written it long before I entered Julia Richman. Riding high, I next submitted a one-act play about judgment in the afterlife, also written on the shul typewriter during the summer lull. As I recall, the thief who stole for his family is sent to heaven, as is a man racked with pain who has committed suicide, but a wicked murderer is sentenced to go back to earth. *"No! No!"* he cries. This time, instead of winning another prize and another impressive book it was no fun to read, as I had expected, I got a very long considered letter from Miss Catherine Jones, *Bluebird* faculty advisor, who explained that they were not accepting the play for publication, because its theological stance vis à vis suicide might offend Catholics. Yossie again thought this was a feather in my cap—how many writers my age were censored?—though I didn't. In any case, my literary efforts didn't impress my friends any more than my grades did. It was somehow just as intellectually contemptible to write stories as to be smart in school, and they kindly did me the favor of not dwelling on the matter.

On a daily basis, the girls, including my intellectual friends, wore saddle shoes, plaid skirts, and cardigan sweaters buttoned up the back not the front. These were clothes purchased especially for school, I soon realized, acquiring some myself instead of wearing formerly "good" clothes that were no longer good enough for dressy occasions. On weekends and holidays in the spring, the style was navy blue suits, with navy blue suede platform ankle straps to match. In the winter, Persian lamb coats, generally gray, or brown sheared beaver. The mothers also wore navy blue suits and ankle straps, but in furs tended toward black Persian lamb, or preferably silver fox. Female jewelry ran heavily toward "cocktail rings," which were gold with twists and swirls set with rubies and sapphires, huge ones for the mothers, smaller ones for the daughters.

But for some unconventional souls styles were changing. Helen Weisgal shifted from page boy and hair ribbon and being crazy about Glenn Miller to hacking away at her hair, wearing a red-plaid lumber jacket, and becoming a ferocious Zionist. (She was the one whose big brother Mendy actually went to Harvard!) But then her father, Meyer Weisgal, was professionally in a different category from the other fathers. He was some kind of big Jewish entrepreneur, though what kind I never knew for sure. Helen and I had fierce arguments about whether you could keep God out of Zionism. Never, I said, loyal to everything in my background. Absolutely, she said, loyal to hers, which was very secular.

Leonora, no longer an overgrown Alice in Wonderland, was now reading a magazine called *Partisan Review,* which I had never heard of, and Proust in the original, and talked knowingly about Rudy Serkin, whoever the hell he was. Maria was getting more and more delicate in her feelings, and urging me to acknowledge that I was the same. There was something going on here, and it didn't fit right. It made me feel funny and squirmy. I was guilty enough about what I was feeling about movie stars and everybody's big brother. Culturally, I was in a very different universe too, cutting school to see Frank Sinatra at the Paramount—with Daddy's permission, he got passes—

and screaming "Frankee!" with the best of them. Daddy approved of him because Sinatra appeared at the shul benefits. And he had actually once come to services, schlepped along by Toots Shor. Frankie was in a tan corduroy jacket, with a little yarmulke perched adorably on his head. I almost fell out of the Ladies Balcony trying to get a good look at him.

But in other ways I, too, was leaving my old self behind. Uncle Cathrael had died, and I lied to my father and led him to believe that I felt worse about it than I did, when I was really crying over some stupid thing that had happened at school. The relatives from Virginia began to seem provincial. Big Joe, who had been imported to Clarksburg to marry a West Virginia Jewish woman, drew smiling faces over everything, notes, poems, you name it, and eventually because of his initials, S.J., began to call himself Stonewall Jackson. (Yes, I now had a cousin called Stonewall Jackson Birstein.) He told me that he was the only Jewish Lion in Clarksburg. Easy was still Easy, still charming, but after his father's death he had to leave New York and go back to Norfolk to take over the family business, and Mama, who never went down the block by herself if she could help it, predicted that small-town life would take its toll on him. Not to mention being under the eye of his mother, Freydel, who began to pop up in New York herself and take me to Schrafft's, where at the end of lunch she would call the waitress over, present her with a nickel, and say, "Here, girlie, buy yourself something." I had to go, out of respect for family, even though my father hated her and said she was the cause of Uncle Cathrael's brain tumor.

Up there with the awful relatives, Herschel's son Seymour, who was my age, now somehow always managed to be in the neighborhood. Daddy, having seen him coming down the street from our window, would hide as soon as the doorbell rang, as did everyone else who happened to be home. But nothing deterred Seymour. "I was in the neighborhood, so I thought I'd drop in," he always said, a puzzle since he lived in the outer reaches of Brooklyn. He also told me he was going to give his brain to science and I said, "Why wait?" But it rolled right off him. He smiled. Out of stupidity or some other mental condition I wasn't sure. After all, his father *had* been hit over the head with a shovel in the Russian trenches, so maybe it was inherited. Mama had a saying that went something like, "You spit in his face and he thinks it's raining," which described Seymour exactly. On Mama's end, the big winner was cousin Bernice, who was famed for taking her newborn baby to Radio City Music Hall, and who, recounting the pain of a gynecological exam to my sister Julia, prefaced her remarks with, "You know, my husband is not a finger, but let me tell you . . ." Julia's eyes went wide as saucers, but what Bernice was talking about I had no idea.

On the plus side, Sookie, now living in the Hotel Taft, where Daddy had gotten Sandy a job as house physician, had a baby, named Beth after one of the Little Women. The baby was absolutely adorable, like a doll but real, and I was thrilled, even though Sookie was all nervous and miserable. She had been that way when she was pregnant too, hating her maternity dresses and sensible shoes. But I excitedly told everybody in high school and anyone else who would listen, about my niece. Since none of the other girls had one, that at least gave me a decided edge. I still couldn't figure out why the person I had formerly known as Sookie should have turned into someone so embittered and un-fun-loving, like a *mother* mother. *I* would never be like that when *I* had a baby, though I never intended to have one, or get married, either. The baby didn't change Sandy, but then he had always been awful anyway, and really didn't like being house physician at the Taft because he was always being called in the middle of the night, sometimes to get some man on his honeymoon unstuck from his fly zipper. Sookie also hated that their waiting room was also their living room, furnished with a maroon leatherette sofa and two club chairs all decorated with brass studs. To me it was thrilling, as was the rumor that Sandy would be one of the first called up into the army even though he was married and a father, because there was a war on, and he was a *doctor*—as if we could ever forget that.

The war was making many other changes as well, and had ever since December 7, which I recognized as a portentous day even as it was happening. I had heard the news of Pearl Harbor on the radio when I was visiting Helen Weisgal's house—her brother was off at *Harvard*—and after we had ascertained that there would be school the next day anyhow, I rode the Broadway bus home, solemnly looking at the other passengers and saying to myself, "This is a nation at war." It was kind of like being my own radio program. I knew I would always remember myself saying that: *"This is a nation at war."* Soon Big Joe told me he had become an air raid warden. They were going to bomb Clarksburg, West Virginia? "It's called the Jewel of the Mountains," he said. Yossie, who had gone down to Norfolk to work in the Navy Yard, had enlisted long before the war actually started, and was now a private in the Army. Daddy was going all out for the war effort, including sending free cigarettes overseas and having big public seders at a hotel that ordinary people paid to attend while servicemen were honored guests. When *Winged Victory* opened, he invited Jewish chorus boys home for shabbos. Julia made her own contribution to the war effort by going to work at the Brooklyn Navy Yard after she had graduated from Hunter College and coming home blonder and blonder. "She's not a blonde!" I screamed. "She's dying her hair!" Julia denied it vehemently. She said it was the chemicals. Mama, who was hardly a scientific genius, backed her up on this.

Uncle Alex, who was as short as Mama, his sister, had talked his way out of the army—by so eagerly claiming he wanted to serve they thought he was crazy. He was now part owner of the grocery where once he had clerked. By what chicanery this had come about I didn't want to think. But the new law said you were only allowed to send twenty-five dollars worth of goods to an armed serviceman overseas and when Uncle Alex recounted the huge packages he was sending and I said it sounded like too much, he said smiling, "Don't worry it isn't worth twenty-five dollars." So this meant that underneath his new-found prosperity, he was still a Communist and Daddy would throw him out of the house if the political climate changed, though right now the Russians were our allies and I staunchly believed in them.

The truth was that we too were getting to be pretty "all-rightnik" ourselves, though not through commerce, like Uncle Alex or my friends' parents on West End Avenue or Riverside Drive. The war was simply ending the Depression and making everybody richer across the board. Soon we had a dinette table in what used to be Yossie's room (the foyer wasn't big enough), and one maid after another—Mama was always scaring them off by paddling along after them in her housedress and apron. But Mama had also acquired a black Persian lamb coat and a cocktail ring. Wall-to-wall carpeting sprouted in the living room and down the hall. With my Upper West Side girlfriends, I dressed up and went to TipToe Inn to eat apple pancakes as large as a small table, and we were sneered at by the German refugee ladies who rendezvoused there and thought we had no manners. Or else Maria and I went to Steinberg's Dairy Restaurant, where we enjoyed baiting the owner, Mr. Steinberg. Maria's beautiful aunt had just married him, and though he always came to chat with us over blintzes, no matter how hard we tried to keep him there, he always managed to vanish just before the check came.

In summer, *cochaleins* had become a thing of the past. We now went directly to the Hotel Anderson, whose pool we used to sneak into. Lifeguards were paid to romance the female guests, there was nightly entertainment in the "Casino" consisting of skits, music, desperate comedians, and kids slipping around on the resined dance floor, and campfires at which dirty English/Yiddish songs were sung, perennial favorites like "Rosh Hashonah Time in Dixieland," which made the older women, including my own mother(!) laugh, but which I didn't get because I didn't know any dirty words in Yiddish. In the winter, a week in Lakewood, New Jersey, had transmogrified into two weeks in Miami Beach, Florida. This was thrilling, first because we got to sit up all night in a train that had a name like the Silver Meteor, and speed southward, finding first daybreak in the dark, mysterious countryside of North Carolina. Even more thrilling was the beach of Miami Beach, which went on and on, practically uninhabited, along a sparkling ocean. No burning your feet on the sand here, dodging bodies. You could walk along, dabbling your toes in the water's edge, or for shade duck under one of the actual palm trees that grew right there. It was all so incredibly easy and accessible.

Which wasn't to say that all of Miami Beach was accessible. No, beyond a certain point uptown Jews weren't allowed to go. That is, we were allowed to walk up there but not stay in any of the hotels. But this anti-semitism was so familiar it was almost comfortable—we weren't in such a foreign place, after all. We didn't need their hotels, anyway. We had our own, kosher, and painted in pink and avocado green, colors that had never occurred in the dreary Catskills, which tended toward Tudor. We had wartime prosperity, we had high rollers, such denizens of my father's synagogue as the man who ran a crooked roulette wheel into order to support his aging, kosher mother in proper style, and others in zoot suits, standing in fancy hotel doorways, twirling watch chains, who sometimes greeted my father with "Hello, Rab," and at other times mysteriously seemed not to know him at all. For shopping we had Lincoln Road, with its Tootsie Rolls, which normally cost five cents, now wrapped in gold foil and selling for a *dollar, twenty-five* dollar hand-painted silk neckties, ladies blouses, also silk and hand painted, but in addition blindingly festooned with sequins. Best of all, the streets swarmed with servicemen, many of them billeted in hotels requisitioned by the U.S. Government. I was allowed to speak to these strangers in uniform, even the handsome young ones, because it was patriotic. And good for the Jews too—they were helping to fight *Hitler*. In between these sanctioned pickups I spent time working on a glamorous tan, but since my hair had gotten lighter and lighter, almost white, and my skin darker and darker, when I got up North I looked like a negative—which either Leonora or Helen or Maria kindly pointed out.

That I should like a vulgar place like Miami Beach was beyond discussion. Izzy and the other fathers had tried to get
them to go there but of course they had refused.

The boy situation hadn't improved any. The ones my age,
who were still too young to be drafted, continued to hate me.
(But why then, did they love Maria, who hated *them*?) Julia, despite the chemically enhanced hair, didn't have much in the way
of real dates either. Among her other uninteresting boyfriends
were two 4F's, one of whom always came by on a Saturday afternoon to tell her about the movie he had just seen, and another reject named Moe who went around with a piece of cotton stuck in his ear because it was runny. Once Moe asked *me*
out, but Mama said I couldn't go, which was a relief, even
though for the honor of it I protested. And Millie wasn't doing
too well with Sandy's doctor friends, either, especially now that
Sookie was no longer her wild crazy self, but was tied down
with a baby and permanently miserable and kept telling me to
wait a minute every time I wanted to ask her something.

For all these reasons the three of us unmarried daughters
prevailed upon our father to use his Broadway connections
and have us made hostesses at the Stage Door Canteen. His
connections worked, as always. If anybody asked why three
rabbi's daughters, one of them decidedly underage, should *be*
hostesses, we never heard about it. The Stage Door Canteen
turned out to be a small space in the basement of one of the
Broadway theaters. It was mildly festooned with streamers
and featured a tiny dance floor and lots of little tables. We
hostesses worked in shifts of about two hours and beforehand
were each given little red-and-blue-striped aprons to tie in a
bow behind our back, and offered such tips as that if we were
shy about approaching a lonely serviceman, to ask him for a

match. It was presumed that everybody smoked, which was why we were also asked to go around emptying ashtrays.

There was a table where tea and coffee and cookies were set out, but no famous stars dishing out food behind it, no Helen Hayes or Lynn Fontanne grabbing hands and saying fervently, "Good luck, soldier boy." The servicemen helped themselves to refreshments. If a big star did come in they were immediately shoved into the center of the dance floor and introduced with great fanfare. But usually we sat at small tables talking, or danced to records. In answer to the question, "Are you connected with show business?" my answer was, "Sort of"—vague enough to be true, and murmured low enough to pass for modesty, as if I were a starlet about to be discovered. Julia liked the talking part best, though she had got off to a scratchy start when a backwoods soldier said he'd like to see a Jew while he was in New York, and she said, "You're looking at one," and he didn't believe her because she seemed normal. Millie as usual settled for a middle way, part dancing, part sitting. But for me, generally, it was dancing, dancing, dancing. The tiny floor was jammed. Anybody could cut in at any time and anybody did. Lunatic dancers, smooth dancers, shy dancers, show-off dancers, soldiers, sailors, coast guard, and marines. After a while, I who started out with Sookie as my mentor, dancing on the tops of her feet, could and would follow every one of them—except the guys who wanted to throw you over their heads when they did the Lindy. Once my cousin from Norfolk, Virginia—Ooshie, aka Oscar Brandeis—came snooping around in his Coast Guard uniform. I didn't see him, but he reported to Daddy that I had been dancing with a *black man*. Daddy's answer is not on record, probably because he didn't deign to respond. We were talking here about a man whose synagogue was annually rescued financially by Cab Calloway and Harry Belafonte at the benefits, and who boasted that Bill Robinson knew him personally.

It was 1944 and by going to summer school I had cut a term off my sentence at Julia Richman. I had written the senior play with Maria, a parody of *Oklahoma* with songs such as "Oy, oy, oy oy Odessa, where the borscht is flowing just like blood," which had cracked us up but flopped miserably on stage. I was about to graduate. Besides theatrical failure, what had I learned? To successfully avoid the head of the English department in his office, who was rumored to deliberately drop things so he could pinch your behind when you bent to pick them up. (A Jew, too, though he certainly didn't act like it.) I had learned the names *Partisan Review* and Rudolph Serkin, though I still didn't know anything about them, discovered that lesbianism didn't exist only in the pages of *The Well of Loneliness,* tried my hand at golf by being taken to a country club with one of the Izzys and his daughter, could follow any guy dancing practically anything anywhere. Every day of my life during these years I had been terrified that Hitler would win the war, and that Jews would go on being killed. I had also learned that when it came to college there were Jewish quotas right here in the United States. The rumor was that the best Jewish students were being turned down by some of the best colleges, and the mediocre ones accepted.

I could probably have gotten a scholarship to *some* college anyway, since I had been named valedictorian of my graduating class, a fact I tried futilely to sweep under the rug where my friends were concerned, but living away from home was totally out of the question, even if money weren't involved. *My* kind of good Jewish girls, not to say rabbis' daughters, didn't do such things. I didn't even make a stab at it. No, I saved my fire for my choice of Queens College, which was *coed*. No more girls schools for me, particularly since my three sisters had all naturally gone to that Jewish nunnery Hunter College. "She's going to school with *boys*?" my mother cried. I looked my father square in the eye over her head, and he nodded.

In my valedictorian's speech, I played heavily on the war theme, and portentously began, after much clearing of throat and greeting all those present, "It is in some ways odd that we, who live in a world of premature good-byes, should balk at yet another." Pretty impressive stuff (up there with *"This is a nation at war"*), I and everyone else who heard it thought, including Millie, who said, "Somebody might almost think you meant it." I did, but now I was ashamed to admit it. I got a donated watch from Lambert Brothers with AB engraved on it, and also a medal from the French department. Daddy almost didn't make it because he was busy with something much more important, but in the end he came too. He wasn't eager because nobody had asked him to present any award. No matter, this was water under the bridge. I was going to Queens College, still misted over in my mind with the ultimate glamour of such as Byron Pearlstein, and so far off in Flushing that I might actually have been going away to school.

Chapter 3

THE FIRST THING I learned in college was that "fine writing" didn't mean it was any good. What it technically did mean I no longer remember, but it was enough to wipe the smile off my face and offer dark intimations that writing would no longer be easy, and that it wouldn't be fun anymore, either. No, sir. This was the academic big leagues, with so many strictures about sentences and word usage and literature in general that nobody writing anything could keep smiling or imagine that they (he or she) could possibly get it right the first time. This all made terrible sense, since to me English was still basically a mysterious second language.

Nor were boys a happy distraction. In 1944, my freshman year, Queens College could hardly be considered coed. Potential male students, eighteen and over, had all volunteered or been drafted. The boys who remained were young and callow, or older and self-consciously obnoxious on account of being 4F. One of them, who could have fallen into either category, was a suitably unwashed artist named David who was greatly interested in painting me. At last a boy who didn't mind my not looking like Doris Day, I thought, flattered until he said, *"Nude."* Creep. I believe bourgeois prude was how he characterized me. Never mind. I knew better than to knuckle under to *that* one, though it did end the boy possibility for a while. I muddled on through the first term, learning all about research papers and footnotes from another married teacher with three names, and in between semesters headed down to Florida again to join my parents, leaving a protesting Julia to register for me for my spring courses. (As it turned out she took a fiendish delight in picking Basketball and Tumbling for my gym course.)

As usual the Silver Meteor was crowded with soldiers, sailors, marines, and large Jewish families, who were eating salami and chasing children up and down the aisle. But this time I struck oil in the shape of a trim, blond, and gorgeous naval officer, who sat down next to me in the morning right after the train had pulled out of Jacksonville. That this male vision of delight was obviously Gentile was made even clearer by his courteous, gentle, and considerate manner as we began to talk. After a while, gold braid shining, he invited me to the diner for lunch, and after that to the club car, where drawn ever closer by the passage of time and endless bottles of beer, we separated only to stagger to the toilets at either end of the car. I was in my Sookie's wedding mode and pretending to be a college *senior*, which even so, judging by his sweet smile, made me years younger than he. He was in turn not only a naval officer, but a doctor, from the Midwest (fascinating, a true American), and not only that but also, as he had made clear from the beginning, married. This last part mattered to me not at all. I had no desire to marry him, only to be in love with him forever. It was wartime, and I had seen enough movies to know how these things worked.

Actually, there *was* a fly or two in our ointment. For one thing, he was not only Gentile, but a Catholic. And not only

Catholic, but a German Catholic. As he asked if he could see me again, perhaps take me to dinner (yes, yes, yes!), there arose a nagging vision of Mama and Papa waiting at the train station, ready to whisk me off to their strictly kosher fuschia-colored hotel. Maybe I could slip him past them. Better yet, slip myself past them. "Henry," I said, sighing. "My friends call me Harry," he said, smiling. Harry? Strange. It was a name that I had hitherto associated only with uncles. I asked him his last name. "Weiss," he said, rearing back a bit when I cried. "Weiss? Your name is *Harry Weiss?*" Oh, there was a God. As the train pulled into the station my parents waited for me in their Miami Beach outfits. Mama in a wide, flowery, mumu type of garment and Daddy in a sports jacket, his rabbinical head covered by a golf cap. (Had I told Harry my father was a rabbi? I could no longer remember.) My mother's jaw dropped as I poured down the train steps with my naval Adonis. "Harry Weiss," I said clearly. "*Doctor* Weiss," deepening my mother's incredulous stupor. My father extended his hand in a manly welcome-to-the-family fashion. Unfortunately, if there was a God, he was a malignant one, with a very Jewish sense of humor, since my father was now inviting Harry to dinner at our hotel the next night and Harry was delightedly accepting.

This time he appeared in his *white* naval uniform, and my mother came out of her fresh swoon long enough to look around triumphantly at the other mothers with daughters sitting in the hotel lobby. My father, on the other hand, seemed tentatively to be putting two and two together. I no longer remember all the particulars of that dinner, only a terrible few. My father respectfully called Harry Doctor, but Harry also respectfully called my father Doctor. What actual Jew

ever addressed a rabbi as Doctor? Then Harry, offered a piece
of pumpernickel, said graciously that he had always been fond
of black bread. What normal Jew had ever addressed a piece of
pumpernickel as black bread? I dimly heard Harry further graciously advise my father that the lobsters in southern waters
were even better than those in the north. Why not bring up his
wife while he was at it? What Mama made of all this I'm not
sure, since she was still staring at Harry besotted. My father,
however, looked squarely at me as I brazenly said after dinner
that Harry and I would now go off and have a good time. The
look said, you got me this once, *ketzele*, but only because I'm a
patriot. Harry and I wandered off down to the beach hand in
hand and watched a silvery ocean in flux. It was all so incredibly perfect. The softly hissing sea, the tropical moon, the black
palm-tree fronds waving overhead. The tacit understanding
that we would never see each other again. Only, wartime had
nothing to do with it, whatever Harry thought. From my point
of view, it was that damn pumpernickel.

In April of 1945 Roosevelt died. An unbelievable tragedy. I
had never known any other president, and I had assumed I
would be voting for him in the next election when I would
have turned twenty-one. This was the first death in my family
since Zayde died, and it was far more serious and far reaching.
Obviously puny little Truman would soon be impeached, replaced with another grand patrician who would be a father to
us all, give fireside chats in an aristocratic accent. Then in
May the war was over. First in Europe. But this was hard to
believe too, since it seemed like a miracle. I whooped it up
and hollered in the living room with Julia and Millie, even
Mama, who came waddling in. But Daddy was missing. I

went into my parents' bedroom and there he sat very quietly tearing up the pages of a telephone book and dropping them out of the window. He was crying.

That window, as did all the windows in our apartment, looked down on Broadway where strangely, though it was midday, there were no cars or buses. Only pedestrians, flooding the avenue in increasing numbers, from all directions, as far as the eye could see. All kinds of people, civilians and servicemen, milling about and tooting New Year's Eve horns, grabbing each other at random and hugging and kissing. I went downstairs and got grabbed by a sailor in his whites and kissed too. Oh, it was glorious! For that one day, the best of all possible worlds. The world was safe again, Nazis would kill no more Jews, and all the brothers and husbands could come home. In July, the same joyous hysteria was repeated outside our windows on Broadway. Truman had dropped two big bombs on Japan and *poof!* the Japs had surrendered.

When things quieted down that summer, working again on the shul typewriter I wrote a story about a secretary in a synagogue. I called it "The Fruit of His Goodness," and I didn't know what to do with it, so I did nothing. I had sent Yossie the "Carousel" story in installments on V-mail to cheer him up when he first went overseas, and he had written back that it wasn't really a story, it was a vignette. This didn't cheer *me* up, but I was still under the impression that my big brother knew everything because he was a boy, and that his big words meant something. *Vignette* was right up there with *kudos*. Adding to my sense of strangeness and unease was the fact that my freshman research paper had now been chosen as a model and was being distributed as required reading in freshman English. The authorship was disguised with a pseudonym,

Judith Gordon, but that didn't disguise the reality that I couldn't answer the study questions now appended, such as "How does the author transcend the rules of punctuation?"

Never mind. The good news was that the servicemen had finally started to come back from overseas. Julia in fact had just even been reunited with her *basherte*. An infantry soldier named Israel Glasser. Characteristically, she spent the night before her wedding washing and ironing his underwear, which was khaki colored. The wedding ceremony itself was small and informal—she wasn't supposed to get married at all yet because Millie, older, was still unmarried, but wartime conditions were still deemed to prevail. Julia wore a short yellow brocaded dress. At Mama's insistence, I was maid of honor, in forest green satin, and walked down the shul aisle to cries from Irv's army mates and and old friends of "Shake it, but don't break it." Millie finally too married her soldier boy, an Army lieutenant whom she had originally picked up at Camp Tamiment, and went to live in Philadelphia, where her life got even dimmer than before, and she was renamed Midge. Best of all, from my own point of view, the boys were coming back to Queens College, servicemen on the GI Bill, older and if not wiser at least with military experience and travel under their belts. For a while, they even wore their uniforms to class, and it was very exciting to walk in and see soldiers and sailors seated at the school desks.

With this fresh restocking of the male population came a new vitality and excitement, especially in the art, music, and drama departments. By now I was well on my way, God help me, to being an outstanding English major, plus getting good marks in everything, even calculus, and trying to hide them.

But my social life was with the newly returned veteran arty crowd, some of whom were required to read my research paper and groused about it, though thank God they didn't know I had written it. I did try for a while to write a play with a boy named Myron Rubin, who had already bobbed his nose, and now changed his name to Mike Stewart. But our play, even before the first act was finished was clearly a total disaster, which didn't bother us much since the world was still all before us. It was wonderful not to regard boys as dates anymore, to see them on an equal basis, not have to dress up for them, to be taken as you were.

However, Mama was right about one thing. Proximity bred familiarity, and familiarity bred a lot of other things that weren't contempt. I fell madly in love with a gorgeous, stupid nineteen-year-old tenor, formerly of the U.S. Navy, who had glossy dark hair and big white teeth, often shown when he was doing his breathing exercises, which could have been taken for a series of agonized smiles. Gerald Muster was six feet four inches tall, which made him over a foot taller than I, and a foot and a half taller than Mama who, when she finally met him, looked up from the end of his necktie and said amiably, "Oy, I thought maybe a giant!" Gerald's mother took a less kindly view of me, perhaps because now that he was back from the war she wanted to keep him back, and because she had very high social standards. The Musters had once lived in the Bronx, but now lived in Forest Hills in an apartment with a dropped living room reached by descending several steps because, as Gerald said, quoting his mother, "We are not Bronx people." With Grandma, who had once lived in Harlem when it housed a prosperous white community, Gerald loved going to Schrafft's and eating sundaes from dishes resting on lacy white paper doilies. The father, a traveling furniture salesman, was away most of the time. The mother wore platform ankle-strap shoes and a silver fox jacket and a little hat with a big rose tilted over one eye, but she snottily asked Gerald if *I* always dressed like that. Like what? He couldn't say, only repeat cheerfully that Mommy disapproved. A typical Jewish arriviste yenta, I would have thought her, familiar with the type from my high school days, but Gerald had told me they weren't Jewish at all but Episcopalian. This news, far from extinguishing my ardor, made our relationship all the more titillating, since it wasn't encumbered by doomsday thoughts of marriage. There was also the guilty excitement of keeping the news from my father, whose antennae strangely didn't seem to be working in this case as they had with Harry Weiss.

I was making other forays into a Gentile world that I had only read about before, but that seemed to be thriving amid our faculty. There was Dr. Dighton, an elegant Shakespeare professor, who waved off a custodian bothering us when we stood talking overtime in the classroom with the words, "Away with you, my man." He owned a house in Princeton. He had a friend there named R. P. Blackmur to whom he said he would send one of my stories for evaluation, if I was seriously thinking of becoming a writer. There was Dr. Emery Holloway, who was an expert on Walt Whitman, which didn't match since Dr. Holloway wore a Hoover collar and pince-nez.

Above all there was Dr. Phyllis Bartlett, Oxford graduate, who walked in academic processions wearing what she called a mangy rabbit hood instead of ermine. She had perhaps the last of the boyish bobs and a space between her front teeth. She told me that as a mark of rebellion she had come out at a tea instead of at a debutante ball, and that her much-married absentminded father failed to recognize one of his ex-wives when he passed her on the street. Could one get any more Gentile than that? From time to time she invited me to dinner, just the two of us. Her husband, some kind of traveling academic overseer, was often away. She referred to him as John, a far cry from my aunt Big Sarah's *"mein man Pollack,"* and smiled fondly upon John's Yale chair, which was featured in the living room. An original by Mary Cassatt, a painter I had never heard of, hung above the fireplace, and Dr. Bartlett gave me tips on how best to polish brass and also clean old family diamonds. She also plied me with martinis which she mixed in a little Italian earthenware jug and kept cold in the fridge. They looked innocent, but were so potent I staggered after her into the dining room for a dinner that featured avocados cut up in a vinaigrette sauce (I had never tasted avocados before) and a large broiled steak, dripping blood, that she cut in slices and served from the platter. I had never seen a steak big enough to cut in slices before or served that way. Oh, this was it! This was what one should aspire to! Would I ever be able hold the martinis? And what about this sudden feeling of loneliness, this sense that I had awakened in a place and didn't know how I got there?

My friends also wanted to live lives they had only seen in the movies, be great painters, great conductors, composers, actors. (Only I harbored vague ambitions of being a published *writer* some day, and this was hush hush anyway.) My best friend was Rosalie Golden, a plump, lusty and busty girl, who wore heavy pancake makeup and mascaraed her eyes all around in the style of Theda Bara. Her burning ambition was to be a chanteuse in a nightclub, which meant abandoning her widowed mother to a solitary life in the Bronx, no easy matter, since the mother had many pretensions of her own, including fancying herself a Russian aristocrat. Rosalie's boyfriend was an older man, in his late twenties. He came from a rich Jewish family in the South, which he had just left to move to New York, and he wore a suede jacket that impressed us very much and for which he kept a brush in his pocket.

Rosalie and her boyfriend and Gerald and I went tea dancing at the Plaza. This we considered the height of social elegance, what with the potted palms and string ensemble renderings and all. Except that we were so drunk Rosalie's ankle-strap shoes were splayed off to the side as she waltzed around. When it snowed Gerald and I walked from Flushing to Forest Hills, no matter how heavy the snowfall, because it seemed such a romantic thing to do. Or else, equally romantic, we wandered around Greenwich Village at night to and from his useless singing lessons. (Gerald's tenor was unalterably terrible, which didn't faze him a bit.) Then there were Balanchine's new ballets at the City Center, which was only a block away from where I lived, and new versions of old operas translated into English, which caused raging controversies in the college music department. We also went to any number of free Easter and Christmas oratorios in churches, where Gerald showed me how to behave, when to stand up and sit down, put money in the collection plate. (I refused to kneel.) The most romantic times were in Town Hall, at the early Sunday evening chamber concerts presented by the New Friends of Music, after which Gerald and I would repair to Rumplemeyer's, as the right thing to do. We also heard Lotte Lehmann in countless final farewell recitals. At the end of them someone always came running down the aisle to present her with a silver rose, in honor of *Der Rosenkavalier*, and she always acted surprised.

Though I was on the E train, often traveling back and forth several times a day, it felt as if I really had gone away to college. Flushing certainly acted like the country. When it snowed, the bus that met the subway couldn't get up the hills. In spring, students lay sprawled out sunbathing on the quadrangle lawn. Cocks crowed in the agricultural school just beyond campus. Trees budded, flowers bloomed. Gerald and I held hands when the lights went out in art history. I was dying to have Gerald relieve me of my virginity, but there was no place to do it. My parents were home all the time. His apartment was often empty, but he wouldn't dream of doing such a thing in "Mommy's house," as he put it.

Rosalie finally provided the solution. In a desperate effort to establish her independence from the Bronx and her mother, Rosalie had secretly rented a tiny little room with a shared hall bathroom on Eighth Street in a building across from the red adobe Whitney Museum. She lent me the key. Gerald agreed that we should try it. After several false starts and stops, including an intermission to go out and buy Vaseline at Whelan's, it *happened!* It hurt like hell, there was blood on the sheets. I had never been so happy in my life. To be so conjoined with another person, to be so conjoined with my gorgeous Gerald. To my surprise he immediately fell asleep, though I was incredibly wide awake. He explained groggily on the subway uptown afterward that this happened with men. Another mystery unveiled. The next day, to my further surprise, I found it was hard to sit down. Again, a wonderful revelation, a souvenir of the extraordinary thing that had happened. And then in the college cafeteria at lunchtime, Gerald greeted me with a husbandly kiss on the cheek. Did all our friends understand what this signified? I wanted to tell the whole world.

Unfortunately, the little kiss on the cheek was a bad omen,
since like many husbands Gerald turned out to be not faithful. In fact, in his eagerness to get ahead in the music world
my boy was something of a whore, I discovered. Aging divas
delighted in him. But that wasn't all. One night, when my
parents were out for a change, and we had made love on my
pullout sofa bed, he told me he was gay. Since he appeared
quite depressed at the time, I was surprised. He explained the
term. I told him not to give it another thought. Who of us in
adolescence, which we were both just out of, hadn't had some
unwelcome thoughts, even maybe experimented a little? Sighing, Gerald began to take me on walks along Lexington Avenue, point out bars frequented only by a male clientele. He
explicated such terms as "cruising" and "rough trade." None
of this made the slightest impression on me. I cheerfully consoled him, confident that I could easily cure him. Anyway, it
wasn't men I was jealous of—I couldn't even imagine what
that was all about—only other women.

Meantime, Yossie's *basherte* had also miraculously appeared.
He too had come back from the Army having risen to the exalted rank of private first class, and was now occupying the
maid's room in a big way. Sometimes he didn't emerge until
three in the afternoon. He was part of what now was called
the problem of the returned war veteran. Except that Yossie
had never known what to do with himself. For the present he
had abandoned the Great American Novel and was applying
himself strictly to the visual arts. And the little maid's room
was now littered with abandoned oil paintings and abandoned

clay heads from whose detritus Mama happily made miniature challahs and tea sets the way she did with the melted
Chanukah candle wax.

From the time I was quite little, Yossie and Sookie and
Millie had schlepped me to Group Theater productions of
Odets and I had instinctively understood what these plays
were about because my sisters and my brother were so totally
Odetsian themselves. Dreamers defeated by the Depression.
Yossie continued in this vein, actually the only remaining suffering practitioner. Millie was now out of the running because
she lived in Philadelphia and Odets was strictly New York.
Sookie, being married to a doctor, no longer counted either—
maybe if she had married a dentist?—or rather counted too
definitively. She had proved that artistic aspiration and personal yearning were doomed to failure and nobody else had
better try it. And so Yossie continued to sleep late, then wander off God knew where. Nobody asked him because he was
a boy. When he was home and not painting or sculpting he
would busy himself inventing quite clever things, such as
packages of Kleenex small enough to put in your pocket or
canned gefilte fish, which he was sure would make his fortune.
Maybe they would have, but he never pursued them, feeling
that having dreamed them up was enough. Or sometimes he
would decide to take me out to dinner as if I were a date—
though it was actually Daddy's money—and we would go to
some place on Broadway called Trader Something and get
stinking drunk on concoctions complete with parasols, fancy
names, and lethal ingredients. We considered getting so
drunk very funny and marveled at Yossie's daring in ordering
such drinks in the first place—it was kind of like the way he
was always the first to use big useless words.

And then, lo and behold, one day Yossie, who had previously contented himself making unwelcome passes at his sisters' girlfriends, brought home a girlfriend of his own. She was a refugee, from Austria via England, young, almost exactly my age, nineteen. In fact we kind of resembled each other, except that she was heavier and had strawberry blond hair. Beyond that any resemblance ended. Sylva not only had a strong Germanic English accent—I loved to hear her roll out the words, "b*rrr*usell sp*rrr*outs," a vegetable she had long experience with—she had a million relatives named Herta or Hans, who all lived in Washington Heights. Above all, she had a mother, but *no* father, a condition unfathomably awful to me. She had last seen her father when she was twelve, and he was released from Buchenwald on condition that he leave Austria immediately. She opened the door to an old man she didn't recognize, and then he vanished into Shanghai, where he died. I couldn't imagine having a father who had turned into an old man without my knowing it, I couldn't imagine a father who vanished, either. I didn't want to imagine it.

But Sylva quickly became Americanized, certainly as far as consumer goods were concerned. This included acquiring a new wardrobe from Daddy's wholesale connections, and a good-sized diamond engagement ring. Daddy had also bought me, unasked, a rust-colored suede coat, and Sylva wanted one too. Desperately. Her yearning was kind of reminiscent of my aunt Goldie and the coat with the silver fox collar. But here Daddy stood firm. Sylva didn't understand that Daddy's devotion to family was to *his* family and anything he did for her was only for Yossie's sake. So poor Sylva's attempts to find another father failed, both in respect to my brother who was fifteen years her senior but was too busy being a son to be anybody's father, and Daddy, who considered that she was trying to poach on my turf. Personally, I would have been only too happy to get him off my case and on to Sylva's. But it didn't work that way.

Sylva was also unsuccessful in trying to join Yossie on his exalted intellectual level. She dutifully accompanied him to the Museum of Modern Art and tried to make the right noises. But when it came to art appreciation on her own, standards plummeted. Once she told me she had gone to the Radio City Music Hall to hear Erno Rapee and his orchestra and though she didn't remember the name of the piece or the composer it was so beautiful. When I looked at her dubiously, she said, "Don't you like music?" A war casualty all right. A perfectly good-natured, very pretty girl adrift in a sea of neurasthenic Litvaks. She would have been so happy back in Vienna with her doting father the accountant, who gave her a charm for her bracelet every time she passed a school test. She still had the bracelet and there weren't that many charms on it. What bemused me most was that her last name was Sperling, and that when she filled out applications it had to come out Sperling, Sylva. But these speculations didn't last long. After much sturm und drang on Yossie's part, she and Yossie finally got married. But there were so many names crowded onto the invitation—this was no genteel WASP wedding, after all—that a lot of the invitees, who didn't know my real name anyhow, assumed that I was the bride and sent me checks. Since they were meant for me, there was a moral case to be made for my keeping them, but Yossie didn't see it that way.

Then, while Yossie was still off on his honeymoon, there was another bolt from the blue. A letter came from a DP camp in

Bari, Italy. It was written in Yiddish in a spidery hand and
signed Josef Birstein. Not only was the first name the same as
that of my brother and several cousins, incredibly, the last
name was spelled exactly like ours too. To clinch the matter,
the letter was accompanied by a small, but clear photo of a
young man who bore a strong resemblance to my father. Josef
said he was the son of my father's brother Shlomo and that he
was the only one left. He gave his weight in stones and described his eyes as beer colored.

I kept staring at the picture. Viennese refugees marrying
among us were one thing, but I had never counted our own
real family among the six million, never realized that any survivor might actually be related to us. My parents' relatives left
behind in Europe had become ancient history to me. "It's a
miracle, a miracle!" I cried to anyone who would listen, as
usual taking the spiritual uplift of the matter on my own
shoulders. Daddy's response to the sudden emergence of this
nephew was surprisingly subdued. It took awhile to dawn on
me that though I had forgotten my father's side of the family
my father never did and had instituted the search for survivors
in the first place. Never mind. Insufficiently ecstatic as everyone else might be, I would be Josef's savior. I studied the picture, found out how many pounds were in a stone, translated
beer colored to hazel. I would make it up to poor Josef. I
would be the one person who understood him. He would be
my cause. Nobody else was left at home anyway. Also, Gerald,
Rosalie, and all the rest of them, though respectful when I
spoke of my intentions, began to seem hopelessly shallow, college not a part of real life, real history, real suffering.

Finally, my father's connections came through. The man
who had managed to get bottles of Canadian Club during the

war, a new Buick right afterwards, at last succeeded in ex-
tracting his nephew from the DP camp. The day of Josef's ar-
rival I cut classes and stood with my parents at a huge cold
pier, surrounded by other waiting relatives, watching the mea-
ger trickle of refugees emerge from the ship. They were all
sizes and all ages, shabby, but somehow more formally dressed
than they were in the newsreels. They were all even wearing
proper hats. But they had also all been tagged, like children,
orphans, flotsam and jetsam tossed up from the sea. Then our
name was called and there was Josef in a raincoat and brown
fedora, carrying a single suitcase. There were kisses and greet-
ings exchanged in Yiddish. He looked just like his picture,
and in that raincoat and fedora might have seemed romantic
and mysterious like someone in a foreign film, except for that
stupid tag dangling from his lapel. When we settled into a
cab, the first thing I did was unpin it, a gesture that startled
him. "You won't need this anymore," I told him in English,
my speaking command of Yiddish having left me on account
of the drama of the occasion. Josef had very little English but
he gave me a long look, then a smile. We had leaped over language barriers. We had connected.

After dinner, at which Josef agreed with my mother, who
insisted on showing off, that the food and the furniture and
everything else was *"shayne, zayer shayne,"* he answered some
of the questions that hadn't been asked in our letters, and
some that had. Yes, he was the only one left. Did he ever go
back to Brest-Litovsk, I wanted to know, and find his old
house? Find his old house? He couldn't even find the street. It
was all ruins. He talked a bit about the DP camp and how
they would wander around the streets of Bari and say, "It's a
beautiful world, but not for us." Then he opened his suitcase

and began to extract presents. Heartbreakingly many presents it seemed from one small bag that otherwise contained all he owned. Among other things was an embroidered linen table-cloth, which Mama loved though Daddy was frowning. A gold pen, but Mama didn't write very much. A cameo, but Mama had a bigger one with a diamond. Then a small gold watch that Josef handed to me directly. Daddy snatched it away. Horrified, I tried to snatch it back again, but Daddy was adamant. "Save it," he told Josef, "save it for someone else." I couldn't believe how cruel and insensitive my father could be. I was really having to revise my opinion of this man all the time.

Josef was installed in Yossie's now vacated maid's room. He emerged in pajamas and a hairnet to wish us all good night. He smelled faintly of pomade. His hair had deep waves up front, and he was evidently anxious to preserve them. He also had a long pinkie nail, like Fu Manchu's, that he said was very useful as a kind of tool to press things down with. These were details I passed over quickly.

What I imagined Josef would do with himself now that he was installed in our apartment I have no idea. But it was a shock when I returned home from college the next day to find him sitting in my room, in my armchair, reading a magazine. He put it down and smiled expectantly. I greeted him cordially and then didn't know what to do. This was when I usually set-tled down to do homework, write papers. Could I ask him to read his magazine in the living room until I had finished? That didn't seem polite, and besides he had clearly been waiting for me. In my broken Yiddish I tried to tell him about school, that I would bring him with me to meet my friends and professors, but what he understood was uncertain. He kept smiling. That night Daddy said he was trying to find Josef a job, which seemed a bit premature, except what else was Josef supposed to do all day? The next afternoon I again found him sitting in my room, the room I had out waited the marriages of four siblings to claim for my own. He was also there the next day and for days after that. By now in spite of myself and all my grand intentions, my heart sank when I saw him. He was inert, heavy, like original sin. Also a kind of smart alec quality had crept into that smile, especially when he refused all subway directions for a visit to some relatives in the far reaches of the Bronx, saying he would walk, and most especially when he claimed that he had conned the Germans into accepting him into the German army. How was this possible? Daddy was by now wondering if this guy was his nephew at all, which was absurd. There was that unmistakable resemblance.

Then one night, I suddenly awoke to the distinct smell of pomade, and the silhouette of somebody sitting on the edge of my bed in pajamas and hairnet.

"Josef?"

"*Yuh.*"

"What do you want?"

"You're not afraid that I sleep in the next room?"

"No."

"I am."

Oh, my god. I could almost hear that smile. I could certainly feel a hand on my blanket, in fact on my leg, but I buried myself under the covers and pretended that nothing had happened, that I had fallen asleep again. After a while Josef went away. In my high school yearbook I had said I was going to do reconstruction work in Europe, but that night all my humanitarian impulses fled. In the morning, I am ashamed

to say, I blabbed to my father. That day when I came home
Josef wasn't there. He had been exiled to another relative in
Brooklyn. I felt guilty. I felt stupid. Worse, I realized that
Daddy had been right again. Obviously, Josef had assumed
that my father would never expend all that money and energy
to bring him over except to palm off the last remaining unwed
daughter. I supposed my father had suspected this all along,
but he certainly knew it when he grabbed that gold watch
away from me—I, the genius who had tried to snatch it back.

Returned from my exalted plane, more puzzled than wiser, I
was now back to helping Gerald write his term papers, which
continued borderline illiterate. But by now my reputation as
a hot shot English major was no longer a deep secret. (Gerald
was furious when a paper I had written for him in its entirety
got a C, when he was perfectly sure that if *my* name had been
on it, it would have gotten an A, which it probably would
have.) In my senior year I even sold my first novel—by mistake, as it were. I had written it as an honors thesis under the
guidance of Dr. Bartlett, who said merrily, "There are four-
teen weeks in the term, so you can write a chapter a week for
thirteen weeks and use the last week to revise." Which I did.
The next term, removing a notice from the English department bulletin board, I entered a contest I never expected to
win, and won. The Dodd Mead Intercollegiate Literary Fellowship, given for the best novel written by an undergraduate
in the entire country. ("Boy, are you lucky," Julia said, as if I
had won a lottery.) The news was in all the newspapers. My
book was called *The Fruit of His Goodness*, and contained the
short story I had written the summer before college on the
shul typewriter and didn't know what to do with. It was about

a rabbi's secretary and a synagogue. I didn't want to think about what my father would say when he read it.

Actually this problem was far fetched because it didn't look as if anyone was ever going to read it. On account of the fourteen-week schedule, the thing was very short. It wasn't even a novella, though, but a kind of shrunken-head little piece of fiction and I had no idea how to make a real book out of it. Nevertheless, it was the talk of the whole campus. A boy in one of my English classes said, "But we know who the real writer is, don't we?" Paolo Milano, a short, fat, bald professor of comparative literature, who managed to get the more intellectual girls interested in him, advised me sagely to keep the faith, not to sell out. Since Dodd Mead was most known for its august backlist, which featured George Bernard Shaw and Winston Churchill, I wasn't sure how I would sell out even if I wanted to. But I didn't want to, that was the point, and, deeply moved, I told him I wouldn't.

Everything was turning into a movie or a novel anyhow, including the lunch at the Yale Club with Dr. Bartlett— thrilling enough in itself—when I was actually called to the phone by someone who wanted to interview me. There were many more interviews. At one, under the supervision of my publisher Tommy Dodd, but also under the influence of too many martinis amid potted palms at the Hotel Vanderbilt, I complained about my Chaucer professor, who had spitefully given me a C because I hadn't ever finished my term paper, though all the other English professors had excused me. The Chaucer professor, and his name, Robert Pratt, was amusingly mentioned in the column, leaving me to wonder how many martinis I had had, and where was Tommy Dodd when I was shooting my mouth off? Laughing, probably. There were also radio interviews, to which Mama and Daddy accompanied me, Mama wearing a big orchid, for reasons that are now obscure. The Jewish press got in on it too. In the *Forward,* my photo was vague and fuzzy, my father's loomed large and clear. The quote from Daddy, in Yiddish, was: "If I could be a rabbi at twenty, why shouldn't my daughter be a writer at twenty-one?" He still hadn't bothered to read the work in question. I had carefully left the manuscript on his desk but, after about six weeks, dusted off the binder and took it back.

I waited until I actually had turned twenty-one to sign my book contract, not wanting Daddy to get in on this act too. It turned out I hadn't actually won prize money, but gotten an advance of $1200, which in fact could be asked for back. Then it was graduation time. A very goyish-sounding professor called to say he was Master of Ceremonies of the occasion and as such would have the honor of inviting my father to deliver the invocation and benediction. Would I mind telling him what seminary my father had been ordained at, so that they could order the proper robe? I took a certain grim pleasure in saying, "The Slobodka Yeshiva," and having to repeat it several times, until the Master of Ceremonies said, "Yes, of course." Then I sat down to write the necessary invocation and the benediction—"fix them up," as Daddy put it. There followed a discussion about whether he should wear his yarmulke under the mortar board or quickly put it on when he had to take the mortar board off. He could never not wear a yarmulke, of course, and there wasn't a chance in hell he'd eschew the mortar board. He decided to wear the yarmulke underneath and grab it if it started to slip off.

After we graduates had all assembled in our rows, the academic procession filed in, my father in robe and mortar board right up near the front. The gown they had produced was interesting. It had long peaked sleeves, like a medieval alchemist's robe. I think they rented it from a road company doing Molière. I won many prizes, and my musician friends in the chorus, including Gerald, clapped and whistled every time I stepped up to the podium. But the big winner was my father, who afterward introduced me to President Klapper and told him how smart I was, rather like Mama on Open School Night, then walked off for the faculty and dignitary reception to which I was naturally not invited, airily waving good-bye as he left, Mama waddling alongside. I'm not sure what I did afterward. I probably went home with Gerald, and probably we celebrated. But underneath was the dark knowledge that what I had to do now, graduation or not, was turn that goddamn little shrunken prize winner into a novel.

Not having school to go to—most of my friends, especially the veterans and also Rosalie, who kept failing courses, were still there—I was incredibly lonely, damning the novel I was doomed to finish, and hating the day I had taken the literary contest notice off the wall. But it wasn't only my college years, but the whole world that seemed to be coming to an end, or at least turning upside down. For openers, Leonora Pearlstein, who somewhere along the line had transferred back to Queens College from a college in the Midwest, went crazy. She wrote a term paper in two different voices, alternating them line by line, and then was found on top of one of the lions in front of the New York Public Library, singing "Give a cheer for the Jones Junior High." Scared that we might be crazy too without knowing it, we all started to go to psychiatrists. I wound up with a swarthy Greek, and after my first session, I asked, thinking I was being cute, "Aren't you going to say God bless you, my child?" He, on the other hand, had a predilection for saying, "It takes two to tango," a strange thing for a Greek. Gerald's was a Negro *woman*.

In other realms, Mike Stewart had written chanteuse material for Rosalie, which went over big at Queens College, but flopped miserably in an audition at a real nightclub. Rosalie's boyfriend had started a little magazine and was giving parties in the brownstone where he lived and where people kept going out to the dark stairwell to smoke what they called "tea." At one party everyone was adulating an extremely loony-looking guy with a weird expression and eyeglasses, who had been released from the bin for a weekend, a poet named Allen Ginsberg. Gerald's mother got cancer and begged him not to let her die. He took pictures of her in a skeletal state and showed them around. But then the whole world seemed to be full of death and skeletons. More and more of what had happened in the concentration camps was revealed. Stacks of cordwood corpses. Horrors beyond any imagining. Also, the bombs that had been dropped in Japan not only incinerated people on the spot, but were making the survivors die for years afterward.

For the eighteenth time I broke up with Gerald, and this time I meant it. He still wouldn't stop seeing the fat opera star he said smelled like a fish. After consultation with my shrink, I gave him an ultimatum. *His* shrink, the Negro lady, said he shouldn't accept ultimatums. His mother died and was buried from Riverside Memorial Chapel, the same place from which my father got a lot of referrals and that was the source of my first diary. Gerald said he was now composing a kaddish. I asked Gerald what an Episcopalian woman was doing being buried from Riverside Memorial Chapel, never mind the kad-dish, and naturally he confessed, laughing, that he was really Jewish. Hadn't I always realized it? Aside from wanting to kill him for lying to me for so long, this fact made Gerald sud-denly available and therefore no longer a forbidden passion. We broke up dramatically wearing evening clothes, having dressed formally to see a performance of *Kiss Me Kate* at the Ziegfeld Theater. Gerald's idea. (The musical was a sell out. Daddy had got us house seats.) We stayed up all night after-ward, and parted dramatically at dawn.

Then I slept with Leon Klein a few times, another Queens College music major, though unlike Gerald extraordinarily gifted. We did it in his car, which he drove out to hidden places in Westchester. However, I seemed not to know *what* to do. He was lying on the backseat, pants down, in the dark-ness. "Touch it," he said. *Touch it?* Was he mad? Actually, he was exasperated. I had thought he was the solution. We had never gotten on well when we were in school together, and so I assumed that as with Scarlett and Rhett our old antagonism would flame into passion. But it didn't quite work out that way. We also had sex on my sofa bed a few times, while my parents slept away in their bedroom. (I think. I hope.) The last time, Leon came inside me. "You *what?*" "Don't you want me and the baby?" "Are you out of your *mind?*" I got my pe-riod. I fell in love with Leon all over again, but he had gone away to teach at some music camp for the summer.

Somewhere along the line I met a young psychiatrist who introduced me to his friends, also young psychiatrists, still in training, and through some weird process of transference I began to go out with them singly or in a group. One of them kept getting analyzed for a bad cough—they had worked it back to his feelings about his father—until it turned out he had caught whooping cough from one of his child patients at Mount Sinai. Another one turned out to be in love with Maria, my old friend from high school who hated men. Another one had had a nineteen-year-old girlfriend who had been living by herself in her own apartment since the age of thirteen. She had recently committed suicide. The one I saw most often was George Shafler, a sober-minded, very literary type who took me to dinner at the Harvard Club, a fact that I relayed to my approving father. Mama, of course, couldn't get straight what kind of work George actually was in, until I explained that he was not only a doctor but a *specialist,* which did the trick. George and I went out quite often even though he had a bad habit of saying, "If you don't finish that novel I'll kill you," which wasn't his business. One night I took him to a party at Mike Stewart's apartment. Mike had left Queens and was now living in a Park Avenue studio with a very nice guy named Shelley. George seemed to be having a good time, so good that when I came back from getting a fresh drink in the kitchenette, I saw him in plain view, necking with a dancer on the sofa. A male dancer. Okay. Once I got over the shock—the guy was a *psychiatrist,* for god's sake—this merely confirmed the fact that I would never get married, since most of the guys I was likely to meet would be gay, anyway.

Luckily, my parents weren't around to pick up on this bleak vision of matrimony, since the congregation had sent them off to visit the new state of Israel. Daddy carefully studied from a modern Hebrew phrase book such sentences as, "What is the price of these tennis shoes?" They took a ship to France, visited Paris, and then sailed on to Israel. My father, of course, was in constant communication by cable throughout. It was all very exciting and scary. When they came back, Daddy was carrying, in addition to a million other presents, a lavender hat box. In it was a Paris hat for me. I had asked for a Paris hat and he had dragooned the wife of one of his show-business congregants who happened to be there to pick one out for me. It looked like hell on me, but it was beautiful to gaze at—black, sprinkled with some kind of jet bead stardust, and covered with veiling. Mama's view of Paris was not as glamorous. For one thing, she didn't see why all the fuss about French cooking. They had eaten in only kosher restaurants and so as far as she was concerned the French ate what we did: gefilte fish, chicken soup, stuffed kishke. She was also deeply disappointed in their hotel, which was very old and had old plumbing. She was right again, since the Hotel Crillion on the Place de la Concorde was indeed made over from a very old palace. Israel of course was the real point of their trip and that was unarguably marvelous. My father, an ardent Zionist since the advent of Hitler, had made a point of going everywhere, seeing everything, meeting everyone. Among the many souvenirs they had to prove it was a silk scarf for me, dense with Yemenite embroidery. ("They go blind making this," Mama said happily.) The only drawback to the trip as my father sadly reported, was that no matter where they were going or whom they were about to meet, including, as it happened, David Ben-Gurion, Mama only said, *"Ich muz gayn pishin."* (I have to go piss.)

I had already handed in one revision of my book, which was deemed lousy by my editor, Elizabeth Stille. In her report she called my secretary heroine "a husband hunter of the clumsiest variety." This was devastating, even worse than finding out in my freshman year that "fine writing" wasn't a compliment. I cried a great deal, and spent the next whole year trying to learn how to write. One thing I did was put the epithet about the heroine into the mouth of her boss, the rabbi, where it worked to great effect. Elizabeth thought so too, though she didn't remember she had written those scathing words to begin with. In fact, she thought the whole book worked now, and after some spitting and polishing, my novel was scheduled for publication. Naturally, the title, *The Fruit of His Goodness*, had to be changed because it sounded too religious, and we wound up with *Star of Glass*, which didn't sound like anything. And then there were long slippery sheets called galleys to contend with and printers marks I had to keep looking up in the back of the dictionary, and still got wrong. My novel was scheduled for fall publication.

That summer I went to the Kenyon School of English in Ohio, at the suggestion of my publisher, Tommy Dodd. It was a graduate summer program in literary criticism and why Tommy Dodd imagined I would be interested in literary criticism I didn't know, because I wasn't. In any case, the subject was immaterial. I had never actually been away to school, no matter what Queens College felt like, and the reality turned out to be as thrilling as I had anticipated. A real campus, in the heart of the Midwest, just as in the college musicals, and buildings covered with ivy. A tower clock that at intervals chimed bars of what someone explained were the same as Big Ben's, putting them all together on the hour. Normally Kenyon College was not coed, and so they housed the females in the Divinity School. The males were scattered in various dorms. Since I had been hanging around with pretty dopey music majors during my whole college career, I had never really known any serious academic heavy hitters. And these were very heavy—postgraduate students at that. The boys especially were even more intellectual than Leonora Pearlstein and Maria Shulman had been in high school, if that were possible, and they too, this time for academic reasons, considered that my having actually written a novel that was about to be published made me sort of primitive.

I supposed they were right. They certainly seemed to know much more about literature than I did. Irving Schmuckler said he intended to prepare for years before *he* wrote *his* first novel. I asked him what his favorite novel written by someone else was, and he told me *The Great Gatsby.* "Listen," I said, briefly snapping out of my humble state,"you wouldn't even say hello to a guy like Gatsby if you met him, much less write a book about him." Irving shook his head and went on to his next course. My humble state returned. Like most everyone else in the student body, Irving was in awe of our illustrious faculty and had read their critical works, though naturally I had never heard of most of them.

There was Arthur Mizener, in white buck shoes, who had just published a biography of F. Scott Fitzgerald, and William Empson with a long Chinese beard, who had written *Seven Types of Ambiguity*, and Kenneth Burke, who seemed to be a happy tinkerer, and an exponent of do-it-yourself criticism, L. C. Knights, an English critic who had written god knows what. (A midsummer ball game was played between the L. C. Knights and the Empson Ambiguities.) Plus two writers I *had* heard of, Robert Lowell and Delmore Schwartz. In Arthur Mizener's novel course I studied William Faulkner and Henry James. When we got to *The Ambassadors,* Lambert Strether's business was vaguely alluded to but never named, as if there were something infra dig about it. I wondered briefly if, like Izzy Pearlstein, he could be a furrier. I also took a course on the short story with Delmore Schwartz, who walked into class dripping cigarette ash and mumbling about Pogo in the comics and the New York Giants, who were his favorite baseball team. But with all the mumbling and ash dripping he made some memorably illuminating points about the art of fiction. Irving Schmuckler said, shaking his head again, "You're taking the easy courses, all you have to do is read the work," as if that were shameful.

Besides going to classes, we had a very active social life. Students and faculty had lots of parties in which they mingled and wound up getting drunk a lot of the time. Robert Lowell in one fit of madness chased his wife, Elizabeth Hardwick, across the campus. Kenneth Burke had to be shoveled out from under the sink in somebody's house where he had passed out from too much booze. Biancamaria Bosco, a visiting student from Rome, was late with a paper and we spent some time teaching her a real Italian accent—which she didn't have, but such as I had learned on Forty-seventh Street—to make her instructor believe she was a helpless foreigner. There was much visiting between the male dorms and the Divinity School, and at the end of the summer I drove home with Martin Williams, a Southern gent who was scared of Jewish girls, but thrilled with them, and who circled me like a lit match around a cigar, hoping and not hoping I would catch fire. He deposited me somewhat disdainfully at West Fifty-fourth Street.

Biancamaria, who came to stay for a week on her way back to Italy, delighted my father who called her "I Go Bianca" because of her willingness to go anywhere, try anything. Once, though, she had to call from Macy's to get directions on how to come back because the first five people she asked didn't speak English. Leon Klein seemed to be out whenever I called him at his new job at NBC Opera. Finally, actual copies of my book arrived. Ten free ones, as agreed on in my contract. The front cover was terrible, all muddy green and brown with a Jewish star stuck in the middle. The picture of me on the back cover was equally terrible. It had been taken by Bachrach, a connection of my father, naturally, and a celebrated photographer of engaged girls. But it made *me* look as if anybody who got engaged to me had to be crazy. Inside the front cover was a list of previous winners of the Intercollegiate Literary Fellowship, including Frederick Morton of City College. Bound into the back was a full page ad for another Dodd Mead book, *Good Morning Miss Dove.* I gave away four of my free copies to my siblings, who characteristically remained wary and silent, and inscribed a fifth copy to my parents, who were already the recipients of a fulsome and lying formal dedication. I waited for the shoe to fall, and finally it did.

One day, my father looked up from his desk in the living room as I was passing by. He had read my book. He was pissed. *Hurt,* he put it. "Is this what you think of me?"

"No, it isn't. It's fiction." (My first use of this defense.) "But why didn't you read it before?" I said. "That manuscript gathered dust on your desk for six weeks, and you didn't even notice when I took it away."

I didn't point out that he had nevertheless been happy enough to stick his two cents into all my interviews.

"I'll tell you a story," my father said. "A young man is engaged to a beautiful and cruel young woman. 'Cut out your mother's heart and bring it to me,' she says. 'Otherwise I won't stay engaged to you.' So he goes and cuts out his mother's heart. But on the way back to bring it to his fiancée, he trips—"

Long pause. My father looked at me.

"—and the mother's heart cries out, 'Are you hurt, my child?'"

Dirty pool. But he always had a way with parables.

Big Joe from Clarksburg, West Virginia, wanted to know if my book was going to be in Macy's window. *Macy's window?*

"Local girl," he said.

Chapter 4

$\mathcal{M}$Y BOOK HAD COME OUT to no acclaim whatever. Nothing in my life had changed. I was applying for fellowships to graduate schools, and for a Fulbright. The Fulbright application was one of two new attempts at fiction. The first was another novel—though I had sworn to myself never to write another novel—frankly autobiographical this time, about a twelve-year-old girl in a poor New York neighborhood. After some thought I named her Cookie. I was still writing mostly in longhand, though I had gotten a Royal portable typewriter as a graduation present. The Fulbright was a more serious fictional attempt, since I wanted to go to France—Sookie's *"Lafayette, je suis ici!"* had made its mark on me. But on what basis could a former English major, whose only claim to fame was one published novel, also in English, ask for a fellowship to go to France? I thought and thought and finally came up with a study of post-World War II American expatriates in France. I didn't know if there were any, but it sounded good, even if it was probably meaningless.

Otherwise, life was at a standstill. I was still living at home. Leon was totally out of the picture, I heard he was going out with his boss's daughter. Gerald, who was still in college, called once for help with a term paper, which I did not give him, to

his astonishment. This had never happened before. I sub-
scribed to a clipping service, which fetched up tiny items here
and there, and also a very long review of my book in *Commentary*, which I didn't understand. I couldn't even tell if the
reviewer liked it, since it really wasn't about my book at all, but
seemed to be some kind of treatise on rabbi's wives. But it was
written in an authoritative tone by somebody named Midge
Decter. So authoritative, it seemed impossible that she might
also have come to Midge by way of Malke Leah, aka Mildred.
Aside from that, zero. This was not how it happened in the
movies, or for that matter in other novels.

Perhaps my editor felt this way too, because in October
she called and said that I wasn't getting enough literary attention and that I should come to dinner and meet a critic she
knew. This didn't sound very appealing, since she also said he
was rather humorless and a hypochondriac. Added to that was
the fact that the invitation was for the thirteenth. But obviously it was an invitation I should accept. There was the usual
question about what to wear. I decided on a mustard-colored
knit dress Daddy and I had bought wholesale, but took off the
bow. It made it less stylish, but this was a serious occasion. I
also figured I should bring either flowers or candy—I decided
on flowers—because that was what you did when somebody
invited you to dinner. Otherwise there was no precedent for
this in my experience.

Elizabeth's apartment was unlike anything I had ever seen
before, in Greenwich Village, up several flights of carpeted
stairs. We were not talking about a railroad flat in a tenement
here. The furniture was light wood and modern—not mod-
erne like Julia's sectional sofa that kept separating under
you—airy, with caned chairs and bits of chrome and leather.

The walls were painted white and had abstract prints and paintings on them. It was all quite spare, with nothing extra. In keeping with this theme, Elizabeth was stirring an old-fashioned with her finger. Her husband, on the other hand, was short and pudgy, and quite abundant in other ways, including his over juicy Italian accent. It was Italian like Biancamaria's, not like the ones on Forty-seventh Street. His name was Mischa, odd for an Italian, because his family background was Russian. Also Jewish, as it turned out. To me, weaned on Irvings and Abes and Hymies, Mischa was as much an odd name for a Russian Jew as it was for an Italian.

Elizabeth accepted my flowers with pleasure, if some surprise. In return she offered me an old-fashioned, stirring this one with her finger too. Obviously, in advanced circles bad manners were good manners. It was a small apartment, but there were no signs of cooking or of dinner. Elizabeth had put copies of my book on all available surfaces, including the coffee table. Mischa said that Elizabeth liked my book a lot, and I took this as a great show of noblesse oblige on his part. There was no hint of *his* liking it or intending to read it and I would have been amazed if there were, since in spite of his name and the juicy fruit Italian accent, he was acting very much like a Jewish husband toward Elizabeth, which was to say as if she were an inferior species. It was interesting that Gentile wives with important jobs could also be treated this way. A half hour later, there was still no one else there. Had I been mistaken about the critic as well as the dinner? If so, it was a relief. The three of us were talking easily by now and laughing about something, when Elizabeth finally went to answer the doorbell. A man came in behind her and said, accusingly, "What were you laughing about?" Then, accepting a chair and coughing, added, "I have a cold." Humorless hypochondriac seemed to be accurate.

The critic's name was Alfred Kazin, and he was scary. I didn't understand all he immediately started talking about. He talked very fast, but though he was okay with Elizabeth, he addressed Mischa in the same superior manner in which Mischa addressed his wife. Mischa took umbrage, and soon they were in an argument, about what I couldn't say. Artists, literature, or maybe politics? The sound of it was a little bit like Daddy and the Communist uncles, though of course that was a stupid idea under the circumstances. Trying to mediate, Elizabeth chimed in. By now I didn't really know what anyone was talking about, but it didn't matter. I might just as well not have been there, though I had been sitting in the same place for well over an hour. I decided that I had been wrong about being invited to dinner—in a normal household we would have been finished eating by now—and was wondering if I was maybe expected to leave, when the argument abated, and Mr. Kazin took a quick sidelong glance at me, and said, "Nice legs."

I had been introduced back into the company, though not quite the way I had expected. Elizabeth immediately shoved one of the copies of my book that she had carefully placed on the coffee table toward him. He immediately shoved it away, saying idly, "Is this the first novel that was panned in *Commentary*?" Panned? Had the review that wasn't about my book at all been a pan?

"It's a wonderful novel and it hasn't been getting sufficient literary attention," Elizabeth said, pushing *Star of Glass* back toward him. Mr. Kazin shoved it away again.

"What about dinner?" he said. "Just because you're Italian, Mischa, doesn't mean we all have to eat at midnight."

It turned out we were going to dinner in a restaurant. This was a new wrinkle too, to be invited to somebody's house to eat *out*. Elizabeth had a car and we all piled in and drove to a place in Little Italy I have ever since thought was called Alfredo's, though it probably wasn't, a very busy restaurant with lots of noise and waiters hoisting trays. We sat down and eventually ordered. I still wasn't a major player in the conversation, but Mr. Kazin was seated opposite from me, talking when he wasn't eating, eating when he wasn't talking, sometimes doing both at the same time, and so I had a chance to study him. He seemed pretty old, which to me he was. But so did Mischa and Elizabeth. Thirty-five, he told me later. His dark hair was close cropped, his nose was large, there were two sad lines running along either side of his face from the edge of his nostrils down to his chin, and his eyes, though a piercing light hazel green, were Oriental in shape. Was he handsome? No, not like Gerald, or for that matter Leon, and certainly not like a movie star. But he sure was authoritive, and so absorbed in whatever he was saying, that at one point I was impelled to lean across and save the cuff of his jacket from dipping into his spaghetti sauce. He glanced at me briefly, then glanced away, still talking. He also, since everybody smoked in those days, pocketed my package of Philip Morris, which happened to be lying on the table near his. After a while, I timidly asked him for a cigarette. He gave me one and said, "Why don't you buy your own?" I said, "Those *are* my own," and he said, "Possessive, aren't you?" I didn't know what to say. If somebody took something away that was yours, was it still yours if they gave it back as their gift? Almost as puzzling was the fact that he kept referring to himself as a writer. I had been given to understand he was a critic.

But the evening was more and more thrilling. I had never met any people who talked like this before, who eschewed good manners, intellectual or the other kind, as it pleased them. I had never met in a purely social situation any kind of a real writer before, critic or otherwise. Around midnight, we piled back into Elizabeth's car and she drove me home, swerving every once in a while so that I was thrown against Mr. Kazin, who was sitting in the back seat next to me. Each time he accepted my polite apology. Maybe it was the old fashioneds, or the wine, but after a while I kept hoping that the car would keep swerving.

I went to bed, imagining the day maybe ten years hence— yes, it would take at least ten years—when, now a famous writer myself, I would run into Alfred Kazin at a literary party and say, "You won't remember this, but we met one evening long ago at—" And then I fell asleep. When I woke up, late in the morning, the phone was ringing and it was Mr. Kazin, and my life had changed forever. And so had his.

We made a date for the next day, Sunday. He was going to a cocktail party nearby and said I should meet him afterward at the Barbizon Plaza over at Fifty-sixth and Sixth. No picking me up at home and meeting Mama and Papa for this man. That was understood. He looked even older than on Friday night, in a navy blue raincoat with the collar turned up, the clown lines running from his nose to his chin sadder and deeper. We went to dinner in a French restaurant nearby, and he introduced me to a drink called a Gibson, which was like a martini, only with an onion instead of an olive. I kept my pack of Philip Morris near me. I was still puzzling over that one. The Gibsons seemed to be stronger than martinis, stronger than the old-fashioneds. Soon we were telling each other we liked music. He began to tell me about his life. *My* life, the Broadway rabbi's daughter part, which fascinated most people, he had early on dismissed as not sufficiently interesting or consequential. His own young years had been spent in grinding poverty in Brooklyn, his mother a struggling dressmaker, his father a struggling house painter. Those years and the Depression had made an indelible mark on him. He had already been married twice, once to a wonderful woman he appeared to have outgrown, the second time, briefly, to a coldhearted bitch from whom he was legally separated. This union had produced a son, now a little boy of two and a half. (A *son*. He was a father! Thrilling.) His most terrible memory was of leaving the house and looking back to see the child, diapers hanging down, clinging bewildered to the doorknob. Only a passion for books had kept Mr. Kazin going. His passion for books would always be his only salvation. It was incredibly moving to hear of this lifetime of struggle, a lifetime of being misunderstood.

"You're not eating," Mr. Kazin said accusingly.

I wasn't. Anything could distract me from food, and this was more than distracting. But he was frowning, clearly there was something frivolous in my indifference to my dinner. I half-expected him to tell me people were starving in Europe. I ate as much as I could—I hadn't imagined that food would matter to someone so rooted in the life of the mind—and then, dinner over, he suggested a walk. He loved to walk, he said, and actually so did I. We wandered over to Central Park South, a few blocks away, and into the park itself, a safe thing to do in those days. It was a beautiful fall night, made romantic and hazy by the lamplight. We stopped to look at the ducks silently swimming past in the black pond. All time was suspended. I didn't know what to do or feel. Then he kissed me. It was a long close-mouthed kiss.

"Oh, Mr. Kazin," I said. I didn't think that the kissing with our mouths closed had put us on a first-name basis.

We started to walk again, this time to his apartment, which was on the ground floor in a building on East Fifty-eighth Street, near the Queensboro Bridge. He let us in, but didn't turn on the lights. We kissed again, no longer with closed mouths. My coat wound up on the floor. He put his hand underneath my skirt and my panties and made me come standing up.

"Do you always come so easily?" he asked.

Wasn't I supposed to? The subject had never been discussed before. We were moving back toward the bed, whose dark bulk I could make out against the wall.

I was now in my slip, perched on the edge of the daybed. The lights were on. Alfred (I supposed I really couldn't call him Mr. Kazin anymore) was in a maroon paisley bathrobe seated in the only arm chair, a manuscript in his lap. It was only a one-room studio apartment sparsely furnished, a sublet since his separation. But he was indifferent to the meagerness of his surroundings. "I want to read you something I'm working on," he said.

He started to read from the loose typewritten pages he was holding. After a few sentences, I realized I'd never heard anything like it, that is, which wasn't already bound in some famous book. It was part of an autobiography—an autobiography of all things, at his age!—about his young boyhood in Brownsville, about his mother's kitchen, and his father's scrubbing the paint from his hands, about relatives and neighbors, and himself wandering the familiar streets and beyond. It was incredibly rich, full of sights and smells and sound, teeming with life. Actually, I'd never heard anything like it from a bound book either. It was singular, a masterpiece. That naked man in the maroon paisley bathrobe is reading me a masterpiece, I thought. Alfred finally finished and looked at me. He could see from my expression what I was thinking and was clearly moved. "I'm calling it *A Walker in the City*," he said. "Colon. *Notes from a Writer's Journal.*"

"You don't need the colon stuff," I said.

"No? You think *A Walker in the City* is enough?"

"Definitely."

He looked at me with profound gratitude, tears beginning to form in his eyes. "Marry me," Alfred said.

I wanted to tell my mother, and Julia too, that for their information it was a big lie about guys sleeping with you and then leaving you in the lurch. If anything, they seemed to get more attached. I was thinking about Leon saying, don't you want me and the baby? About Alfred Kazin asking me to marry him first time out. On the off-chance that he was serious, I said no immediately, of course I didn't want to get married—which was the absolute truth. I also didn't know when I would see him again. He was going off to a place called Yaddo to do more work on that extraordinary book. Yaddo, he told me, was an artist's colony in Saratoga, a place which had saved his life on more than one occasion. It was also clearly a place where he could easily forget all about me.

But in a few days a letter arrived, typed on a yellow second sheet. A friendly letter, lightly affectionate in tone—

telling me about Yaddo, the other artists in residence, the Saratoga pines. I had never gotten a letter from a writer before—Gerald's had been semiliterate, Leon had confined himself to short postcards—and I was impressed out of my mind. More letters followed, he wasn't playing a game and waiting for an answer—and they were all spectacular, not love letters, but little finished essays in themselves. I answered as best I could, writing several drafts of stilted prose before I copied them on my Royal portable and sent them off. He also wanted me to send him a copy of *Star of Glass,* which I was very reluctant to do. I was nowhere near in his league. It would ruin the friendship, if that was what it was. Kill the romance, if *that* was what it was. Mix apples and oranges. I could have gone on and on, thinking of reasons not to send it, but obviously I couldn't keep my novel from him forever.

I sent it, he read it, made measured critical comments, none too favorable, though with some hope. I wasn't offended. It had the welcome flavor of Rhett Butler giving advice to Scarlett O'Hara. And that was that. He still obviously liked me, and in fact had grown so lonely at Yaddo—how loneliness plagued this remarkable man, which of course was only to be expected—that, what with an oncoming cold and the increasingly bleak weather, matched by the increasingly bleak company of the other residents, he had decided to come back home early. He was eager to see me. He was so glad we had met. That was another amazing thing about him. He wasn't like the other boys I knew—of course, he wasn't a boy— careful not to reveal his feelings. He led with his chin, never stopping to worry first about commitment or rejection. I couldn't get over that.

Meanwhile, Elizabeth called. "I think Mr. Kazin liked

you," she said. "I think you'll be hearing from him." I acted surprised. I didn't want to lie to her, and I wasn't even guarding some secret. But my connection with Alfred had become too special in my mind, too private to share. Besides, thanks to dear old Clara I was very superstitious about good fortune.

He came back, and I was immediately catapulted into happiness, a world I had never known before and where Alfred was always there. He was a living antidote to all that I had been mentally force-fed about male-female relationships and had willed myself not to believe. "You can let down your brains with me," Alfred said. Infelicitous phrase, especially coming from him, but heartening nevertheless . . . Boys won't like you if you're too smart? Ha ha, what boys? Don't kiss on the first date. Kiss? What about sleeping with somebody on the first date without even thinking about it? . . . The list went on and on, down to and including never let him see you without makeup. All now and forever null and void.

"He says he loves me," I told Dr. Zaphiropoulos, my Greek shrink, still wary about falling for *that* line. "Maybe he does," Dr. Z said, to my surprise. I began to think maybe he did, though for what reason I couldn't fathom, and after a while believed it completely, though still not knowing the reason. But I felt totally safe with him, as he said he did with me. We told each other everything. No subjects were out of bounds, from Faulkner—I more or less repeated to him what I had learned in Arthur Mizener's course—to constipation. He was so moved when we got to that last one, it was almost like the first night, when he read to me from his book.

He was on the homestretch now with the *Walker,* and we went over it painstakingly inch by inch, on the table in his studio apartment after making love, in various cafeterias in my neighborhood, where you could sit for hours over a cup of coffee. He was very receptive to my small criticisms and suggestions, amazingly grateful, though serious literary discussions immediately seemed to make him feel sexy, which they didn't me. It was hard to switch gears like that. But Alfred was very ready to help me with my writing, too—I still couldn't call it work. Right at the beginning he had given me a big leatherette notebook, and told me I must keep a journal, write in it every day. It wasn't my habit to keep a journal, except for recording odd snatches of this and that which I was afraid I would forget. But I kept at it, mostly writing ecstatically about him, with flights of fancy about snowfall in the city and that sort of thing thrown in, made for somebody to read after I died. Even I knew this wasn't my best writing, but Alfred said, "You must write every day"—which the teachers who said you must only write about what you know about had never told me. "I couldn't love you if you weren't a writer," Alfred said. This was a bit more worrisome, as any sentence beginning "I couldn't love you if—" would have been. What if I decided not to be a writer, an idea I often toyed with. I had only become one because I had won a contest by a fluke. Then I realized that my world really had changed when my book was published, though not in the way movies had led me to believe. But without *Star of Glass*, I would never have met Elizabeth, and if I had never met Elizabeth I would never have met Alfred. Actually I wasn't so sure about that one. I would have had to meet him somehow, somewhere. He was so clearly my *basherte*, much as I hated to admit my mother was right about anything.

Every day led to some kind of private adventure. We

would meet in the afternoons, after we had finished writing, outside of Tiffany's, which was midway between us. Often we wound up at concerts, mostly at Carnegie Hall, easy to do since it was only a few blocks away. We had established early on that we both loved music, though Alfred automatically assumed he knew more about it because he actually played the violin. I didn't think so, but I played no instrument at all, and had really learned all I knew about music through the boys I had slept with, a point I could hardly bring up under the circumstances. How far away all that seemed anyway, those silly days of trying to check into the Algonquin and tea dancing at the Plaza and trying to be sophisticated. The life I was leading now was truly grown-up and sophisticated, even when we just went to the movies, which both of us had early on admitted we loved too. Also, we walked and walked and walked all over the place, I often in high heels. Alfred particularly liked walking across bridges, especially the Brooklyn Bridge, which turned out to have a certain literary cachet I hadn't thought about before, and whose history he told me about as we crossed it, high above traffic, like walking into glory.

Bed too could be glorious. Alfred taught me quite a few things I had never dreamed of, and I was a totally willing pupil. In for a penny, in for a pound, was how I saw it. The days of poor Leon pleading with me to "touch it" were long over. There *were* a few problems. The close-mouthed kiss had never reappeared again, and now his spittle tended to run down my chin when we kissed too long, as we often did, and I really didn't like that. Also, at the height of passion, Alfred often said, "Be still. Let me catch my breath," which tended to put a damper on things. But then what did I know about all this sex stuff, really? Alfred often spoke of a *"grande amoureuse"* in his past who did. And there was one other thing. He *always* made me come now, manually, sometimes sighing patiently until I did. It never happened spontaneously anymore. Sometimes, for no reason, I thought about that package of cigarettes, taken, then grandly given back. But after I came, I always loved him passionately, and watched over him as he fell asleep, which he did at once.

Inevitably Alfred met my parents, a meeting which, for all his trying to avoid it, didn't make much of a dent on him, though it did on Daddy. "How old is he?" my father had asked beforehand. "Thirty-five," I said, ready to parry objections about a twice-divorced man with a child. But, "In his prime," Daddy said, always the one to be impressed by intellect—male. This went back to the days of revering the *Talmud chochem* of which he himself was one. But religious learning left Alfred cold, even repelled him, as did Judaism in general. He didn't want to be caught in any of the old Jewish traps. He had been brought up a Socialist, defiantly eating on Yom Kippur, singing Young Peoples Socialist League songs. This indifference to my family was okay with me. Not the defiantly eating on Yom Kippur part, which seemed stupid. But Alfred was, after all, my own defiant way of getting away from home too.

I also met Alfred's younger sister, Pearl, who up until that time had been in the south of Italy, sharing a house in a place called Taormina with the writer Truman Capote. Imagine having a sister who did things like that, instead of marrying a doctor or running around with a carpet sweeper or moving to Philadelphia. I liked Pearl at once, a female Alfred with the same Asian eyes and impressive intellect, but much kindlier in manner, and only five years older than I. I began to feel that this was my true sister, the one I should have had in the first place. For her part, I think Pearl was happy to have any sister at all. Though, speaking of sisters, I suddenly realized that, though she clearly adored him, Pearl wasn't mentioned in Alfred's autobiography at all. When I remarked on this to Alfred he said of course he knew about the omission, so I assumed there was some aesthetic principle involved. I had also long since met Alfred's little son, Michael, who was on loan every Saturday, when I would zip him into his fancy snowsuit— sometimes backwards by mistake—and with his father take him to the zoo. Michael was adorable, a miniature Alfred with the same Asian eyes—there was a very dominant gene here— and very amiable in conversation. When I asked him what he did in nursery school, he said, "Pway," and he identified a piece of fruit I had just peeled for him as an "Onch." I also voyaged out to Brooklyn to meet Alfred's parents, who were still in Brownsville exactly as he had left them. I was taken with his father, a shy, gray-haired version of Alfred again with those same eyes—and much less so with his mother. The Jewish mother had yet to be born that I could cotton to. But clearly she was beyond criticism, as were basically his father and sister. This was totally different from my family where we all criticized and laughed at each other all the time. But perhaps Alfred's family was of some higher order of being. He certainly gave that impression.

The Christmas holidays were coming and Alfred was going to join his editor and the editor's wife in Key West. He wanted me to come there too. Daddy grandly got me train tickets to Miami, which were very hard to get, and from there I took a little plane to Key West. This was not the Florida that I knew. There were no dressed-to-kill Jews wandering around, no handpainted neckties, no dollar Tootsie Rolls, in fact no Jews at all that I could see, no fancy hotels crowding up the beach front. There was only one right on the water, small and elegant, where Alfred's editor and his wife were staying. I wasn't jealous of their well-heeled exclusivity. The hotel where Alfred, and now I too, were staying, was on a street right in the middle of slatternly old Key West. It was white, had sagging balconies, tiled floors, and brass beds—we had adjoining rooms—and was where Ernest Hemingway himself had stayed. We also drank at bars where Hemingway had drunk, and ate at restaurants where Hemingway had eaten. (Alfred had already met one of Hemingway's ex-wives before I came down.) This was *literary*, not fancy shmancy Florida, authentic, the real thing. Caribbean. We also ate turtle burgers, toured the Coca-Cola factory, and walked the town endlessly. New Year's Eve was the best New Year's Eve of my life—the days when I worried about not having a New Year's Eve date seemed far, far behind me. We went to an exceedingly seedy striptease nightclub with the editor and his wife, who were the epitome of refinement. Once more it seemed that in the best circles low-down was high class. It was December 31, 1950. I had met Alfred in mid-October, but could no longer remember life without him. Sometimes he was apologetic about having been married twice before. But that was silly. He had to do *something* before I was old enough for him to meet me.

We flew to Cuba for a few days, my first trip out of the United States, and again stayed in a hotel that no member of my family would have recognized as such. Havana was something like Key West, but even more foreign. There were outdoor cafés, just as in pictures of Europe, and all signs and speech were in Spanish. The place was run by a dictator, Batista, who could possibly arrest us for no reason at any moment. But Alfred was both indefatigable and intrepid. He dragged me by the hand down dark streets and alleys that it scared me to death just to put a foot in. In the Havana airport somber customs officials in uniform rifled through our luggage before we were allowed to board the plane and descend in the tacky freedom of Key West, which, though I didn't confess it to Alfred, I was relieved to see again. He would have found this attitude very provincial.

The trade-off for our great adventure was that on our way back to New York we had to stop off in Miami Beach and visit Mama and Daddy for a few hours. They had been in a car crash and were both pretty banged up, the effects of Daddy's atrocious driving—Daddy had decided to drive all the way down—though Daddy gave short shrift to the injury part, preferring to show us clippings about the accident from local Georgia newspapers, which mentioned his name prominently. My mother made sure that all the other ladies saw that I had come with a boyfriend. It wouldn't have occurred to anybody that Alfred and I were sleeping together, except possibly—no, probably—my father. We boarded our train comfortably, knowing that for a few weeks we would have a choice of two apartments to make love in. There was a huge pile of someone's expensive luggage occupying four Pullman seats at the end of the car. I snuggled down next to Alfred. He was holding my hand, murmuring sexy things to me. The car door was pulled open and a porter and then a handsome man in a brown suit and brown homburg stepped in, and my jaw dropped open. "Puss," Alfred whispered to me, his favorite endearment, "Puss . . . *Puss?*" But I was beyond hearing, beyond even knowing who was talking to me. The man I was staring at was Clark Gable.

Alfred might just as well have been Peppy.

Alfred had now moved back to an old apartment he had always kept to lend out or use as a studio, on Pineapple Street in Brooklyn Heights. It was on the top floor of an old tenement, dark brown and evil smelling, with stairs that sagged and creaked. It looked to me like what we had managed to escape from on Forty-seventh Street, but everybody else, Pearlie included, said it was *marvelous*. So clearly I was missing something. Feeling himself at home, Alfred began to give little parties. Refreshments involved bologna slices, which he slapped on a plate—I would then daintily arrange them in overlapping circles garnished with cocktail onions, which Alfred didn't get mad at because he never noticed—and a bottle of whiskey, generally something called Guckenheimer's Reserve. The friends were all Alfred's age, or older, a distinction that at first was lost on me since they *all* seemed old—and sat around happily on the decrepit daybed or on the sloping floor, eating the bologna slices, which soon vanished, cocktail onions and all, and drinking the Guckenheimer's Reserve, which lasted longer. It was a big bottle.

And they talked. And talked and talked and talked. I had never heard such talk, high flown and passionate, about art, music, literature, politics. Also what they were working on. Sometimes they said to each other, "Did you work well today?" I had always thought of writing as something private, and this sounded as if they were inquiring of each other's bowel movements. "Were you a Litvak, or a Galitzianer?" I never said that, though, or much of anything else. I was way, way out of my league, and it would have been hard to get a word in edgewise in any case. Even if I had felt I had something to say, I hadn't developed any timing. I liked them, though, and they seemed to like me, especially Isaac Rosenfeld, who was round faced and jolly and wore round eyeglasses, and who smiled a lot, as did his chubby kind of amiably sloppy wife, Vassiliki. I think he had published one novel, but had a story in PR, which turned out to be *Partisan Review*, a magazine they often mentioned and that, of course, I had still never read, though Leonora Pearlstein had.

Isaac's best friend was Saul Bellow, they had both grown up in Chicago. Saul had published two novels, which I had never heard of either, naturally, and was working on another that he was calling *The Adventures of Augie March*. Saul had dark curly hair, almond eyes, a handsome mouth. He was stunning, the ultimate beautiful young Jewish intellectual incarnate. Wherever he happened to be, in no matter how crowded or noisy a room, I knew instinctively where he was. He was also very funny, unusual among these intellectuals, Alfred foremost among them, who tended to be glum on account of the burdens of the life of the mind—but did being a novelist make you an intellectual?—and laughed at his own jokes so hard that he could hardly get to the punch line. Alfred and he had a very sticky relationship, based on mutual admiration and rivalry. They both played the violin, and when they got together for duets it soon became a question of who would win. Another of Saul's friends, whom he palled around with a lot was Ralph Ellison, former short-order cook and jazz trumpeter, now working on a novel called *Invisible Man*. He lived in Harlem and was the only Negro in the group—coffee colored and suave with a beautiful speaking voice and carefully enunciated Oklahoma accent.

Harold Rosenberg, another regular but of an older generation, worked in advertising and wrote brilliant essays on the
side. He was a big guy, with a big black mustache and a big
stiff leg held out in front of him as he sat, and had a wonderful way of taking ideas out of a muddled intellectual argument
and propping them up to be looked at. Alfred, embarrassed by
my youth and also marveling at it, said to Harold, "This girl
was born in 1927," and Harold said after a thoughtful moment, "I was kind of born that year, myself." All the men were
married, but the wives, also present, were dim, even cheerful
Vassiliki was very much relegated to the background. I was
amazed to see shtetl conditions prevail in a group so intellectually advanced, especially since to top it all off, most of the
dim wives seemed to support the husbands financially. Really,
for all practical purposes, except for living in such a heady mi-
lieu, the wives could have been my sisters. But, on the other
hand, none of this applied to *me*. I wasn't a wife, and if I too
was in the background, it was only because I was very young.
I could never be one of those wives. And even if I could—per-
ish the thought—Alfred would *never* have wanted me to be.

Alfred's friends gave as many parties as he did, and we went
to lots of them. Isaac and Vassiliki's were in Greenwich Village,
crowded and full of commotion. It was like being invited into
one of those lit apartments Gerald and I used to pass on our
romantic walks in the snow. Harold Rosenberg lived in a walk-
up on the *east* side of the Village, a part of New York I had
never been to before, and which didn't feel very safe. These
parties, presided over by his long-suffering wife, May, who had
big teeth and many complaints, were full of artists, who called
themselves abstract expressionists. But the artists weren't half
so voluble or interesting as the literary intellectuals, despite the

discussions about "action painting" led by Harold, most of which I didn't understand. Extremely avant-garde drawings and paintings covered almost all the walls, helter skelter. They were all inscribed to Harold and May.

Another one of Alfred's oldest and best friends was Richard Hofstadter, a charming man who taught history at Columbia and lived in a different sphere from the others. Dick and Bede, his very pretty wife, who didn't have an air of being put upon, lived in a real apartment on Claremont Avenue, with nice furniture and a big living room and a big separate dining room, and they invited us to what was called a dinner party, a big step up from those meals with my high school friends in the foyers of West End Avenue. First we had drinks and canapés in the living room, about eight of us, evenly divided between sexes, and then after an hour or so we went into the dining room, which was set with beautiful plates and silverware, and Bede served up delicious stuff I had never tasted before, or versions of things I *had* tasted before but didn't dream could be this good. The male guests seemed to be all people who also taught at Columbia, including a young historian named Peter Gay, a bachelor whom the Hofstadters had more or less taken under their wing, and Lionel Trilling, a courtly gentleman married to a homely yenta of a wife named Diana, who looked and acted like my Tante Freydel. Dessert we ate at the table—everybody told Bede what a terrific cook she was, which seemed to please her—and then we went back into the living room for coffee and more drinks. At some point a woman came in through the back door and snuck into the kitchen to clean up, which was a good thing because there was a tremendous amount of mess left over from dinner and it was hard to see how Bede could have managed it on top of the cooking and serving and looking as if she hadn't done any of it.

Alfred also took me to a *Partisan Review* party, a bewildering occasion in spite of my having got used to the fact that when Alfred took me to a party, he more or less tossed me in at the door, and left me to sink or swim on my own, a custom that all the other men seemed to follow also, including with their wives, who then clustered in the shallow water. To me this pool was as large and roiling and as frightening as the one Peppy's mother used to take us to at Brighton Beach. It wasn't simply a matter of not knowing who anybody was, but of not knowing anybody, and certainly no one was making any attempt to be friendly. With relief I spied Delmore Schwartz and timidly went over to him. He remembered me from the Kenyon School of English. I told him I didn't know anyone there, and he looked around and mumbled that he might introduce me to Alfred Kazin. I said I already knew him and Delmore Schwartz said he thought I had said I didn't know anybody, and we were back to square one. Luckily Mrs. Schwartz was nearby with several other wives, but they all laughed when I addressed her politely as Mrs. Schwartz. I retreated to the couch and sat there forlornly, knowing that it would be bad form in these circles to go and attach myself to my date. Alfred himself wouldn't understand it. A few feet away several men were having an important intellectual conclave, including two I later learned were the editors, William Philips and Philip Rahv. They all threw an occasional glance at me. Finally, one of the men came up and introduced himself as Will Barrett. "Can we look at your part?" he said. "We were wondering if you were a real blonde."

Bad as this was—Alfred consoled me by saying said they

were a rotten crowd anyway, but then why did he go to their parties?—there was a far more serious fly in my ointment. Somebody Alfred did like, passionately, an ugly, bossy German refugee named Hannah Arendt who had bad teeth and short bushy hair, and a flood of pronouncements rather than opinions. Lots of other German immigrants, like the people who had snubbed us at Tip Toe Inn, had been equally arrogant, but we felt sorry for them anyway, because they had come fresh from Hitler. Russian immigrants of my parents' generation had been almost embarrassingly humble when faced with the American world. But humble was not in this lady's vocabulary, certainly not when it came to American culture, which she clearly regarded as beneath contempt. In fact, even the word *arrogant* didn't begin to tell the story. She had written a book called *The Origins of Totalitarianism,* and Alfred had not only helped her greatly with the English, but also helped her get it published. This no one would have guessed from the offhand way with which she treated him. To me she said there was no such name as Ann, the real name was Hannah. Her husband, Heinrich Blucher, was, on the contrary, a very sweet German, if such a thing were possible, but so lofty in his thinking and expression it was hard to do more than smile as if I understood.

What Hannah Arendt called a party at her house was more like a convocation in a principal's office. Everybody sat in a rigid semicircle and put forth ideas. Perhaps if Alfred hadn't had to explain to me afterward who the guests, such as Paul Tillich, were, I would have been more impressed, rather than turned into stone by terror and boredom. There was also an acolyte woman named Ruth, who every time Hannah put forth a thought would happily chime in with, "And not only that . . ." The first time we had finally got out of there, Alfred asked me if I liked Hannah. I said yes, though "like" was an awfully puny word under the circumstances. He said, "Good. Because if you don't like her, I can't love you." Another condition, and a very close shave. He also said that he had had an affair with Ruth, the acolyte, and proposed to her, but she had turned him down. He also said that he had wanted to sleep with Hannah, and she had laughed and turned him down too. Neither of these rejections seemed to bother him, but they bothered me on his behalf.

After all this social life, Alfred said that Carol, Michael's mother, had told him that his friends were worried about him since he was being seen around with a glamorous young blonde, which sounded worrisome to me too until I realized to my astonishment that she was warning him about me.

Early in the fall, I had turned down two fellowships, one to Cornell and the other to Duke because I had unintentionally started my new novel and felt homesick at the thought of going away with it. It had occurred to me many times since that if I *had* accepted either, I would have been in Ithaca or North Carolina in October and never have met Alfred. Incredible thought. I had almost forgotten about the Fulbright, but amazingly I got it. Another daydream come true. A whole year in France, my first trip abroad, everything, travel, books, living expenses paid for. I was waiting for Alfred in Rockefeller Plaza one day, when my former teacher Paolo Milano came by and I told him all about it. He was suitably thrilled, and when Alfred, actually an old friend of Paolo's, popped up, he said, "This girl has just won a Fulbright." Alfred said he already knew, which somehow put a damper on things—Paolo wanted to be the first to spread the news, and besides, Paolo hadn't realized Alfred and I even knew each other. After Paolo left, Alfred said thoughtfully, "I admire you. It isn't every girl who would leave her lover for a year to go abroad." There was something in his tone that made it sound less than a compliment, which was absurd. Of course it was meant as a compliment. Alfred was totally on my side in these matters, not like my family. (My father had already promised me a red convertible if I didn't go away and, when I turned it down, had taken to his bed for three days.) What troubled me, though, was Alfred calling himself my lover, a strangely delimiting word when he was all the world to me.

My Fulbright wasn't starting until the fall, and we decided to travel together in Europe first for the whole summer. Daydreams were coming true all over the place. Name a contest and I won it, Alfred being very much first prize in the man category. I thought of the little Southern missy, whom I had met at the Kenyon School of English, Melanie Thornton, with whom I'd meant to travel to Europe for the first time, but whose parents didn't think I was a suitable companion for her. (trans.: dirty Jew.) Now *they* weren't good enough for me. Alfred had made everything turn out right. More than right. I'd won the maiden voyage to Europe contest too.

So we sailed away for a year and a day, spiritually speaking. Relatives and friends ganged up in both our cabins. We were on a great ocean liner, the *Île de France*. There was champagne, and I was wearing the spray of pale green orchids my father had sent me. It was all just as in the movies, and to top it off, the next day would be my twenty-fourth birthday. When everybody had gone, amid the hooting of the steamship, the same incredibly romantic sound I had listened to on Fifty-first Street, Alfred and I leaned over the railing, looking at the departing skyscrapers of Manhattan, the swirling ocean waters below. Total, ideal perfection. Had little Honey from Hell's Kitchen ever imagined this would really happen to her? I wanted to tell her it had. Hug her, jump up and down together, let her know she was safe with me, poor little kid. Then Alfred and I went inside to explore the wonders below decks, the shops, bars, beauty parlor, dining salon.

At dinner, to which we had been summoned by a steward striking a gong, Alfred seemed depressed rather than exuberant. I asked him what was the matter. Well, Hannah Arendt had said my father was a vulgar man and to stay away from him. Alfred took it as an edict. But wasn't it vulgar to repeat this remark to me, not to mention vulgar to make in the first place? In fact, she had said more or less the same thing to me about *his* parents too, but I hadn't dreamed of telling him. Why should I? There was a damper on my spirits now too. But not for long. No, we were sailing away on a romantic sea, far from all of them.

Paris was beautiful and looked exactly like itself. I couldn't believe I was actually there. We checked in at the Lutetia on the Boulevard Raspail and were shown into two tiny attic rooms. Actually, the hotel was too expensive for us and the management not very polite about it. But Hannah Arendt had said it was the hotel we should stay at, and she was by her own account an experienced traveler. Besides, weren't attic rooms the epitome of Paris? I did, of course, keep making silly mistakes. To Alfred's horror I had fallen asleep on the boat train from Le Havre instead of staring out at the countryside.

But extreme emotion always made me fall asleep. Then for my *petit déjeuner* I wanted to have coffee and croissants in my room, but Alfred said that was ridiculous, everybody in Paris went out to a café for breakfast. Perhaps they did, perhaps like him all Parisians were early risers for whom breakfast was an eagerly awaited meal. Once on my way to the café, I remarked on how *small* everything was, people, cars, et cetera, and that was the wrong thing to say too, though they patently were. Never mind. We were in Paris! Paris! . . . And Alfred knew where to go, what to see, whom to see. He even knew an expatriate couple, who had made their home in Paris for years, had a child who spoke French, and welcomed wandering Americans for *gigot* on Sunday. And the composer Nicholas Nabokov and his young ravishingly beautiful American wife who moved in the highest cultural circles, which included Stravinsky and the Rothschilds.

We went to Chartres, we took a trip to Mont St Michel, which because he had been much influenced by Henry Adams's book, Alfred was surprised to find weren't next door to each other. Then we set off for Italy, which was really the name of Alfred's heart's desire. He had traveled there with Carol. Also, he had never hidden the fact that he didn't like the French or their language, and thought it was affected for people, even the French, to speak French in the first place.

As we traveled, I found surprisingly that sex was getting worse, rather than better. It was taking longer and longer for Alfred to make me come. Partly, I supposed, I was made nervous by all the packing and unpacking of our numerous bags, the complaints of the porters, the mutterings of other train passengers, by seeing all the different places and meeting all the different people. Or maybe it was because in Italy we had begun to stay in one room with a big *letto matrimoniale*, though the passports we submitted at the desk had two different last names, and the concierge called me *signorina*. This last was embarrassing, though I knew it was backsliding to see it that way. For some unaccountable reason, I began to have fantasies about Leon, who seemed in retrospect to have been my sexiest experience of all. I tried not to, but I missed a young body, the body of a boy my age, in his twenties. Alfred didn't have a young body. The fact of money was also getting to be a problem. It had been agreed that we would each pay for ourselves. Alfred was hardly in a position to treat me to a summer in Europe, which I would never have wanted in any case. But because I was not allowed to put down cash on the spot—this would have embarrassed Alfred, and women didn't do that kind of thing—Alfred paid all the bills, for which he kept a running and complicated account, made even more so when there was a change in currency. Privately, I reimbursed him, which wasn't so easy, either. Many of our road maps were covered with his calculations.

But these were minor cavils. I was traveling in glorious Europe with my beloved, who knew every one and everything, and who loved me back. The French Riviera had been glorious, the Italian Riviera even more so. We packed picnics for our excursions, drank beautiful wine from upended bottles, bit into peaches whose juice ran down our chins, quoted Keats. Pisa looked as if it had been kicked in the stomach by the war, all of it leaning, Siena was for fairy tales, cobblestoned and circular, Florence had the Ponte Vecchio and was glorious, Rome had everything else and was glorious. Alfred kept digging up famous people all over the place, most of whom I didn't know were famous. The director Harold Clurman and an incredibly glamorous Stella Adler in Florence, Alberto Moravia in Rome who kind of looked and acted like a petulant adolescent, and also Ignazio Silone, who had an Irish wife, which was fortunate for me because I couldn't speak Italian. Neither did Alfred, really, though nobody noticed it. Italians were altogether different from the French when it came to speaking their language, and if you even said *grazia* told you your mother was surely Italian.

Another worry for me, this time regarding etiquette, arose because Alfred was always the honored male guest at dinner, and I was therefore the honored female, which meant that I was always having to help myself from a proffered dish before the other guests, a situation that at first came as news to me. I didn't know how to handle this, what implements to use, how much to take. Matters came to an unfortunate climax in Silone's house. The maid offered me a platter with a huge omelet, enough for everybody. This seemed simple, but when I started to take a helping, it turned out that the omelet was filled with mozzarella cheese, very stretchy mozzarella cheese. My piece wouldn't come away. The maid backed up. The cheese stretched, but didn't break. The maid backed up farther. This went on for some time, with the mozzarella stretching to practically a thread, which still refused to break. Finally Silone leaped up and severed the thing with a whack of his knife. For the rest of my stay in Italy I had severe omelet anxieties.

In August, Alfred went off to teach in the Salzburg Seminar, which was the way he had managed to finance his trip abroad. I would join him in a few weeks, as we had arranged. Meanwhile, I stayed with my old friend Biancamaria of Kenyon College days, who lived in Rome. She was married now to an engineer named Carlo and they had a baby son, an apartment with stone floors, a very hot sunny balcony, and a slave of a maid. She was still my dear Biancamaria but in a very foreign context, though no matter where we were we could no longer have fallen into the old habits of unattached girls together. It was a lonely few weeks. Bianca went off to the university in the morning, came home to nurse her baby, make raw pasta for the maid to cook for lunch. Carlo went off to his engineer's office, came back to eat the pasta, and then both of them changed into nightclothes and took an hour's nap. I tried to occupy myself fruitfully, in a way that Alfred would approve of, see required sights, visit museums and churches et cetera, but I had never traveled on my own before and I was very conscious the whole time of doing exactly that. Dear God, what would I do when after the Salzburg session, Alfred left Europe for good?

As always, letters flew back and forth. Alfred wrote wonderful descriptions of the little town of Salzburg, the grandeur of the Schloss Leopoldskron, where classes were held and students and faculty stayed, of concerts at the Mozart Festival, and of his famous colleagues at the seminar. Wherever he was there always seemed to be famous people. There was also a young female doctor attached to the place, who, he hinted, had fallen in love with him. This was understandable. Poor woman, I felt very sorry for her, and guilty, since he was mine. As to my letters, they were as cheerful and uncomplaining as I could make them. But Rome without Alfred wasn't the *real* Rome, even though I was staying in a Roman household with real Romans. "Why don't you marry him and end it all?" Biancamaria said, in her maybe too-good English. "God, no," I said, though I was no longer sure in my own mind why getting married was so totally out of the question.

The time finally came when I was to join Alfred in

Salzburg. He himself had a room in the schloss like other faculty and students. I was installed in a farmhouse down the road. A real farmhouse with squawking things in the yard and a huge, snarling watchdog that looked like a dog in a concentration camp. I was scared crossing the yard but Alfred said not to worry about it. We climbed upstairs to my room, and my worries vanished temporarily. The room looked like an illustration for *Heidi* and had a bed piled high with goosedown comforters clothed in snowy white. We had never seen such a bed in real life and dove right into it. A great reunion. At the schloss later on, I met Henry Steele Commager and his wife, and his three beautiful, utterly Gentile teenage children, Steele, Nell, and Lisa. They were a genuinely wacky American family, as opposed to mine, who had only pathetically aspired to be like the one in *You Can't Take It with You*. The palace itself, though, was a disappointment. I'd never been inside one before, without a guide, and there was a museum-caliber quality that was missing here, maybe because the place was busy with students and papers and pencils and books. Then there was the fact that the police dog in the farmhouse yard still behaved as if he were guarding a concentration camp, and that though it was Austria, hearing German spoken aloud was terrifying. I didn't need to voice these thoughts to know that Alfred would find them provincial. So we went on making deliciously cushioned love in my featherbed, walking into the pretty little town of Salzburg itself to hear concerts, chamber music, operas—a music lover's paradise. Breakfast I had in my room, lunch and dinner at the schloss, but once, not finding him around, I went in to lunch by myself, and Alfred was furious. I didn't belong there, what business had I to insinuate myself into the group without his auspices? I burst into tears.

Had he brought me to Salzburg only to isolate me in a farm-house with a police dog for company? Eventually, the storm subsided, Alfred apologized and even began to treat me more like a wife than a girlfriend. He asked me to wash some hand-kerchiefs for him. I stood at the sinks with several wives. I had never washed a handkerchief before. It was not as easy as I thought. The crusty and gluey stuff kept sliding around but never coming off. Still it seemed some kind of honor to have been asked, and the wives gave me sympathetic and helpful hints as they would to a new recruit.

Increasingly over the summer, I asked myself if it had been crazy to accept that Fulbright, and dreaded the day when I would have to do without my love. That day had now come. I was standing on a dock in Genoa in the brilliant sunshine, waving to Alfred as the SS *United States* slid away. My heart was breaking. Tears streamed from my eyes. An Italian cus-toms guard gripped my shoulder and said, *"Corragio!"*

Chapter 5

"WHO WAS THAT HANDSOME MAN bending over you?" Alfred asked suspiciously in a letter written from shipboard.

I explained that I was being counseled courage. And courage was what I definitely needed now that I was on my own. Practically the first word I heard when I got back to France to live as a student was *"Comment?"* A word I was to hear constantly thereafter. I had won French prizes in high school and college. But the French in their own country were absolutely lousy about their language. In Paris they spoke fast, took no prisoners, and never seemed to understand you no matter how many prizes you'd won.

After a brief stay at the Cité Universitaire, a vast holding pen for foreign students that was divided into pavilions for various nationalities, I was sent for the first part of my Fulbright to the Université of Aix-Marseille, in Aix-en-Provence, a small town full of colonial widows and teeming with anti-American sentiments. For example, wasn't Chicago a *"pays de gangstères?"* And, "You want water? I thought Americans drank only Coca-Cola." My landlady wore suits and hats with veils as she peddled to her errands on a bike. My room rent included a *petit déjeuner* of café au lait and croissants and confiture

135

brought up by the Italian maid, who also criticized my French. (Blissfully, there were also letters from Alfred on the tray several times a week.) Baths were extra, and so was dinner, if I chose to have it en famille, including a birthday dinner for a young friend of my landlady to which I had been formally invited, the first time I had ever been charged for a birthday party. Another time my landlord told me cheerfully, pointing up at the sky, about watching air fights between the Germans and the Allies during the war, and hoping that both sides would destroy each other. Also that of course they couldn't let the *Exodus* land because the passengers stank. It was hard to correlate this with my understanding from wartime movies that all the French had been members of the Resistance. But again there must have been something I was missing.

My fellow Fulbrights saw themselves as graduate students, but on a grand scale. The most pimply one told me that Americans were hopelessly adolescent. There were also older expatriates, mostly couples and mostly Jewish, supported by the GI Bill. They looked down on the Fulbrights as pampered children. They themselves were living on what they thought was the cheap, but was self-inflicted squalor. All of them were writing plays or novels. After reading some of their work, I thought it was lucky that I had never taken my Fulbright project on American expatriates after World War II too seriously, and luckier still that the Fulbright people would never check up on me. Expatriate painters were in better shape. It was Cézanne country. Mont Saint Victoire was perpetually in view, country byways were narrow and walled with tan stone, the distant landscape broke up into a patchwork of muted color. But Aix itself had clearly never thought much of its native son, since in its little museum there were only several of his academic nude drawings, plus the rock Cézanne wiped his brushes on. Actually, the rock did look like a Cézanne. But with it all I felt at home, as I had throughout Europe. Everything was so *familiar*. And much of what I had assumed was characteristically Jewish immigrant—attitudes, smells, physical features—turned out to be really just European.

After a few months in provincial Provence, where the favorite phrase of the locals was *"Ça ne se fait pas ici"* (That isn't done here), I was sent to continue my studies in Paris. I hadn't done much studying in Aix except for attending a few canned and uninterruptible lectures by pompous professors whose entrance we greeted by leaping to our feet, and whose finish we applauded by leaping up again and rapping on our desks. I intended not to do much studying at the Sorbonne either, where similar pedagogical conditions would prevail. Mostly, I was trying to work on my second novel, which wasn't easy, since most of my writing was taken up with letters to Alfred, who was still writing me two or three times a week. Of course, *he* seemed to be able to write a lot of other things too. *A Walker in the City* had finally been published, and one day a copy made it through French customs. In his inscription to me, Alfred called it "our book." That "our," that beautiful book, which I read again and again, though I had known practically every word of it in advance, brought us even closer, though I had no idea when—or if—we would ever see each other again. But all of that was part of the great romantic drama that was our love, wasn't it? And where better to be in love than Paris?

Paris, Paris, Paris was a mantra I repeated to myself, in love with the city itself too. I rented a room with a widow who told me she adored quotations, though she could never remember who had said what—her husband or La Bruyère, for example. I did go to the Sorbonne, but mostly I wandered around Paris, trying to memorize it. I couldn't believe I was actually there, it had been part of my daydreams for so long. And like all dreams it was evanescent, because the fact was that I wouldn't, couldn't be there forever. I hopped on the back of buses, got off at the Pont Alexandre III, looked across the Seine at the Île St Louis and beyond that at the spires of Notre Dame, at the mansard roofs on the other bank, hopped on another bus to the American Express office in the Place de L'Opéra to pick up my mail and stopped to look at the Opéra itself, enchanted by the ceaseless baroque curves and swirls. With every turn of every corner, Paris seemed to be striking a new pose, saying look at me. An incredibly accessible city, so unlike New York.

I was lonely, but it was impossible to be personally un-happy for long in a place so beautiful. It would be like being down in the dumps while you were listening to Handel's *Messiah*. Not that I imagined I really belonged in Paris. Everything advised me that I was a stranger, from the continuing sneers at my spoken French—I was even told once when I mistook the gender of sauerkraut that I was revising the language of Descartes—to the many signs and demonstrators saying "Yankee Go Home." But even if they weren't openly hostile it was understood that the French wanted nothing to do with Americans. Nobody I knew had ever been invited into a French home, unless they were paying for room and board.

It didn't matter. Enough expatriates were around to form a welcoming group of their own. There were first the other Fulbrights, with whom I had lunch in cafés, or dinners in the cheapest student restaurants imaginable. Then, almost every

Sunday I went to see Stanley and Eileen Geist in their little apartment on the rue de Verneuil. They had lived in Paris since the end of the war and had a French-speaking little daughter who looked like a Renoir and a *bonne à tout faire* who made a *gigot* to feed the Sunday guests. Eileen, a toothy, buxom, homely but very sexy young woman, cheerfully worked for the U.S. government and probably supported the household, since Stanley was a very serious intellectual, a critic and a writer, who didn't seem to have published much. Most of the other guests were writers too, beginning or otherwise, including a Norwegian lesbian playwright and a young Negro named Jimmy Baldwin, who was finishing up his first novel. We sat around trying to figure out what kind of articles would get us published and Jimmy, who was hilarious, came up with "A Negro Looks at Henry James" for *Partisan Review*. Jimmy and I had wonderful times laughing and sitting in cafés together, but he was a born hard-luck guy too. When he first came to Paris from the United States, rejoicing in his freedom as a black man, he was immediately arrested as an Arab. When a friend lent him a chalet in Switzerland so he could work in untrammeled solitude, he was immediately snowed in by an avalanche. Jimmy's novel, *Go Tell It on the Mountain*, got finished and bought, though, and he went back to America briefly for publication, which excited everybody very much.

There were other expatriates I came to know too, such as Ellen Adler, the daughter of Stella Adler, and Sonia Orwell, the young widow of George Orwell, who palled around together, one dark haired, the other blonde, two gorgeous butterflies. We never got to be real friends, since they lived in very glamorous musical and literary realms. In fact, I was surprised that they talked to me at all. Probably that I was known to be having an affair with Alfred Kazin gave me a little bit of an entree into their world. Astonishingly, the person whom I did become close to was an old childhood friend of Hannah Arendt, of all people. The friend's name was Annchen Weill and how she and Hannah had ever become friends and stayed friends was a mystery: Hannah a high-haunched Prussian martinet, Annchen totally sweet and plump and delicately solicitous of other people's feelings. Annchen's husband, Eric Weill, unfortunately, was obnoxious and opinionated, preening himself on being a professor of philosophy. Hannah hated him. She called him a *"besser wissern,"* someone who always knew better, which of course described Hannah herself exactly. He was her male counterpart, though to call Hannah female was to obscure the issue.

Another couple with the same name, minus one *l,* were Simone Weil's parents. They were a pair of nice elderly Jews, who spoke touchingly of their dead daughter, then having a big intellectual vogue. (Alfred and Hannah thought the world of her work.) They even gave me a few snapshots of Simone to keep. Simone Weil wasn't much to look at, though, unless one liked gaunt features and big eyeglasses. And I confess that much of what I read of her writings repelled me, though it had been made clear to me by Hannah and Alfred and others that Catholicism was in, and Judaism out. The first was intellectually respectable. The second was beneath contempt. This didn't jibe with the memorized catechism I had heard endlessly parroted at PS 17. Obviously, as with so much else I was learning lately there was more here than met the eye. Still, wasn't it as vain to fixate on one's weaknesses as on one's strengths, on one's physical ugliness as on one's beauty? Wasn't all consuming humility the same as overweening pride? I wrote Alfred about my problems with this matter, and he seemed to feel that my provincial, aka shtetl, Jewish background was keeping me from a finer understanding, perhaps always would.

It was a relief to get away from all this in the company of Patricia Nabokov, an expatriate at the totally other end of the spectrum, a young woman still in her late twenties, but in the grandest of styles, a classic brunette beauty with a bun at the nape of her neck, an exquitely sculpted nose, and liquid blue eyes. She had once been a model, easy to believe, and now couturiers lent her their gowns to be worn and seen in on important social occasions. She was the first woman I had ever met whose jewelry matched her clothes—topazes for yellow silk, amethysts for purple, and so on. She was married to the Russian composer, Nicholas Nabokov, and invited me to their box at the Opéra, where Igor Stravinsky dropped in while I was actually sitting there. The Nabokov apartment, overlooking the Luxembourg Gardens, was filled with beautiful antiques, Russian emigrés wafting long plumes of cigarette smoke as they discussed world events in heavily accented French, and elegantly mannered titled Rothschilds. It was common knowledge that at nineteen, Patricia had been the mistress of Camus. Yes, this was much more like it, as far as I was concerned. The real thing, the real high life, what one had read about in every French novel since the beginning of time.

But it actually wasn't that real, after all. As we got to be friends, Patricia (née Blake) told me more about herself. It turned out that with all her sophistication, she was only a few years older than I and hungry, I think, for the company of another American girl. I told her about the elastic mozzarella omelet at Ignazio Silone's house and she told me that early on in her marriage she too had been the guest of honor at dinner, only it was a great banquet at a long table and a footman came to her first with an entire large fish. Patricia said she looked at the thing and burst into tears. She called herself Jewish, but she was only half Jewish, on her father's side. He was a dentist. The beauteous Mme Nabokov was a Jewish *dentist's* daughter? I told her, consolingly, that her father might be a dentist but that she really wasn't Jewish because her mother wasn't. But no, for the highest moral reasons she insisted on considering herself a Jew. My own feeling was that you couldn't elect yourself a Jew for high moral reasons. You had to have it dumped on you. Alfred would have glumly agreed with this, but I didn't tell him about it. I didn't tell Patricia, either. Julia, meanwhile, was taking Alfred's course in American literature at the New School. Patricia went off to New York, met with Alfred, and brought me back a sheer navy blue blouse from him as a present.

When we parted in Genoa in September Alfred had said he didn't know when, if ever, he was coming over again. It had always been understood that he was a busy man with interests other than me. Then he wrote he might be returning that summer. Then in the spring. Then it definitely became in early February, which, amazingly, was almost upon us. After much searching, I gave my quotation-spouting landlady notice and rented two rooms in an ornately run-down hotel on the rue de La Harpe, just off the Boulevard Saint Michel and on the edge of the Arab quarter. The management seemed astonished that I wanted to rent rooms by the month, but after murmuring the usual *"Ah, ces américains,"* they agreed. Although the hotel was certainly seedy, ill lit, with stuffing coming out of ancient upholstery, I was impressed that nevertheless maids were running around changing sheets at all hours.

I mentioned this striking display of cleanliness, very unusual in France, where perfume had been invented, to Stanley Geist, who closed his eyes briefly, nodding, but said nothing.

A joyous reunion with Alfred, whom I met at the ship in Le Havre, and tried to familiarize myself with on the boat train going back to Paris. He looked sort of different, rawer, with a space between his front teeth I hadn't noticed before. By the time we got to Paris, however, he had more or less settled back into himself. I gave him the larger of the two rooms on our sixth-floor hotel walk-up, knowing I would spend most of my time there lit by the rose-colored bulb over the bed anyway. We really were the longest-running tenants by far. (Once, bending over the downstairs desk, I heard a couple behind me rent a room for forty-five minutes.) At first Alfred was delighted with everything, me most of all, and even forgave the French for speaking French. Our stickiest moment was when we ran into a friend of one of my sisters, who introduced me to the person she was with as "Miss Honey Birstein." Alfred's mouth horrifiedly opened and shut. I marched him away before any words could come out of it. My Fulbright days were of course now firmly behind me, though technically they would last through June. I not only stopped going to the Sorbonne completely, I lost touch with the other Fulbrights I had made friends with. To Alfred they were naturally below the salt, too young, too callow. Our teacher and adviser, Michel, he dismissed as a Communist. I tried to go on seeing them by myself but Alfred was offended, especially when I had lunch with Michel. He did consent to see the Geists, since he was the one who had introduced me to them in the first place, and also the Nabokovs, though he distrusted Patricia's beauty,

which he said he didn't find beautiful, and their terribly su-
perficial affinity for high society.

In my memory I pass quickly over the part where Hannah
Arendt arrived in Paris in a great burst of train steam, like
Mephisto. Annchen was there too, standing on the platform
with Alfred and me. "I feel that I am awaiting my judge and
executioner," she had said to me privately beforehand. Need-
less to say, Hannah almost immediately gave us, including
Annchen, the poop on how life in Paris (and elsewhere) should
be lived, told us what to think about everything from the Lou-
vre to Simone de Beauvoir (absurd woman) to the superiority
of *fraise des bois* over American strawberries, and announced
that her charmless hotel was the most charming in France.
Soon she continued on her travels, and soon it was time for Alfred to leave Paris too. One of the ways he had financed his trip
this time was to be a guest professor of Amerikanistics in
Cologne, Germany, to which he was on his way. I saw him off
on the train. We were parting again, but this time when we got
together it would be forever. We had finally decided that there
was nothing else for us to do but get married.

Where was now the question. Paris, my first choice, was out
because of the many typically French bureaucratic impediments
involved. You had to hire a lawyer just to get the ball rolling.
Germany, equally bureaucratic—they wanted our parents' marriage certificates, to make sure, I suppose, that we weren't bastards, was also—well, Germany. We would figure it out when I
joined him. I gave up the last month of my Fulbright, trying not
to feel that I had given up Paris too, and went off to Cologne.

Germany in 1952 was just as horrible as I expected, and even
the word *achtung* made me freeze where I was, heart pounding.

Everyone on the street looked lumpen, gross, and suspicious, men with heavy jowls and big paunches, women with elastics under their chins to hold their hats in place. They had really skimmed off the best, the finest, the lightest of themselves. Where were *you* under Hitler, what did *you* do, I asked silently of everyone I passed. At the University of Köln, faculty and students were either arrogantly impervious to what had happened, or groveling at our Jewish feet. Disgusting either way, though maybe the groveling and the breast beating and the crying was worse. Our landlady, a youngish rather modern type, prided herself on her liberal views, which meant that when there were complaints that some of the inhabitants of the local DP camp were coming into town and stealing, she said pleasantly, "I believe DPs are the same as everyone else. There are good ones and bad ones among them." How they got to be DPs in the first place eluded her. But then simple physical facts staring them in the face eluded many Germans, as obviously they had for years. Both Cologne and the neighboring city of Bonn had been completely destroyed during the war and in 1952 almost nothing had been reconstructed—I once took a half-hour tram ride through the center of Cologne and didn't see one whole building left standing—yet I heard two Germans arguing vociferously, "Bonn is more beautiful than Cologne . . ." "No, Cologne is more beautiful." Alfred was engrossed in his teaching and loved being called Herr Professor Doktor, but I was left on my own in what were increasingly nightmarish surroundings. Once, a copy of *Commentary* magazine was forwarded from New York, and in it there was an excerpt from a newly discovered diary of a little Dutch girl named Anne Frank, and after I read it I couldn't go out on the street for days.

In the midst of this atmospheric horror, Hannah Arendt arrived to resume her rightful place among celebrated German intellectuals. She had been invited by people in high places, the German government, maybe, and accepted this as her due. It was the first time she had come back. This time Hannah didn't bother to set us straight on anything, I think she hardly knew we were there. She was too busy accepting the groveling as her due, receiving plaudits from one and all, including Heidegger, who had been her teacher, but was known to be a Nazi sympathizer. I had never seen her so totally happy, smiling big smiles that made the most of her long crooked teeth, guffawing heartily. It was an awful sight. "How *can* she?" I asked Alfred. "She forgives them," he said grandly. Well, maybe she could, but I certainly couldn't. I didn't ask Alfred if he could. It would have been unthinkable.

Eventually, thank God, Arendt, temporarily satiated with honors and compliments, returned to her new home, the United States, which she considered barbaric. Alfred and I made our final plans to get married, in Basel, the nearest Swiss city, which was Protestant not Catholic, and therefore more easygoing in its legal requirements. We took the train to Switzerland, and though we could have done it all in one day, stayed overnight in separate hotel rooms, my idea. Among other things, I couldn't bear to get off a train and get married without taking a bath first. These were obviously atavistic feelings with *mikvah* overtones, but I couldn't help it. That night before our wedding, though, I had many, many misgivings. In my head I wrote plaintive, pleading letters to Sookie, my closest thing to a mother. And then in the morning all doubts vanished. It was the end of June, the sun was shining brightly as we walked along the Rhine to the beautiful, baroque Basel city hall. I was carrying the bouquet Alfred had given me, and wearing the sheer navy blue blouse, the gift from him that Patricia had brought over from New York. As witnesses we had a clerk from our hotel and a young official from the American consulate. After a drunken lunch we repaired back to our hotel. Were ever two people happier? We were married, on our own terms, just the two of us, no family, no one, in the most romantic circumstances imaginable. "Keep your slip on," Alfred murmured as we came back to our hotel room and fell on the bed to make love, "rub my balls with your wedding ring." A confusing moment—this wasn't part of *my* daydream, which truth be told involved being swept off and carried up a red velvet staircase—but it passed.

The next day I went off to have my maiden name crossed out on my passport and my married name substituted. Another disturbing moment—I had been proud of that passport, which was my very first—but I understood that this was the kind of thing that married life required. Actually, I wasn't feeling very married yet. Because his presence wasn't strictly necessary, Alfred had stayed behind in our hotel room, writing in his journal. But then off we went on another Swiss train to our honeymoon destination in Lugano. It was great to be free of Germany, free of thinking about Nazi horrors. I was ecstatic—until a businessman sitting opposite us in the compartment began to laugh and boast about how during the war the Swiss charged Jews thirty thousand dollars for passports and then took them back immediately. Lugano itself, however, had no dark shadows, it was all bright and sunshiny, really like an MGM movie, brilliant blue lake and all. The next morning I stood on our hotel balcony in the pink lacy peignoir set my college friend Rosalie Golden had given me in case of just such an eventuality, and looked out over the technicolored lake and mountains, hardly believing that fate had actually set me here. Afterward I went for a walk by myself and kept looking at my shiny gold wedding ring and telling myself I was actually married. Alfred was back in our room writing in his journal.

We left Germany soon after our return and set out for Cambridge, England, where Alfred was to take part in a Fulbright conference. Cambridge was beautiful, as majestic and regal as its photographs. I had plenty of time to look around since only the husbands taught and were given rooms in the colleges, where they often dined. All the wives, which now included me, stayed in a small hotel in town, which didn't elicit any shock or surprise, except from me. The wives were very sweet to me though, especially when they learned I had been married only three weeks. They themselves were much older. There was Mrs. Alan Nevins, and Mrs. Henry Steele Commager, whom I already knew from Salzburg, and Mrs. John Hope Franklin. The husbands were nice too, when we saw them. Henry Commager took me and Alfred punting on the Cam and upriver to tea at a country inn. I wore a picture hat and a wide skirt spread out on the seat. Sir Charles and Lady Darwin invited us to a garden party. The invitation actually said "Sir Charles and Lady Darwin request the honor of your company at—— ——" and I didn't know if I had to write back in the third person. I only knew by now that I was the one to answer it. At the party itself, a kind Englishwoman undertook to enlighten me about the identity of various guests grouped in genteel conversation on the smooth green lawn, and when she said, "And that's the Mistress of Newnham," I said sophisticatedly, "Do tell." I didn't understand until much later that there was a Newnham College.

After Cambridge came London, where Alfred as usual knew lots of famous people, as usual not so famous to me. He explained to me before we went to meet them who Arthur Koestler was, and Stephen Spender. I tried to go shopping, thinking that now at last, unlike in Germany, Italy, or France, I could relax into my native tongue. But since I was looking for a pocketbook and an eyelet garter belt, I failed to make myself understood.

Then it was time to sail home. We went back on the *Queen Elizabeth*. The English Fulbright grant was paying for Alfred's ticket, and I had managed to switch my own passage from the French Line. As we stood on deck together, it was hard to remember that I had come to Europe originally on my own, as a Fulbright scholar. Now I was a happily married woman. There were tears in my eyes, nevertheless, as we sailed silently out of Southampton harbor. For what? For the whole part of my life that was over. I would never see Europe again the same way. I would never again be that girl come to Paris for the first time.

Chapter 6

*A*LL FOUR PARENTS met us at the vast pier, which was thronged with disembarked passengers and strewn with piles of luggage. At the sight of our particular welcoming committee I evidently looked so woebegone that a customs official beckoned me into his office. I thought he was going to put me in jail, which at that point would have been fine with me, but he only asked me sympathetically what was the matter. I told him that two sets of parents were out there, each wanting a piece of us and that we had just gotten married. He suggested I rest in his office for a while. When I came back out, the customs official chalked up our luggage with dispatch and we were ready to go. Mama and Papa had planned a big welcoming spread for us, but Alfred shook his head and so I did too. It was time to establish firmly where my loyalty lay. I was going home with my husband.

I didn't realize I was also going home with my husband's parents, until we were all well underway to Brooklyn in the taxi. I didn't understand this—why hadn't Alfred taken the same staunch stand that I had—in short, told them to get lost? I also didn't understand why, when we got to the creaky old apartment on Pineapple Street, his parents should be sitting down to eat the chicken and other food my parents had

151

put in the fridge for Alfred and me. Something here wasn't right, though Alfred seemed to be just normally miserable. When his mother and father finally left, I gave a sigh of relief. Alone at last. I turned to my love, but he was in a rage. It wasn't his parents that had been the matter, but what my parents had done to his bachelor pad. He looked around fiercely. Julia had clearly also contributed her efforts. Flowered pillows were propped up on the sagging day bed. A pipe he never smoked sat prominently in a pipe dish. There were a pink shag rug and matching toilet seat cover in his bathroom. He snatched off the toilet seat cover and threw it out the window, which I thought was very funny. I could see it landing on somebody's very surprised head. Then he marched into his bedroom, saw the stylish new set of peach-colored sheets and pillowcases, and became seriously enraged.

"Get those sheets off there!" he cried. "Put back the white ones!"

I had no idea where the white ones were. I had never made this bed in my life, having mostly climbed out under cover of darkness while Alfred was sleeping and gone home on the subway.

"Or are you too *lazy* to change sheets?"Alfred said.

Lazy . . . And so began Phase One of our married love. Europe hadn't counted at all. That was part of the courtship.

After our wedding in Basel, I had cabled home and asked Daddy to send us his blessing. Which Daddy did in his return cable, wanting also to know who was the officiating rabbi. (He added that Basel had been the site of the first World Zionist Congress.) There hadn't been any rabbi, of course, and soon after we came home, Daddy's mission in life became to marry us under Jewish law. This was obviously under-standable, but Alfred didn't think so. On account of his So-cialist background, anything about the Jewish religion alarmed and threatened him, and also having my father marry us required Alfred to get a Jewish divorce from his first wife, which he was very reluctant to do. After much pleading, weeping, cajoling from the mothers on both sides—my father was stern and stony—the deed was finally done. Alfred went to the Actors Temple, was surrounded by rabbis, and a metaphoric messenger was dispatched to Rochester to tell Al-fred's first wife, who was long happily married and the mother of twins, that she had been cast off. Alfred, actually, kind of enjoyed the divorce, after all. "I think I just exchanged you for a camel," he said when he came home.

In a few months we left the tenement apartment on Pineapple Street, which really wasn't right for two people—Alfred held on to the lease, though, for personal security rea-sons and because the rent was so cheap—and we moved to the upper West Side, not far from Columbia. Saul Bellow, now divorced from his wife, lived nearby, off Riverside Drive. His apartment was tiny, but if you stood on the toilet seat in his little bathroom and looked sideways through the window you could see a beautiful view of the Hudson. We took turns doing this. Often on Sunday afternoons, we walked along the drive, talking about life, Saul and I lagging behind, or else went into one of the ping-pong parlors on Broadway and Ninety-sixth for a few games. Those were the lovely times. I fell in love with Saul without knowing I had. (Without *his* knowing I had.) However, often joining us was Saul's new young girlfriend, who worked at *Partisan Review* and called herself Alexandra Tschacbasov, which suggested old Russian aristocracy in the background. She had big breasts and wore a big cross that hung down between them. Obviously, the combination did something for Saul, since he was always hinting about the hot stuff that went on in bed between them, sometimes, it seemed, only minutes after it happened. This reaction from a man who said they were so poor when he was young that his mother gave them torn up Yiddish newspapers to use as toilet paper, and the letters seemed so holy to him he couldn't bear to wipe himself with them.

Alexandra's father's name turned out to have been Lichterman before it was Tschacbasov, which certainly made the cross, if not the bosom, seem rather dubious. This didn't bother Saul. Nor did the fact that, to me at least, his girlfriend was incredibly stupid. Talking about her job at PR, she told me, eyes wide, that she could have had her choice between Saul Bellow and Philip Rahv—imagine that! She saw them as equally big fish in the sea of intellectuals, ignoring the fact that Saul was gorgeous and sexy and a brilliant writer, and Philip Rahv was a gravel-voiced gorilla, and only an editor, at that. Another one of her habits was to ask in reference to any recent point in history, "How old was I then?" and we would have to marvel at how young she was. Actually, she was only two years younger than I, which didn't stop her from making statements to me beginning with the phrase, "For people of *my* generation . . ." For her birthday Saul bought her a beautiful antique garnet ring. For my birthday Alfred secretly exchanged the Royal portable typewriter I had gotten for my college graduation for another model. He didn't understand why I was crying. "But I thought you *wanted* elite type instead of pica."

Around this time, *Commentary* magazine asked me to come down and talk about my writing something for them. I met with a not very pleasant, heavyset man named Greenberg, or something like that. (Alfred would know when I came home.) He talked about my doing an article, which wasn't exactly my strong suit, I explained. Fiction was what I was interested in. In that case, okay—I should send them a story. When he found out that I was married to Alfred, however, the atmosphere changed. Another editor came in to take a look at me. I was happy, though, and finished the story I was working on and sent it to the editor who had asked me to come down. Within a week I got the story back with a curt, form rejection letter. No note, nothing. Luckily, that same story was lying on my desk when my sister-in-law Pearl came in, read it, and brought it to *The New Yorker*, where she was a copy editor. After some hemming and hawing, they took it. God Bless Pearlie, God Bless America! Who cared about *Commentary*? The Jewish press had always been lousy to me anyway, and a Harold U. Ribalow in a review of *Star of Glass* for some Jewish rag had suggested that I either stop writing or that my father quit the rabbinate. *The New Yorker* was where I really belonged, a special triumph because Muriel Sparkman, one of my professors at Queens College, had once asked me, "If the *New Yorker* won't take my stories, what makes you think they'll take yours?" Yes, I had really entered into an age of miracles.

Alfred had been invited to teach at Harvard for the fall term, and this was as exciting to us as going to Europe. And possibly more foreign. Daddy, as impressed with the idea of Harvard as we were—shades of Mendy Weisgal!—and once more on a friendly, if wary, footing with Alfred, commandeered a Riverside Memorial Chapel limousine and driver to take us and our goods up to Boston. In this way we arrived in great style, at our temporary but elegant quarters on Beacon Hill in a house designed by Bullfinch. The funeral car driver was nice, though kind of surprised to find his passengers capable of speech, not to mention cheerful.

When we were settled, we began to "dine out"—a new phrase for us—almost every night. The Hofstadter dinner parties paled by comparison with what was going on at Harvard. We were hosted by many Cambridge regulars, from Nobel prize winners such as the economist Vassily Leontief and his wife to the cartoonist Al Capp and *his* wife, who looked very like an older version of Daisy Mae. Marion and Arthur Schlesinger Jr. also frequently entertained, though Marion, a chubby woman from an old Cambridge family, who was smiling and bitter, seemed to hate the whole thing. It was Arthur who always called and invited us. The first time, he said, "Don't dress," I answered airily that it was okay, I would probably just wear my red silk. After dinner at the Schlesingers, the ladies arose from the table, and I had to be pried away by Marion. It wasn't voluntary. Also, no matter where we went, all the serving women seemed to look alike, rosy cheeked with a gray braid wrapped around the head. They would slowly take away the fancy service plates one by one, and then after a long wait and in the same manner, serve the next course and the next. It all took forever. But the impression that this was how life was usually lived was so strong, it was months before I realized that all the serving women were the same lady, hired for the occasion. What was called a Cambridge accommodator.

Other visitors to Harvard also circulated at these dinners, such as Isaiah Berlin, whose burping rapid English speech made him completely incomprehensible, at least to me. And often at the Schlesingers there were showbusiness celebrities like Lauren Bacall, because of Arthur's increasing political activity, especially in the Adlai Stevenson campaign. The wives, as usual, were very much in the background, again bound by as many social strictures as Jewish women in the shtetl, it seemed to me, and certainly by more social obligations. Once I was asked to pour at a Harvard tea, but they sat me down at the coffee urn, not the teapot, feeling no doubt that tea and all the accouterments would be too much for me. Which it would have been, though Julia Richman had taken an occasional stab at teaching its girls such social skills, along with always crossing your legs at the ankles. Or maybe being asked to pour tea was considered too prestigious for a young visiting faculty wife. Also true. I had no hard feelings about it, only relief when the coffee stint was over. When I wasn't socializing I was working futilely on my second novel at the same table in the living room where we ate. Proofs of my story came from *The New Yorker*. We had agreed on changes in the manuscript, but now they had made more changes without telling me. I was upset, and waited for Alfred to come home from Harvard and sympathize. He looked at the proofs without reading them and threw them across the room. "What do you want me to do about it?" he said. I was impressed that he cared so much about what they had done to my story, though I didn't quite understand why he had to throw it across the room.

Other than that it was an unmitigatedly glorious few months. We loved Harvard, we loved Boston, we loved being social lions, and could have gone on that way forever. But Alfred wasn't asked to stay, and when we came back to New York, we found that the young academics to whom we had sublet our apartment had taken all the knobs off the bedroom and bathroom doors to keep their little children from locking themselves in, and never put the knobs back.

That summer at Elizabeth Stille's suggestion—she was going there too—we rented a small place for a few weeks in a Cape Cod fishing village called Wellfleet. The beach there beat Brighton and Miami by a mile and was the most glorious stretch I had ever seen. On and on it went, flanked by high dunes on one side and a wild ocean on the other, vast, empty, with no signs of human habitation. Sometimes, walking along it, I thought that when God created the world it must have looked like this. On the other side of the narrow spit of land, which was the Cape at that point, was the bay, equally scrubby and also almost devoid of human habitation. In between bay and ocean were dense pine woods and freshwater lakes, which were called, following local usage, ponds. All of this, this miraculous confluence of land and water made Wellfleet sheer heaven. Our little apartment that first summer was near the bay, and Alfred and I spent hours lolling on the beach, sharing a paperback mystery. Alfred was the faster reader and so he would go first, tearing out about twenty pages or so when he had finished them and handing them over to me, laughing when he was already finished and I was still trying to guess the murderer.

Saul Bellow was renting a little cottage nearby. One evening he came over as I was ironing Alfred's shirts. His face became sadder and sadder as he watched me. I thought this was because in his divorced state he was envying our domestic felicity. But finally he could contain himself no longer and blurted out, "Annie, that shirt looks as if it were washed in the bay and run over by a train." This was hardly what I expected to hear. I asked him haughtily if he thought he could do better.

He could. He whipped expertly through several of Alfred's shirts, long-sleeved ones too, having learned how from being the youngest child and following his mother around as she did the housework. He was also a devoted father, as I found out when his son Gregory, who was about twelve, came to visit, and Saul cooked and took care of him. Alfred's son, five-year-old Michael, came for a stay also and emerged from the plane in Provincetown all by himself, grinning adorably and with his baseball cap skewed sideways. Baseball meant more to him than I suspected, though, because a few days later he had a nightmare, and kept saying "I'm weddy, I'm weddy." I calmed him and held him and asked him what he was ready for. "I'm weddy for the pitch," he said. But soon he was happily playing out on the beach with the other children, and Gregory Bellow, a preteenager with testy moments was very sweet to him to Saul's delighted surprise.

Into this paradise inevitably dropped Hannah Arendt, visiting, I believe, her new friend, Mary McCarthy. Hannah, of course, turned up her nose at the beauties of Wellfleet, which couldn't begin to compare with that mosquito-infested bog in the Catskills to which she herself went in the summer and that reminded her of Koenigsberg. I asked her to come to dinner, but she said no, she would wait until I had been married longer and really learned to cook. She stayed only a short time, but one afternoon as we were in the middle of making love in an abandoned stretch of the dunes, Alfred suddenly leapt up, remembering that Hannah would be leaving right around then. He raced into town to say good-bye to her, panting, and on foot all the way. We had no car.

Back in New York, my first published story appeared. Pearl,

almost as excited as I, and very unlike her brother in that respect—I was still puzzling over Alfred's throwing my proofs
across the room—said that William Maxwell, one of my favorite writers, who was a *New Yorker* editor, liked my work
enormously, which was thrilling. Sheldon Soffer, a former
music major at Queens College, seeing my name in print and
having learned I was married, called to find out how I liked
getting sex all the time. And Rosalie's mother, objecting to the
portrayal of her and her daughter in my story, called to accuse
me of hiding behind my husband.

On another level, though she never mentioned my story at
all, Hannah Arendt stayed very much in the picture. I had still
not been married long enough for her to chance dinner at our
house, but we made command appearances at hers. The dish
she usually made was called *Koenigsberger klops*, some sort of
Teutonic meatballs, which she served with rice and a dessert
called *rote greutze*, for which she defrosted a package of Birds
Eye frozen raspberries. Before, during, and after dinner, and at
all times in between, she freely voiced opinions on everything.
Again, my name wasn't really Ann—that was only a poor
translation—it was actually Hannah. Avoid the parents, both
Alfred's and mine, she cautioned me. Along the same lines, she
dismissed Yiddish as a low German dialect, and so and so as
"only a little Jew." There were quite a few such so-and-sos,
though this was the first non-officially Nazi mouth from which
I ever heard that phrase. Erich Heller, a distinguished literary
critic of Czech origin, was dismissed as a "Viennese hand
kisser." Saul Bellow, she told me, had thin lips and people with
thin lips couldn't be trusted. Americans didn't understand the
genre (whatever genre it was that came up). Bufferin was better
than aspirin. Alfred switched to Bufferin. Henry Schwartzman,

a medical maladroit, if there ever was one, who let his mangy little dog climb around the examining table even if you were on it—this man was a brilliant doctor. So we all went to him, Ruth, Hannah's chief yes-sayer, included.

And, no, Hannah Arendt wouldn't and couldn't sign a political petition because she was a *naturalized* citizen—and of course it made a difference. Americans knew nothing about politics. Toscannini couldn't conduct Beethoven or any other German composer. *The Magic Flute* had the most marvelous comic libretto of all the Mozart operas, it being in German, of course, though to me that libretto had all the wit and sparkle of an elephant dancing. Hannah's husband, Heinrich Blucher, was a genius, which he probably was, but as she repeatedly told us he was unfortunately unable to put any of his profound philosophical concepts in writing. She made this point so many times, Heinrich wouldn't have been able to write anything even if he wanted to. Ultimately Alfred got Heinrich a job teaching at the New School, where students followed him around with a tape recorder. The other thing about Heinrich, repeated by Hannah in a loud whisper, also many times, was that there was insanity in his family and this was why they had never had any children.

On New Year's Eve, the party at Hannah's house, a tradition, involved the usual rigid semicircle locked in her living room, except larger. I thought wistfully of Alfred's and my first New Year's Eve, in the wonderful strip joint in Key West. Still, by now, trapped as I was in that circle of iron, I felt free to venture an opinion from time to time. When I did, Hannah would glance at me and say, "Shut up, little one, what do you know?" and then guffaw heartily. In fact she liked this rejoinder so much, she took to repeating it on many occasions other than her party. When I suggested to Alfred that Hannah was in effect insulting his wife, *he* told me to shut up.

Matters came to a head, though that phrase, "I can't love you if you don't like her," still echoed, when Alfred and I went to see Hannah get a prize from the Academy of Arts and Letters. It was an important occasion—Alfred himself had already received such a prize—with a garden party for guests to follow. As we entered the crowded hall Hannah appeared and began to drag Alfred down the aisle to sit with her. Heinrich avoided public occasions. "You go up to the balcony and sit with Ruth," she said to me peremptorily. Which I did—for a while. Until I asked myself what I was doing up there, relegated to a place where even the women in my father's synagogue were no longer required to sit, planted next to my husband's former girlfriend/cum Hannah Arendt's chief sycophant, looking down at my husband in front row seats with Hannah Arendt. To Ruth's surprise, I got up and walked out, taking the subway to my night teaching job at Queens College, fighting tears of rage the whole time. When I got home Alfred said pleasantly, "Where were you? Thornton Wilder wanted to meet you." I told him that if I had been sitting with him he would have known where I was. I also said, "You tell Hannah Arendt that the next time she wants to borrow my husband, she'd better ask my permission first." This concept stunned and surprised him. He apologized to me, then mulled the whole thing over. Much later on, he picked up the telephone when he thought I was out of earshot. "You hurt Ann's feelings," I heard him say. Which was hardly the point. Hannah hung up on him, loudly enough for me to hear it, and I must say I didn't blame her.

Harvard had been just the beginning of our academic odyssey. Alfred was now offered a special chair for a year at Smith College and, once again subletting our apartment—this time to Alfred's sister, Pearl, and Saul's insistently girlish girlfriend— I packed up pots and pans, books and clothes, and we went up to Northampton. (I'm not sure if once again we were driven by one of Daddy's Riverside Memorial Chapel connections, but it was certainly possible.) Our apartment was on a street called Paradise Road, with a terrace that overlooked Paradise Pond—so named by the Swedish soprano Jenny Lind, who was impressed by its beauty. All in all, what could be better? Another American dream come true. A pretty apartment on a pretty street in a pretty little town with good stores such as Peck and Peck and pretty college girls swarming in and out of them and all over campus. The faculty was congenial and quite distinguished and even included notable female professors, such as Mary Ellen Chase and her companion Eleanor Duckett. One of Alfred's courses was a fiction workshop, which met at our apartment. Why Alfred, who had never written a line of fiction in his life, should be teaching fiction writing, and I, who had just finished my second novel and even had had a story in *The New Yorker*, should not was a question I never asked myself. Neither did anyone else, even though the little group of happy young females that met in our house and for whom I provided coffee and cake, included a smiling Sylvia Plath. No, my big claim to fame was that I had done what every Smith girl aimed to do, snared a great catch as a husband, a comparative assessment of my achievements in life with which I agreed. At home when I was growing up I had fought this concept tooth and nail, but the Ivy League, or rather Seven Sisters setting put a different complexion on things. When I became visibly pregnant, young Mrs. Kazin evolved into an even greater object of admiration, not to say tittering envy.

Sylvia Plath was particularly cheerful and friendly, and I liked her very much. In some ways she reminded me of myself when I was an undergraduate. She was blond, attractive, talented, and made much of by the English Department, which expected great things of her. Like everyone else, I had heard the story of Sylvia's suicide attempt and how she was found unconscious and covered by spiderwebs under her house. But she was so totally cheerful and outgoing now, the episode seemed aberrational. Besides, suicide attempts and breakdowns were not unknown among Smith's hardworking and often fiercely competitive undergraduates, and another member of Alfred's writing seminar, Jane Truslow, had had a breakdown at about the same time as Sylvia. In my own life, a curious confusion between town and gown, as it were, kept happening the more pregnant I got and the closer the publication of my new novel. "When's it due?" people would say. And I would answer either February (book) or June (baby), depending on which I thought they were talking about. It did get a little sticky if people asked was this my first and I said blithely, "No, my first came out several years ago."

My second novel, *The Troublemaker*, did come out in February, and Mary Ellen Chase was wonderfully admiring of it, but she alas was something of a maverick among our literary connections. In fact, in early spring there was a symposium on the novel at which various writers were invited to speak. Alfred figured largely in the proceedings, of course, as did Saul Bellow, who brought his buddy Ralph Ellison along. (This was still an era when other friends of Ralph, seeking to buy a co-op, were told that Negro visitors would not be welcome.) Both of them stayed with us for the weekend, and enjoyed all the meals I provided. I was pleased that they did. My pals. Because of some funny early misunderstanding, Ralph was convinced that I was a trumpet player, like him, and nothing could persuade him otherwise. This seemed to have brought us together and we always laughed when we met. I even laughed when Ralph, seeing I was pregnant, said of Alfred, "Goddamn him." In any case, nobody, including me, thought of my work in connection with the important public discourses being given on the novel. We all knew I had written two of them, but it was a matter politely swept under the rug.

And then, William Maxwell, whom I had never laid eyes on before, but who Pearl had said liked my story, included a long and greatly flattering reference to *The Troublemaker* in the beautiful speech he gave. It was the latest novel he had read. I was overcome, I was flabbergasted, I was in a state of pure bliss. At the party after the last session we were at last introduced, and we smiled in recognition, as if we had long known each other without ever meeting. He asked solicitously about my pregnancy. He and his wife had recently had a baby so he was warmly informed on the subject. And then, when he left, he said, "God bless you. You're a writer after my own heart." At that moment, my whole life came together. I was pregnant. I was a writer after his own heart. I mentioned this to Saul, who said, "Well, he's a very sweet guy." And then to Alfred, who gave an almost painfully embarrassed shrug.

Some days later, I received two letters in the same mail. One was from Fanny Ellison, who thanked me for taking such good care of Ralph. She also said she had been reading my novel *The Troublemaker* and enjoyed it very much. Another

letter was from Saul's girlfriend. She thanked me for taking
such good care of Saul and said she had read my novel *The
Troublemaker* and enjoyed it very much. I started to cry. Alfred asked me why. I really didn't know. I just felt I had done
something wrong. Overstepped the bounds with my admiring
buddies Ralph and Saul, put them on the spot? Made their
wives take the heat for them? Then what about William
Maxwell? Well, as Saul had said, "He's a very sweet guy." Another letter came, this time from William Maxwell to Alfred,
thanking him for his efforts in the symposium and saying in
reference to the impending birth of the new baby, "My God,
what pleasures await you." I had to persuade Alfred that
Maxwell wasn't being sarcastic at Alfred's expense.

The Smith commencement speaker that year was Adlai
Stevenson, whom the faculty was introduced to at a garden
party beforehand and whom I was dismayed to find a sweaty,
red-faced, pot-bellied politician, not a noble patrician at all.
Was this the man who had been chosen in 1952 to lead us all
away from the dark Eisenhower years? I put my doubts on
hold. All the liberal faculty and the activist faculty wives who
were always circulating petitions were there and nobody else
seemed disappointed. The ceremonies began, and soon the
honored speaker rose to address us. The voice was familiar
from campaign speeches, so at first I didn't realize what that
voice was saying. Then I sat up—not easy, since I was in my
ninth month. Adlai Stevenson was telling the entire Smith
graduating class of 1955 that their one, their *only* purpose in
life, was now to go out and be good wives and mothers. The
graduating class, including Sylvia Plath, applauded. The liberal faculty and activist wives applauded. I looked aghast at
Mary Ellen Chase and Eleanor Duckett, and was pained even

more on their behalf and behalf of the other woman professors of that generation sitting there than on my own. What
had it cost them to be professors, how much had they given
up, only to hear this fatuous, self-inflated loser tell them it
meant nothing at all? But nobody talked about it, not in public at least, not then. The liberal faculty and their liberal wives
were all gearing up for Adlai Stevenson's 1956 campaign.

The awaited pleasure was born at the end of June. It was lucky
Alfred was there because for days he had been saying anxiously
he needed to go into New York to see his little son, Michael,
and Hannah Arendt, putting them in inverse order of importance to him, I felt. Hannah and he had had several long-dis-
tance conversations and smoothed things over. When I
pointed out that the baby was due any day, he said that first
babies were always late. But as her initial courtesy in a long
string of them, our daughter Cathrael—she was named after
my beloved uncle—arrived ten days early, kindly sparing me a
lot of anxious weeks and false alarms. As Alfred waited in an
anteroom with Daniel Aaron, another Smith professor and
the father of three, I watched her get born. I had been praying for a girl, so as to avoid all hassles with Alfred about cir-
cumcision and a bar mitzvah, if it were a boy. And there she
was. A miracle from start to finish, even though when they
first put her on my chest, cheesy and white, she fleetingly resembled my mother-in-law and I had to assure us both that
she could always wear makeup. Yes, at last I understood that
thin line between life and death. I was so happy, so fulfilled
that if God had asked me to die then, I would have said okay.
To Alfred, when he was allowed to get out of the waiting room
and was hanging over me, I said, "I gave you a daughter." "I

gave you a daughter," he repeated, moved to tears. It was understood that he would call Saul Bellow with the news first
and then our parents.

The next day he sheepishly brought along a manuscript he
was working on to the hospital for me to look at, along with
some flowers. I understood. He wanted to make sure I was
still there for him and I was. In fact I loved him more than
ever. How could I not? I had never, ever been so connected to
another human being in my life.

We took the baby home, though it would soon be time to
leave our own paradise and Paradise Road. Smith hadn't asked
Alfred to stay on, and he had accepted a professorship at
nearby Amherst College. Anyway, Paradise Road was becoming less and less paradisiacal. A diaper pail stank in the heat of
the bathroom. We were lucky to have it, though. Daddy had
given us two years of free diaper service. Baby clothes hung on
the line on the terrace blocking any view at all, and visitors
had to swat them away when they sat down. (I had washed all
the tiny things myself, rinsing three times, as the baby book
said.) In New York, new mothers generally had baby nurses
for a month. Here I had one only for a week because Henri-
etta was scheduled to go to Tanglewood to take care of the
newborn of "a bandleader named Leonard Bernstein." The
next nurse was with us two days. I fired her because she
screamed at me for picking up my baby, who was crying. She
firmly believed babies had to cry three hours at a stretch to ex-
ercise their lungs.

Baby nurses weren't the fashion in local baby care, anyway.
Which might have been okay except that neither were husbands, as I was soon to discover. (If I had given Alfred a daughter, it was metaphorical.) No, a sisterhood went to work when

babies were born, which involved bringing over casseroles and staying to visit and chat. This made Alfred happy, but not me. Sisterhood had not been the happiest experience of my life. Anyway, I didn't want to eat, or visit or chat, I wanted to sleep. I wanted a helping hand. But Alfred was concerned about his own dinner and woke me up if I did happen to fall asleep at dinnertime to find out where it was. Diapering the baby, which he did try a few times, nauseated him. My parents came up, bringing loads of gifts, but no practical help. There were lots of other presents too. (Hannah Arendt sent her version of a baby present, a big coffee table book on Egyptian art, directly to Alfred.) Calling on literal sisterhood I desperately telephoned Sookie, who had always said she would be there in a flash to help if needed—after all hadn't I helped her out with her first baby?—but the flash never came and neither did she. A few faculty wives, putting down their casseroles, wondered why my mother hadn't come to stay for a while, as their mothers had. But they didn't know Clara. Which was probably a blessing. The real blessing was that my little baby for all the commotion around her was absolutely adorable.

Amherst, town and gown, was only seven miles from Northampton, but it could have been, and after a while I thought, should have been, on another planet. Northampton for all its small size and geographical isolation, had a cosmopolitan and intellectual flavor. This was largely owing to the late William Alan Nielsen, a Shakespeare scholar who had been Smith College's president for many years, and who had a swift eye for the highly qualified refugee scholar, and other intellectuals, men and women, who would appreciate having a sequential three-day teaching schedule so they could work uninterrupted on their own books the other days. There was also the fact that Smith College was an educational institution only for females, and therefore could hardly put on airs or imagine itself of any great consequence. Amherst, on the other hand, with a faculty that couldn't hold a candle to Smith's but that was all male, and with an all male student body, held itself most dearly. Scenically it was certainly beautiful, so much so that as my time there went on I began to think of it as Shangri-la in reverse. Here in this valley, everybody was staid and dour and lifeless. Outside, people were laughing and happy. Certainly, Amherst was one of the smuggest places on earth. It made even little Aix-en-Provence seem cosmopolitan. That Amherst was also anti-Semitic went without saying, without even being noticed.

We had been set down in a twelve-room house, which was way too big for us and for which we had practically no furniture. Since there was also a coal furnace and a two-acre yard that was planted with asparagus for some reason, we also acquired as a furnace stoker and sometime gardener, a Mr. Harold White. Mr. White, as we called him, though everybody else, I learned, called him Harold, looked at us and said in his slow New England drawl, "Yes, we had some of you people around here once." Braving the menace of New York and people like us he installed himself in the Hotel Dixie once a year and went to the flower show. I kind of liked the picture of him in a dive like the Hotel Dixie, especially since on his own turf he was a compendium of terse opinions. Such as, when I politely asked him to take his dirty cap off my clean line of babies clothes, which now dried in the cellar: "They say babies have to eat a peck of dirt."

For me, as time went on, things got worse and worse and more isolated. I had now become totally faculty wife and mother, a woman who was supposed to have no other interests. In the tobacco fields nearby, peasant women squatted to give birth, and then went on with their field work. The local faculty wives, though often graduates of Smith, Radcliffe, and Wellesley, seemed determined to emulate them. They were vocal about dedicating their lives to husband, house, baby, and cooking, but their houses were filthy, and their babies often dirty and sickly. When I walked out wheeling a carriage they laughed about how fresh and clean my baby was. And although they themselves were as unkempt as their children, again almost as a matter of principle, they were not above some academic sexual hanky panky and mate swapping. Alfred didn't understand what I was complaining about, or why his former young darling had become a full-time nag. The other wives weren't complaining. "What do other women do?" he kept asking, truly puzzled, especially when I wouldn't type his manuscripts for him the way the other wives did. I pointed out that he should type mine, since he was a touch typist and I wasn't, which also didn't sit well. But then to him Amherst truly was a New England Shangri-la, and he was happy being a male college professor in a male universe. (The University of Massachusetts, though coed and technically also in Amherst, was way out at the other end of town, and socially infra dig. We went there to see the ice sculptures.)

We did have visitors from the outside world, of course. Pearl came up, a doting aunt, and so did Michael, who was very patient about his new baby sister, except when she crawled over to his big jigsaw puzzle spread out on the floor and extracted pieces with a pincer movement she had just learned. Jason Epstein, a young publisher, and his wife, Barbara, came to visit, wearing resort attire because they had assumed they were off for a country weekend. Mama and Daddy made unannounced, and unappreciated appearances with presents that were now verging on the insane: a tricycle for a child who couldn't even walk yet, solid silver diaper pins. Alfred's parents came and managed to sit out on the lawn and not speak to each other for hours and hours on end.

Another frequent visitor to Amherst, though he wasn't exactly a visitor but an honored native son returned, was Robert Frost, who stayed at the local inn called the Lord Amherst. He sometimes came to our house for dinner, and though I was in awe of him—he looked just like his pictures, granite faced and seamed with a rustic white cowlick—I was very fond of him too. He wasn't at all the genial old man whom he was assumed to be, but a tough old bird who knew his mind and spoke it. He was also, contrary to popular belief, a night person, not an early riser at all, and he would sometimes stay on after dinner until one in the morning. Being basically a night person myself, caught in a world where this was considered immoral, I appreciated this in him and loved his telling us that when he was a farmer he would milk the cows at noon and at midnight, because morning had nothing to do with it, they had only to be milked at twelve-hour intervals. Sometimes he took me out to tea and then we would walk around town and he would tell me strangely personal things, such as that his daughter was a terrible anti-Semite. Also, once we stopped at a wall in town and he said that when his wife died he stood there and suddenly threw all the change in his pockets over it. He didn't understand why.

Things between Alfred and me were going from bad to worse. Trying to recapture our early bliss we decided to go back to France that summer. We took the baby with us, though traveling with a thirteen-month-old, as any fool could have told us, was not exactly the way to ensure any kind of carefree passion. Eileen Geist, our old Paris friend, got us a tiny apartment whose owner was away, and a darling *bonne à tout faire* to go with it. Renée made delicious French meals for the baby which were hard not to steal for oneself. For a while, Paris was its old romantic self again. Beautiful, misty as an Impressionist painting. We ran into Ralph and Fanny Ellison. What they were doing in Paris, I don't remember, but Fanny said they were staying at the Hotel de Fleabag. Both of them doted on the baby. Evidently they had tried for years, unsuccessfully to have one. Ralph told me privately, laughing, how he would produce the sperm, stick the container into his breast pocket to keep it warm and run down to the doctor's office with it.

After Paris, we went to Nice, where Alfred had got a job teaching to finance our trip. And soon the old pattern repeated itself, with a French accent. Alfred off teaching, me stuck at home with the baby, no sitters, and therefore no way for *me* to get out at night. This lasted for six weeks, and then home on the *Île de France,* which we had booked for romantic reasons, in a tiny cabin equipped with a chamber pot.

Back in Amherst, the jailhouse conditions still prevailed, with their New England accent. In Aix-en-Provence, the phrase most used was *"Ça ne se fait pas ici."* In Amherst it was "That isn't done here." Henry Steele Commager, our friend from the Salzburg and Cambridge days was also a professor there, and one of the reasons Alfred had accepted his job. But if I had thought that Evan, his wife, would be my friend in court, I was mistaken. Underneath the family tradition of gentle lunacy, she was a Southern lady, and brooked no malcontents or rocking of boats. By now even the dentist felt free to tell me to stop writing for a couple of years because it was making me so nervous. When the Hungarian Revolution occurred and some of the faculty made a move to support it, the response was that The Ladies of Amherst, a social club, which usually took care of teas, "handles that sort of thing." There were obligatory dinner parties that took days to prepare for, since besides the shopping and the cooking there was the necessity of making the house, and especially the bathroom, look as if no one had ever lived there. One day in the winter I had been so enraged with this relentless domesticity, I threw all the dirty dishes out the window into the snow. When the snow melted and there were the dishes embedded in the lawn, I knew I had to get out of there. The Amherst version of the American dream wasn't for me. I was going back to New York where there were cleaning ladies, and where no one ever said that isn't done here, because it was.

Chapter 7

$\mathcal{W}$E HAD TAKEN AN APARTMENT on the Upper West Side. Where else? In the late fifties in New York that was the place to be, just as the Left Bank of Paris had been earlier on, though this neighborhood hardly offered the same aesthetic pleasures. But apartments were big—ours accommodated all the furniture from our entire house in Amherst, granted that the house had been pitifully underfurnished to begin with—and rents were pretty reasonable. The area, though, still had a leftover flavor from the old *allrightnik* days. Katey (née Cathrael) and I were very happy as I pushed her stroller down streets where there were friendly doormen, lots of shop windows to look into, and Jewish storekeepers who popped lollies into her mouth at the slightest provocation. The storekeepers were also friendly and flattering to her mother. "Mrs. Kazin, you look so good today I thought you were going to a bar mitzvah." Cheap, if unreliable houshold help was readily available, and you could sit in a playground keeping one eye on your child and reading a good book instead of being cooped up in a little yard with some woman you had absolutely no connection with except that you were both young mothers and on top of that she kept quoting from Dr. Spock. I was so delighted with this new

175

state of affairs that I wrote an article for *Mademoiselle* about
the pleasures of bringing up a child in the city, by implication
as opposed to the suburbs, which were then the fashion. I
called it *The City Mouse,* and never identified the community
I had left in any way, including as a college town. But there
immediately appeared a major article in the Springfield, Massachusetts paper that compared the shock and horror of my little piece to *Peyton Place.* Amherst rides again. The Springfield
reporter who was assigned to call me kindly told me that I
could say no comment. Which I did. It was all, happily, very
far away.

We were back on my turf and my family's. My sisters, now
that I was a married woman and a mother, welcomed me into
the fold. We had lots of family parties at which we threw all
the children into the pot, including Michael, and which also
often included Pearlie, who felt so much a part of our family
that she had taken to referring to my father as Papa, which I
never called him. Even Alfred's own father, who was five years
older, said he thought of my father as a father to him. All this
meant that Daddy was back in the picture in a big way. Not
only as the reigning paternal figure, but as a man who, as
usual, had connections for everything. Whatever needed
doing, whatever needed getting we called on him for. Painting, built-in bookcases, liquor, fancy foods, theater tickets,
luggage, wholesale clothing. Our shelves were filled with
booze and dainties from the 21 Club, whose owners were,
naturally, Daddy's parishioners. One time Saul Bellow needed
a tuxedo and we consulted Daddy about it, who naturally sent
Saul to one of his connections. Unfortunately, the guy talked
Saul into a midnight blue outfit, very much the rage at the

time. Then Saul went off to his formal party and Philip Rahv asked him in a gravel voice, "What kind of a color is *that?*" and Saul, deflated, thought bitterly, "It's Annie's fault."

The *allrightnik* strain on the West Side was only a minor one though, rapidly fading. Naturally, Mama, who had to worry about something, and who had worried about our living in Amherst now worried about what to wear to visit a daughter who lived on Riverside Drive. There was no persuading her that it really wasn't Riverside Drive anymore, or West End Avenue, or Central Park West. The neighborhood hardly boasted the same population as when I was in high school. The Jews now weren't jewelers and dress manufacturers, and they weren't exactly fancy, either. In fact many of the local Jewish denizens were somewhat bedraggled intellectuals, many late of City College, like Alfred, and drawn by the big apartments at low rents. Mama quieted down about what to wear and my parents visited often on a Sunday, when I made them tuna fish. Or else I brought Katey down to Fifty-fourth Street where the crib my parents had installed in their bedroom for when we visited from Amherst was still standing. Other than that, Mama never took on any child-care responsibilities—"I suffered enough in my life," she was fond of declaring. But Daddy, who was the one who had taken care of us as kids, anyway, had no compunctions about wheeling Katey down Broadway in her stroller, though Fifty-fourth Street was no longer uptown and the neighborhood was now graced with legitimate theaters and the Stage Delicatessen. Sometimes Daddy took us for drives in his big black clergyman's Buick on Sunday, at great risk to limb of daughter and granddaughter, though fortunately we never thought of it in quite that way.

Palisades Parkway was his favorite place to go, possibly because he imagined the trees (= fresh air) would do Katey good.
His Buick also boasted a small plaid car blanket, which Katey
assumed was for her alone, though I tried to explain there
were nine other grandchildren. "I am the only *gramchile!*" she
insisted. "This kid is out of the world," Daddy, laughing, pronounced in his not always accurate showbiz lingo.

By now, Alfred, like everyone else, loved my father, and
Daddy of course continued to hold Alfred in the deepest admiration and affection, not to mention awe. But on one point
Daddy wouldn't yield an inch, and that was to Alfred's exceedingly scathing views on Jews in general and Israel in particular. They were always having huge arguments on the subject—Daddy quoting scripture and historic suffering, and
Alfred Hannah Arendt's *The Origins of Totalitarianism,* which
was Alfred's bible. It was a good thing I had never told Daddy
how Hannah Arendt had laughed at me the first time I went
to Europe because I had an Israeli visa, of all things, in my
passport. And it was a good thing that I had never told *her*
that the man in the consulate when I went to get the visa
asked me if I would have room maybe to carry a little package. We were already in her mind too utterly below the salt.

The Arab cause was far more elevated. She (and Alfred too,
despite my raging tears) had both defended Ernest Bevan's
stance vis à vis the DPs on some sophisticated ground of
realpolitik. And in fact Hannah had told me proudly that she
was on the hit list of the Irgun, and if she ever went to Israel
they would try to get her. By then I was wondering why they
couldn't get her here. The arguments about Jews between Alfred
and Daddy were getting worse and worse. One day they were
sitting in our living room having a real knock-down drag-out.

Then suddenly there came a terrific bolt of lightning and a huge clap of thunder. It shut them both up. It was probably the only thing that could. They stared at each other, each probably convinced that God had been ready to smite the other.

Along similar lines, Alfred had always refused to come to Daddy's shul for services, citing also his Socialist background, though this was one of the few signs of it still left. Finally one Kol Nidre night I persuaded him to come—we had already been married seven years. We listened as Daddy gave his Kol Nidre appeal, his last as it happened, since he was already very ill with cancer. His face was white and pinched as he looked up at us sitting in the balcony along with Mama. Not at us, really, but at Alfred. He talked his heart out, rambling as always, mispronouncing such old hazards as "sinews." He wanted Alfred to love him, to see him as an intellectual equal. I don't know what Alfred felt, except the usual boredom, I suppose, at listening to an overlong sermon. But I told Daddy that Alfred had been much impressed, and Daddy, a believer, believed me.

Before that Jewish year was out, in July of 1959, Daddy died. My mother, saying "My friend is dead, my king is dead," laid out a little square black dress before falling into a deep sleep, heavily sedated by the fight doctor, who was now the synagogue president. That night, my aunt Big Sarah, said to me from an adjoining stall in the ladies room of Riverside Memorial Chapel, where people had come to pay their respects, "Your fodder was a very sexy man, Chana." The next day, the day of the funeral, Forty-seventh Street came to a full stop. The cops put little hoods over the parking meters and the sidewalk and synagogue were jammed with mourners, many of them famous, others not so famous, including the widow of Singing Sam the Barbasol man, and those members of AGVA (The American Guild of Variety Artists)—my father was their chaplain—who were not working in the Catskills. George Jessel gave the eulogy dressed in a cutaway. When we sat shiva, among the infinite number of visitors, including Peppy, was my sister-in-law, Pearl, who came over every day on her lunch break from *The New Yorker*.

Three weeks later, Alfred went off on a State Department junket to Russia, which was still a scary place to go to in those days. People could disappear and did. For a while, I didn't know where Alfred actually was, or how to reach him. Then I got a couple of postcards saying he was experiencing Russia full in the chest. They were the only things he had ever written to me that I destroyed. Meanwhile, Mama, who hadn't wanted to stay one night alone on Fifty-fourth Street, was being utterly miserable in Brooklyn in an apartment Julia had found for her practically next door. When I went to visit, Mama in tears couldn't stop eating, and I in tears couldn't start. What made it even more heartbreaking was that Mama was eating broccoli, which she hated but was consigned to because she was too fat.

After that came another academic gig in Puerto Rico, best left largely undescribed. I was once again an isolated faculty wife in miserable housing, surrounded by transported pots and pans and trying also to take care of a little four-year-old daughter, this time in intolerable heat. The summer that my father died seemed never to want to end. Alfred's mother was now dying of cancer too. I kept wanting to ask Daddy what to do, how to handle it, just as I had about his own dying. The big local celebrity was Nathan Leopold, now finally out on parole, but with the stipulation that he couldn't leave the island. He was asked everywhere, and women especially made much of him, as if he were a Dostoyevskian tragic hero instead of a coldblooded murderer. Somebody brought him over one night and he sat on our balcony talking about what he would do if he were ever allowed to go to New York. One place he mentioned going to was Romany Marie's, another was Delmonico's. His favorite book was James Branch Cabell's *Jurgen*. It was like falling into a time warp. Besides, he still had the personality of a smart rich Jewish kid, so spoiled he wouldn't have been beyond committing murder for the hell of it. Another example of immigrant adaptation, I supposed. Alfred's mother died that fall. And there we were, Daddy's girl and Mama's boy, with a dark empty wind whistling behind us. My own mother died a couple of years later. With all of her endless nagging and complaints about my father she literally couldn't live without him. And without him the rest of my family had already disintegrated into warring factions.

Meanwhile, in New York the West Side intellectuals were flourishing and multiplying. Anti-Communism was a big thing. Suddenly all the outcasts were incasts, people who because they had once been radicals were now in the know, which sometimes seemed was all they'd ever wanted. Personally, I didn't quite see what the fuss was about or why it required violating other people's civil liberties. Viewed in a certain way, my father would probably have been called a premature anti-Communist in these circles: witness the uncles sometimes allowed and sometimes not allowed to come into our house when they were borrowing money. Alfred said I wasn't political. But that wasn't strictly true either, since we had always been registered Democrats, and the Democrats, as I understood it, constituted one of the two major American political parties.

Anyway, there the West Side intellectuals all were. Diana Trilling, always absurdly self-important, writing letters to *The New York Times* along with Stephen Spender and others, saying, "We view with disdain and repugnance," et cetera, some insufficiently anti-Communist attitude. I also remember her giving a speech at a Congress for Cultural Freedom meeting— the first time I realized that any organization with freedom in the title was against it. There was a banner behind her saying, "One World or None." Diana was firmly planted in front of the *None*. Sidney Hook wrote articles about "Can Our Teachers be Trusted?" (Ans: no.) And Norman Podhoretz, recently married to Midge Decter, the same one who had written her first review about my first novel, was practically in tears as he said, "It's not my fault I was too young to grow up in the thirties." The Irvings diverged sharply. Irving Kristol, back from England and saying "flat" and "lorry," edited *Commentary* on a sharp swing to the right, and Irving Howe held the line on being a Socialist, just as he had always, to his credit, independently held the line on being a Jew.

Political differences or political agreements aside, however, or maybe because of them, we all met and argued happily at one another's houses. For some reason parties (of the purely social kind) had become the big thing and the parties themselves were getting bigger and bigger. Not least, mine and Alfred's, since we had moved to a larger West Side apartment and could accommodate more people. Space, though, wasn't the only need, and so Bea Kristol (aka Gertrude Himmelfarb) and I swapped back and forth my big coffee urn and her dozens of drinking glasses. (There was no point in owning double all that stuff.) Food came from Zabar's around the corner, which was only crowded and not yet an institution, and so Mr. Klein was happy to consult about how many salamis sliced thinly, and how many pounds of chopped liver were needed to feed fifty.

The guests were always basically the same at everyone's party, or so it seems in retrospect. The same brightly colored pieces shaken up into different designs. Among the regulars in our house were the Kristols, the Howes, Robert Lowell and Elizabeth Hardwick, Jules and Judy Feiffer, Jason and Barbara Epstein, Harold and May Rosenberg, Daniel Bell, Dick and Bede Hofstadter, Delmore Schwartz, Harold Rosenberg, Herbert Gold and his latest blond shiksa, also Patricia Blake, no longer married to Nicholas Nabokov, but now a Russian specialist at *Life*. Francis Steegmuller and his new fiancée, Shirley Hazzard, provided the much needed leaven—though that probably isn't the right word—of elegant Gentiles. And then there was that distinguished Gentile gent, Murray Kempton, wry and clever and unvaryingly courteous, who scooted around town on his bicycle like an Oxford don. Alfred's sister, Pearl, often came, of course, and sometimes my sister Sookie and her husband, Sandy. I remember Sookie shaking her little behind provocatively and saying to Harold Rosenberg, head uptilted, "But aren't you generalizing?" And Harold, genially, "If you don't generalize you gossip." If it was a cocktail party, and she was still up, Katey ran around in a scratchy party dress tripping people up underfoot, and later on tried to drink up all the dregs from the abandoned glasses.

Another big party occasion at our house was Thanksgiving, because it was the one holiday besides July Fourth that Jews could celebrate without guilt. Not that we had ever had turkey and trimmings when I was a kid. Brisket and chicken were what my mother complainingly, not thankfully, produced on all occasions. But all those *Ladies Home Journal* illustrations and articles, and the cut out pumpkins and Pilgrims in PS 17 had made a mark on me nevertheless. So we always had a big feast, with lots of guests and nicely mannered children, if possible. One year, Ralph Ellison, who had been a short order cook, expertly carved the turkey.

There were also the Columbia parties, farther uptown, provided mainly by Columbia faculty but spreading tentacles outward. Daniel Bell, a foremost host, producing singlehandedly enough boeuf bourguignon—an academic dinner party standby—for at least thirty people. Naturally, some of the Columbia faculty were never to be found in our house. These included the Trillings. Lionel and Alfred had never liked each other, though it was hard to say which one had led off in this matter. Actually, though I kept my opinion to myself, I personally liked Lionel, finding him courtly and well-mannered, quite a sea-change from the usual Jewish West Side intellectual, though one didn't think of him as Jewish, only intellectual. I must also admit that at first in these circles I had come as something of a surprise, not to say a disappointment. Mrs. Kazin, being a small young blonde, wasn't built on the same scale or with the same accoutrements as Mrs. Trilling, and for a while I wandered around feeling like a little ship without a prow. Lionel soon unbent, though. Once he showed me how to do the Black Bottom, a popular dance of his youth. Another time he said, rather darkly, "If I liked Alfred even less, I'd invite you to lunch."

More strictly literary and less academic, though again there was an overlap, were Jason and Barbara Epstein's parties in a big duplex on West Sixty-seventh Street, which had originally been one of a series of artist's ateliers. (The Lowells occupied another.) Jason was now an important editor at Doubleday, and Barbara was an editor at *The New York Review of Books,* which had been started during a *New York Times* strike, when the book section wasn't available. With these connections, the guests at their parties looked like a compendium of Contemporary Authors at Play. Into this group one evening stepped a young woman, with an olive complexion and lots of dark wavy hair. It was Susan Sontag, making her first public appearance. Though a newcomer to the scene, she worked the place like a pro. Finally, she and Alfred and I wound up in the same elevator going downstairs together. "Oh, my," she breathed, "so many celebrities." Then, after elaborately clapping a hand over her mouth, she gaped at Alfred and said, "I beg your pardon—are you a celebrity too?" Aside from the fact that nobody in the literary world looked like Alfred Kazin except Alfred Kazin, I would have bet that she had a complete dossier on everybody who was there. Alfred, nevertheless, was smiling like an idiot, until I said, "He's Rock Hudson and I'm Doris Day"—which he didn't think was funny at all.

Another great partygiver was Lillian Hellman, though we weren't invited to her town house for a very long tme. She moved in much higher echelons of celebrity, which included generals and celebrated musicians, besides notable literary figures. Dashiell Hammett, her very ill lover, was ensconced in the basement level. Lillian was known to be very much a snob. A Jew from the South, but unlike my own Southern relatives such as Cousin Ooshie and Tante Freydel with a lot of dough and breeding presumably in the background. You had to pass muster to get to her house. One of her bigger parties was right after the annual Academy of Arts and Letters bash, the one I had years before walked out of because Hannah

Arendt had appropriated my husband. Now Alfred was himself one of the immortals, who all sat onstage like the picture on a box of Dutch Masters cigars, with an occasional immortal, like James Dickey, for instance, so drunk he was practically falling sideways off his chair.

At the garden party afterward, the Academy members and other luminaries were gathered. Ralph Ellison was there, along with his friend Al Murray, who was a major in the Air Force and originally appeared wearing his uniform. It was an impressive and unusual sight, a black officer, the only one in our midst. On one occasion I had on a white bouclé cardigan suit with orange-and-gold-braid edging—a Chanel ripoff that I had bought at Shapiro's, a discount place on Broadway, for twenty-five dollars, and that probably wouldn't withstand many cleanings. Even then Lillian's eyesight was probably not of the best, because when she came by she nodded approvingly at my suit, taking it for a real Chanel, and we were invited to her party forthwith. This phenomenon fascinated me, and at another one of her parties I stuck out my hand with a ring on it, gold and diamonds, that she admired greatly. I admired it myself. Katey and I had got it out of a plastic bubble that came out of a machine in the supermarket. It was one of the better ones, since it had cost a quarter.

What was actually talked about at all these garrulous parties, it's hard to remember, except that aside from the usual backbiting and attempts at memorable wisecracks, it was more a question of taking positions—for example, how far to go vis à vis anti-Communism—than actual discussion. Of course, I wasn't an intellectual, only an unknown fiction writer, but even well-established novelists were given short shrift in these circles, that is, if they were alive and writing in

English. Saul Bellow remembered overhearing Philip Rahv say over the phone that nothing had come in for the next issue of *Partisan Review*, all he had were the stories. But then Rahv himself proclaimed openly that no important fiction had been written since the thirties. Criticism was where it was at. Criticism about criticism. Articles appeared with such titles as "The Critic as Prophet." It got to the point where when once at a party there was a big argument about some review of a novel in *The New York Review of Books*—an easily accessible novel, incidentally—and Dwight Macdonald asked me if I had read the review, and I said no, I had read the book, Dwight said, "You're kidding."

Alfred, of course, was at the center of this literary circle, for good reason. He was absolutely brilliant and an extraordinarily gifted writer. Books were his whole life, the clue to his whole life, his text, his bible. He could never see them, as I did, as just someone else's opinion. Granted, I had been taught from childhood on that we were the People of the Book. But these books were something else, most honored if they were written by Protestants, preferably of the nineteenth century—no matter that some of these guys were blatantly anti-Semitic. Catholic thinkers, as I said before, were also much in vogue, and some Jewish intellectuals, like the critic Richard Gilman, even converted to Catholicism, though they later snapped out of it. Of course, in a sense, my father had also considered books other people's opinions too, and was always poring over the huge tomes in his library as preparation for sermons, *beth hamedrash* study, et cetera, consulting other rabbis over the phone for their interpretations. I suppose, in his heart, Alfred considered himself a rabbi too. But Hawthorne and Melville, and certainly Hemingway and

Faulkner were hardly sacred texts, and also pretty damn easy
to understand without any exegesis. Even Faulkner couldn't
give the Talmud a run for its money.

Still, now that my father was dead, I began to see Alfred
as more and more like him. There was his learning, his dedication to books, even though they *were* pretty easy to understand and written in English. Alfred had also become quite
handsome, certainly more and more distinguished looking.
Like Bede Hofstadter, who had said it about her husband,
Richard, I would sometime look at him while he was giving a
lecture and think, "I sleep with that man." That women were
always throwing themselves at him, only emphasized my own
good fortune. And I knew, of course, that without him I
would never have moved in such exalted literary circles. He
was my passport to my own life. But I was also vital to his, as
he never tired of telling me, especially when I was down in the
dumps for what seemed to be no good reason. Brilliant writer
though he was, Alfred Kazin truly depended on my literary
judgment, and he never sent anything out without my going
over it. Not only was this flattering, it was also comfortingly
familiar since I had performed the same anonymous service
for my father with his sermons and benedictions.

Sometimes, though, basking in the literary limelight, the
parties, the general brouhaha and cachet, I would think, "I
got rich quick," and a goose would walk over my grave, warning that I would one day have to pay for these unearned
riches. But I pushed the thought aside. Who could I have confessed it to, anyway, without sounding like an ungrateful Jewish nag, a shrew? And meanwhile Alfred's celebrity grew. By
now even salespeople in department stores were recognizing
his name on my charge plates. Books came in the mail every

day—there wasn't any book that we wanted to read that we couldn't have sent over—an average of at least thirty a month. And all kinds of interesting writers washed up on our shores, wanting to connect with Alfred.

Once Bernard Malamud came over, an old City College classmate—they had both gotten Bs. He had written a baseball novel called *The Natural*. A shy guy, pretty bald and with glasses, a real sweetheart. He had more protective coloration than any writer I knew, right up there with Southern women, and if I'd met him on the subway I would have assumed he was an accountant. We got to be friends, he and I, and when Roger Straus of Farrar, Straus took him up and invited him to a formal dinner, he felt free to come and borrow a pair of black evening sox from Alfred, which he had forgotten to bring along from his home in Oregon. Being meticulous, Bern returned the sox the very next day, assuring us he had washed them out.

Then there was Elie Wiesel, whose novel *Night,* originally written in Yiddish, had just been published in English. He was a dour, skinny young man, who smiled only in pain, and was kind of scary. A blackbird of misery. A very different kind of immigrant. The living embodiment of the Holocaust right in our living room. He lived in a single room at the Masters Institute, which was a kind of minor league Y, where I took ballet classes with my sister-in-law, Pearl, and Bede Hofstadter, but no such light pleasures were allowed into Elie's ken. It was darkness all around and through and through. His book was stunning, surreal, like a Chagall painting. But so was his conversation. I could never tell what was real and what was a dream. And then the same thought always returned. If I had gone through what he had—and it was only by an immense stroke of luck that I hadn't, we were even the same age—what torments would have raged through my mind and heart?

During the summers, the intellectuals gathered outside of New York, but didn't actually take a vacation. In the Hamptons, people stood around on the beach with drinks in their hands, though they didn't need drinks to make it all seem like a vast cocktail party. Sometimes we stayed with Harold and May Rosenberg in Springs, a less pricey Hamptons outpost, populated mostly by artists, who in those days still didn't have much money. At dinner there were continuing fierce discussions with Harold and his painter friends about Abstract Expressionism. That was the great thing about Harold. There was always something to argue about, but he never took it personally. Still, aside from Harold, the Hamptons were a place for impecunious artists or the nouveau riche, who later became collectors. Alfred and I were neither. His lawyer was, though. When I first met him and his wife, they were living on West End Avenue, with decorated plates on the wall, and for refreshments a huge platter of cold cuts wrapped in yellow cellophane. By now they had gone through a series of upwardly mobile addresses, and were not only art collectors, but specialists, swapping a Renoir for two Prendergasts, or something of that order. At Hamptons parties, they and other collectors stood meekly to the side, happy to be condescended to by the same artistic circles they were buying their way into. In a way, oddly, another Jewish success story.

The great summer love of our life, my life anyway, wasn't the Hamptons, it was Wellfleet. I was still as ravished by its beauty as I was in the beginning, though it was a different kind of life now with taking care of Katey, keeping house, needing to find baby-sitters, and trying to keep Michael from being too unhappy during the week or two when the divorce agreement required him to visit. And keeping Katey from being too jealous. One night when we went to Edmund and Elena Wilson's house for dinner, bringing Michael along—the Wilsons had a young daughter Michael's age—Katey said, "I hope you have a mizzible time."

And, of course, it wasn't only the beauty of the place, but the company inhabiting Wellfleet that made it all so exciting. Edmund Wilson was the reigning presence, as well he might be—he and Elena were among the most longtime Wellfleet residents—formidable but unpretentious—willing to talk to anyone, including me, about his latest enthusiasm, which was the Dead Sea Scrolls. The fact that my late father had been a rabbi intrigued him, and he often asked me questions about Hebrew that I could never answer, but that it was immensely flattering to be asked. Actually, he came to the beach itself rarely, and when he did was accoutered in white, with a Panama hat and cane, kind of like a literary Sidney Greenstreet. Elena Wilson was the real beach regular, a tall elegant woman, née Mumm, as in champagne, to be found there every day, swimming into the waves, walking along the surf with their dog Brown. After much discussion, and brilliant sugestions thrown out by others, this was what Edmund had named him. It was kind of like the Wilson version of the Edsel.

The Wilsons' small dinner parties kept up until midsummer, when Edmund left for his ancestral home in Talcottville in upstate New York, eager to get away from what had become for him "the fucking Riviera." The dinners took place in their pretty, conventional, white clapboard house in town, and when we left after a visit Elena would give me a little bag of salad greens fresh from their garden. Edmund, aside from being the ultimate man of letters—I tremendously admired both him and his work—was also literally an entertainer, being an amateur magician. Saying of Katey, "Ann, that's the best behaved child I've ever met—except for two Hungarians—" he offered his services for her seventh birthday. Everybody came out of the Wellfleet woods for the occasion, invited or not, to see Edmund perform, with an array of props that didn't quite work, and his young daughter Helen, head wrapped in a Turkish towel, as his assistant. That his patter was so literary as to be imcomprehensible to the other seven-year-olds, or that he usually didn't get the right card, didn't bother them at all. The performance kind of ground to a halt, anyway, when he asked me for some newspapers that he could tear up and I directed him to the pile of them in the kitchen. About twenty minutes later, I found him absorbed, reading them.

The Wilsons were year-round residents. But there was a large summer community living all over the place, many deep in the woods, near the beautiful freshwater ponds. They included Marcel Breuer, who lived in a simple house of his own design, Dwight Macdonald and his family, who occupied one of an old pair of Quonset huts set years before on Slough Pond—the first time I met Dwight he unfolded his long self from the water stark naked and formally shook my hand. The Schlesinger family occupied the other Quonset hut set farther along on the pond. And after he had made a bundle on *The Last Hurrah*, Edwin O'Connor, who had formerly rented a single room in town, had commissioned a supermodern house on a hill with the only blacktop road in the woods. Ed was one of the funniest people in the world, with the voice of a radio announcer and a general showbusiness bent, and one of his best friends was Abe Burrows, who often came over to visit from Provincetown. On a less light-hearted level, Mary McCarthy, a vicious smiler, rented a house one summer, some said on purpose to plague her ex-husband, Edmund Wilson, and inevitably Hannah Arendt came to visit her. People asked if it wasn't an unlikely friendship, but it seemed to me that if ever a pair was well matched it was these two. Personally, I think they scared the hell out of each other.

Different people would also pop up year after year, taking over the house of someone who maybe had gone to Europe or maybe just needed the extra money from the rental—rents were climbing sky high. One summer found Norman Mailer and his wife, Adele, occupying one of the Quonset huts on the pond. They invited us for a drink, and there was Norman sitting, as he thought, provocatively, on a bench, stark naked, legs apart. (This was very different from Dwight, who had merely been skinny dipping, as old Cape residents often did.) I glanced at what looked like a little curled thumb nestling against Norman's thigh. Was this what all the fuss was about, his self-advertised machismo? Why carry on about a thing like that?

Alan Tate also turned up renting in the woods with his then wife, the poet Bel Gardner who utterly adored him. Alan was the perfect Southern gentleman, except in his cups, when he remained merely Southern. One night, when we were all pretty drunk, and Alfred had gone off to the john, Alan leaned closer to me and said confidentially, "Alfred is hopeless, but *you* could pass for a Nashville debutante." He didn't understand why I burst out laughing, or why, his anti-Semitism aside, a Nashville debutante was the last thing I ever wanted to be.

With all its celebrated male intellectual heavy hitters, Wellfleet was actually a very domestic scene for the women, no matter whether they themselves happened to be intellectuals or writers. We all had children of various ages—the Schlesingers had four, including twins—and devoted much of our time caring for them. Once I caught Elena Wilson smiling at me as I watched Katey filling up her sand pail, and saying approvingly, "You look like a mother hen." This watchfulness was particularly necessary on the beach, where the men, who tended to look lousy in bathing suits anyway, clustered importantly together, while we wives, some blankets away, peered out to make sure no child had run into the waves. We also provided breakfasts, lunches, dinners, entertained guests, gave cocktail parties, provisioned beach cookouts, and of course had dinner parties. Most of the other families but us owned their houses, and I was getting tired of renting a different place each summer, having to get rid of other people's detritus before we could decently move in, and then even worse, having to pack up our sheets and towels when we moved out and abandon all our lovely summer aquisitions, including rubber rafts and ketchup. But Alfred's Socialist background, as he made clear, mitigated against his owning property.

In between these summers our academic travels continued, always with my having to pack trunks full of pots and pans and linens, and needing to set up house once again in somebody else's house (twice in California) find a school for Katey and all the rest of it. We also took a trip to Israel, leaving Katey behind with my sister Sookie, both things I was reluctant to do. I didn't want to leave Katey behind, nor spend a lot of money on my fare when we could have used it for more household help. Alfred's fare was being paid for since he was going as a guest of the Israeli government. This too seemed bizarre since he had spent so much time attacking the country, but I silently thanked my lucky stars that at least the Arab League hadn't asked him first. Oddly, in the end Alfred was the one who became passionate about Israel and I, for the time being, was the one who fell out of love with it. I was astonished by the local chutzpah, their constantly referring to us Americans as Jews of the Diaspora, when they were only a dot in the Middle East; Their incredible condescension toward women, turning me almost immediately into a "little lady." The forcible way they were dumping terrified busloads of North African Jews in the middle of the desert so that new towns could be created.

That trip we didn't meet many writers—I suggested to Alfred that maybe we were getting the tour for the Mayor of Cleveland, since each day we were scheduled for at least one greeting from some municipality or other. But that was only part of it. All my life I had thought about Palestine, dreamed of Palestine, then of Israel. When the Hebrew letters lit up on the El Al plane I thought they said something like, "Lift up your heads, oh ye gates," instead of smoking wasn't permitted and fasten your seatbelts. When somebody tried to get by in the crowded aisle and said, "*Slicha* (excuse me)," I wondered why he wanted us to grant him atonement. Only, now that I was here, although the land looked the same—extraordinarily beautiful and uncannily like the illustrations in the Bible—it didn't feel the same. It was relentlessly claustrophobic, not only because of the official selling of the party line, but spiritually claustrophobic as well. Especially in Jerusalem, whose very light and stones were endlessly demanding. Of what, exactly, I

couldn't say—my soul?—and I fought against giving in to it. I
was haunted by Jerusalem, afraid of it. I couldn't wait to get
out of there and back to the prosaic pleasures of small newer
cities like Haifa and Tel Aviv, which were both open to the
blue Mediterranean. Later, when Alfred wrote about our trip,
he forgot to mention me at all, and said that some official had
presented him with flowers. Since this was likely to give a
wrong impression, I suggested he either take out the flowers or
put his wife in the picture. He took out the flowers.

In the United States, the big news was all about John F.
Kennedy, and about almost every other Kennedy as well. We
all identified with the Kennedys. Jack and Jackie were more or
less the same age as Alfred and I, about two years younger
down the line, and this was also true of Katey and Caroline.
Arthur Schlesinger, our old Harvard and Cape friend, had
been knee-deep in Kennedy's campaign. Now he had a post as
Presidential Assistant, and an office in the White House. We
went to see him in Washington, taking Katey with us, who had
somehow broken the strap on her patent-leather Mary Janes
and was limping along with one shoe coming off. Arthur was
very sweet about it, having those four children of his own. In-
formality aside, I was filled with awe in Arthur's White House
office by being that close to the President of the United States,
that close to someone who was so close to the President of the
United States. (It was like that song: "I danced with the boy
who danced with the girl who danced with the Prince of
Wales.") My father would have been beside himself with pride
at this proximity, though no doubt he would have claimed that
JFK knew him. Being an American had meant everything to
my father, and when I first went to register to vote he said he

would come with me because he was a citizen. When I explained that I was a citizen too, having been born here, my father shook his head and said, "*I* have papers." Even I, in my arrogant young adulthood, understood what this meant to him and, swallowing my pride, I let him come along.

The Kennedy clan had also changed the face of the Cape. Besides in the traffic jams in Hyannis, their presence was felt everywhere, even when least expected. In one of our rented houses Alfred and I gave a party to which Arthur Schlesinger brought Richard Goodwin, a big muck-a-muck in Presidential circles, and he in turn was accompanied by Secret Service men who staked themselves out in the woods. It was very strange to look out from the deck and see men in dark business suits stationed stolidly among the scrubby trees where everybody else ran around in shorts. Personally, I kept wondering what the hell to wear if I ever should get invited to a party at the White House, or maybe Hickory Hill. It didn't happen. Arthur had said he'd like both of us to meet JFK, but as usual Alfred consigned the *both* to that part of his mind where such things were buried, and went off to a White House lunch by himself, afterward writing a piece that so riled up the President he told Arthur, please, don't bring any more of your friends to meet me.

The parties in New York continued, getting more and more far reaching, even in some cases out of control. Norman Mailer's mother called one day to invite us to a party Norman was giving. I was the one who happened to speak to her, and declined, without even waiting to ask Alfred, who I knew wouldn't want to go. It was just as well, since at that party Norman stabbed his wife, Adele, in the back, enraged by some sexual infraction on her part, I believe. Luckily for Adele, she didn't die, and luckily for Norman, Adele didn't press charges. For me that party had something of a sequel, however, which occurred at another party, this one in honor of Jimmy Baldwin's birthday. Jimmy was now something of a celebrity, but beyond that people loved him personally. There was music at this one—unusual in itself, since most literary parties were purely talk—and lots of dancing, including a dance I had never seen before. An actor named Roscoe Lee Brown told me it was called The Twist, and taught it to me, or tried anyway. I couldn't believe it. This dance was as close to having sex standing up as I had ever seen on a dance floor. At some point later on, Elia Kazan started to speak to me and interrupted himself to say, "You're a beautiful woman, or don't you give a shit?" Another shocking first. Nobody had ever said that word to me in public before. Never mind beautiful. Norman, having recently been sprung from jail was there too, being made much of. Male guests were slapping him on the back. A hero. Why? Because he had stabbed his wife in the back? He said to me that he had been thinking about me when he was in jail. My heart turned cold. A horrible thought. I told Norman that to me he was no hero at all. I thought he was a monster. Norman interrupted. "Don't say that," he said. "You're my—" And then someone interrupted *him*, and I never found out what I was to him. And though I confess I was curious it was probably all to the good.

A new face on the New York scene, or rather the part of the scene I knew, was Truman Capote, Pearlie's old friend, the one she had been sharing a house with in Taormina when I first met Alfred. Pearl knew a fantastic number of people, and they were all crazy about her. At that time she was living in a small apartment on the West Side and she asked Truman Capote to dinner, which the four of us ate in the kitchen. He was kind of freakish, of course, what with being so small, and having that high voice, but very funny and very nice. Since I admired his work greatly, it was easy to like him too. Another one of Pearl's literary friends to whom we were introduced was Dylan Thomas—more than a friend to Pearl, actually. This time Pearl brought him over to our apartment. He was totally drunk when he came in, and got drunker as time went on. "Spare me your meat, give me drink," he said loftily, if woozily, to my offer of something or other on crackers. He was, however, ineffably and ineluctably Dylan Thomas, his round head covered with sweaty curls, his Welsh accent making everything he said sound like poetry. In fact, when I went out into the hall with him, showing him to the bathroom, possibly, he did quote poetry to me, though not his own. "But only God, my dear," he said, gazing at me drunkenly as if I were a shiny party decoration, "could love you for yourself alone, and not your yellow hair."

With all of this socializing, traveling, setting up house in various academic communities, I had never stopped writing, of course. Usually in difficult circumstances—in Berkeley, for instance, I sat on the edge of the bed and typed on the vanity table—and often, it seemed, writing on water. Most of our intellectual friends who did know I was a writer assumed that I had been Alfred's student and that was where I had gotten the idea, which probably hadn't been a good one. Others had no idea after all these years what my writing name was, or wanted to know why I didn't use Kazin. Murray Kempton was one of our few literary friends who not only knew my work, but admired it openly, even in print. Francis Steegmuller was another. I wondered if this had something to do with their not being Jewish and therefore not worried about losing their manhood to literary women. But beguiling though it was I put the thought aside. It left out and took in too many people. Other writers had worse troubles, I told myself, thinking along the lines of "Eat. People are starving in Europe." So I just kept at it, working on a third novel, doing stories and pieces for *Mademoiselle* and other magazines. Still, sometimes I decided to throw in the towel and get a Ph.D., which would give me my academic visiting card and a crack at a good job. And after all, hadn't I been a straight-A student, graduating Magna Cum Laude with honors in English? Didn't I have a Fulbright to my credit, six credits toward my masters, two published novels? I went up to Columbia and met with the department chairman, one Louis Leary, to discuss the matter. I presented what I thought were my impressive credentials. At which, Professor Leary laughed and said, "What's the matter, can't your husband support you?" Alfred laughed too when I told him, and I felt guilty, as if in some way I had insulted my husband and he was being nice about it.

John F. Kennedy was assassinated. It was an unbelievable shock and horror, and a personal loss. Roosevelt had been a father, Kennedy and his family was *us*. The glorious and brief reign was over, we finally understood. Arthur Schlesinger transferred his allegiance to Bobby almost immediately. Dick Goodwin went to work for Lyndon Johnson. But for the rest of us that heady sense of being young and close to the thrill of power was gone for good. Ironically, an invitation to the White House finally did come, though in a peculiar form. A card arrived in the mail asking us to tea with President and

Mrs. Johnson on what happened to be the very next day. I called and said politely and regretfully that we couldn't, the invitation had come too late. A Southern lady on the other end said cajolingly, "Oh, why don't you all just hop on a shuttle and come on down?" The style had certainly changed. But I thought, could little Honey from Hell's Kitchen ever have imagined herself casually turning down an invitation to the White House?

The next year found us at a small party where Jackie Kennedy was present. I talked to her for a while. In a way it was easy. She was softspoken, utterly well bred and utterly charming, and looked exactly like herself. I remember that she made some laughing remark about Kenneth Galbraith and other Harvard types. But it was also like talking to a living and incredibly moving piece of history. She was wearing a black dress with a white collar—still in mourning. The ring that she had put on her huband's finger, then taken off again, was back on hers. Alfred, who had to leave early to teach a class at the New School, ran into her in the elevator and naturally appropriated her entire presence at the party for himself. He dined out on the encounter—as we had learned to say at Harvard—endlessly repeating what he said and what she said. In a way, it was as if I had lost not only President Kennedy, but Mrs. Kennedy too.

My third novel, *The Sweet Birds of Gorham* was finally finished and sold to a young editor at David McKay and Company named Phyllis Grann, who hopefully sent it out for blurbs. To our astonishment a postcard arrived from somewhere in Kansas, signed Truman Capote. Truman Capote loved my book. *Vogue* printed an excerpt, then asked me to review

movies for them. I had been a movie buff all my life, but I had
never reviewed one and I was scared stiff. It wasn't like reviewing a book, after all. You couldn't leaf back through pages
and check on what you'd missed. The first movie I was sent to
review was Laurence Olivier's *Othello*. I sat next to Brendan
Gill, who reviewed movies for *The New Yorker*. Other film
critics, experienced ones, were scattered about the screening
room. Public relations people were smiling at us, nervously
expectant. The screen was still blank, as was my mind. "Brendan," I said, "how do you review a movie?" And he answered
kindly, "Well, to begin with you know the plot of this
one . . ." Actually, reviewing movies wasn't at all like just
going to them. You couldn't sit back and relax, be there for
fun. It was far more stressful than that. Certainly nothing like
going to a double feature with my friend Peppy. You *could*
make a few notes in the dark, but afterward you had to carry
your impressions around like an egg balanced on the top of
your head, until you had got it all down. Sometimes, I needed
to look at more than one movie in a day, which would leave
me with time to kill. Once, in between screenings, I went to
the Russian Tea Room to have a drink and sat myself down at
the bar, where I had often waited for a table with Alfred. They
said, sorry, no unaccompanied women were allowed at the
bar. Great, then I would sit in one of the booths. The booths,
all empty, were also all reserved. Evidently a woman alone in
those days was ipso facto a professional whore.

The greatly sustaining factor in all of this, and life in general,
was my daughter, Katey, who had turned from an adorable little girl into an adorable early teenager—yes, such a thing was
possible—as American a child as I could have wished for.

Michael was an American child too, of course, but in a way this had always been in the cards for him—brought up in the suburbs, his mother a member of an old, wealthy *German*-Jewish family that had been in this country for ages. Katey was ideal company at a screening and knew to keep her mouth shut about the movie until I had written a draft of my review. In fact, she was a pleasure to be with on any occasion—whether we were hanging out at home, going for a walk, out to dinner, to the theater, anywhere—pretty, funny, kind, all at the same time. She couldn't imagine having a mother who didn't know English. She could barely remember how my father had doted on her, which in its way was an even greater loss to her than it was to me. I had counted on him to fill in the gaps in her history. I had always assumed that he would intruct her in Judaism, religion, Hebrew. Now, there wasn't anyone. I was too ignorant—having been brought up as an Orthodox *girl*—and Alfred wanted only to wash his hands of the whole business.

Katey went to a private school called Dalton. Actually, I had sent her there by mistake, thinking it was the progressive place it famously once was, and that she would spend her time knitting afghans or something. I figured that the intellectual atmosphere at home was rigorous enough. She didn't need it in school too. (Bede Hofstadter's daughter attended Brearley, some steps up on the social ladder, where she was a schoolmate of Leonard Bernstein's daughter, and the two of them, according to Bede, adorably argued over whose father was more famous.) In fact, I was horribly mistaken about Dalton. The school had just been taken over by a new director named Donald Barr, who seemed to hate children but love wealthy arriviste parents, the spiritual kin of Alfred's lawyer and his wife, the art collectors. The mothers were particularly eager to be seen as having it made. Katey and I used to call them Dalton mothers, and they were recognizable anywhere in their expensive gray suits and leopard hats and matching belts and makeup that had taken hours to put on. Under Donald Barr, the children were pitted against each other competitively and the curriculum soared to new heights of pretentiousness, made for the parents to read and exclaim over. One day Katey's sixth-grade class had been studying Proust(!)—or were under the impression they had—and when she strolled over to the Dumas French Bakery nearby afterward, the saleswoman said, before Katey could even open her mouth, "We're out of madeleines, Mademoiselle."

Literarily speaking, there was now another new kid on the block. But, miraculously, he not only wasn't a kid, he didn't even write in English—or French, or Spanish, either. It was Isaac Bashevis Singer, a later immigrant, who had been put on our cultural map by Saul Bellow's translation from the Yiddish of *Gimpel the Fool*, a story published in *Partisan Review*. Before that Singer had been known only to readers of his little tales in the *Forward*. Now he had become something of a small celebrity, and Yiddish something of a fad. Irving Howe had always done important and dedicated work in Yiddish studies and literature, but there weren't many like him. Suddenly people who had pretended not to know Yiddish were pretending to know it. Alfred, who in one of his books had made the crack that Yiddish was a language where you broke all the windows to let in a little air, wrote a glowing introduction to the stories of Sholom Aleichem. I myself had met Isaac at a party, where in an accent thicker than even my Uncle Max's he told me that it was a *mitzvah* to eat dairy products on She-vuoth, cheese blintzes being a prime example. Shevuoth was coming up, which was why he had made that point, and a few days later he called. Alfred answered the phone, but Isaac Singer asked to speak to me directly. He started with what had to be one of the great come-on lines in history. "Hello, Mrs. Kazin? Singer here. How's about our blintzes?"

That time he took me to Steinberg's Dairy Restaurant on Upper Broadway, where my high school friend Maria and I used to torment her uncle, the owner. Sometimes the scene of our meetings shifted to the Eclair, on Seventy-second Street. Isaac was a confirmed vegetarian—for moral reasons or not I never discovered. But he kept telling me wonderfully racy stories in a Yiddish accent that made me think he was my benign old Zayde, which he emphatically wasn't. Actually, my Zayde hadn't been all that benign. It was the accent that made me and everyone else sentimental, and obfuscated his real personality. He told me he had once had bright red hair, not too much of a surprise, since though he was now bald, his skin was that whitish redhead's color. He also told me how while he was waiting his turn in a Warsaw whorehouse, he would sit there reading a book. How else was he to pass the time, he asked me slyly? He was also eager to know if I had ever had any supernatural experiences, with ghosts and suchlike, which I had, but didn't want to talk about. After a while I realized that another thing he wanted to know was if I would help him translate his stories. He would roughly put them into English, and I would then put them into good English. But I refused. My Yiddish was too lousy to catch subtle nuances, and I had better things to do with my time. He said tauntingly, "If Saul Bellow can do it, you can't?"

One year, for my birthday, Isaac said he would take me down to the old *Forward* building on the Lower East Side and show me around. The *Forward* was moving uptown and he needed to clean out his old desk. That day I called him and said, Alfred wants to come too. He said sighing, so did his wife, Alma. She was a saleslady at Lord and Taylor, in a dress department I used to frequent but now tried to avoid because I didn't want her to wait on me—which, incidentally, she would have been perfectly happy to do. One day, when Alma and I happened to meet on the bus, she told me what an easy husband Isaac was. He never fussed about dinner but was perfectly agreeable to eating out when she came home from work. After Isaac and I had been friends for a while, and had spent some time eating whipped cream desserts and feeding the pigeons that flocked around him on Broadway, I sent him my new book. And wasn't too surprised when he wrote back that he hadn't had time to read it yet, but that Alma liked it very much.

Around the same time a guest at one of our parties, pointing to my books on the living room shelf, said to me, "Oh, I love her work, don't you?"

I might have felt I had lost Mrs. Kennedy, but I hadn't lost Truman Capote. Far from it. One day in the mail there came an intriguing invitation. It was to a ball that Truman was giving in honor of Katherine Graham, the publisher of *The Washington Post*. Guests were to come dressed in black and/or white and wear masks. Everything about this invitation was amazing, not least because I had never been invited to an actual private ball before—it was like being asked to Twelve Oaks from Tara. Then there was the matter of what to wear—easy for the men, who had only to put on their tuxedos—and then of course finding a mask. Where did you get one? Levy's Stationery Store on Broadway, Katey's old Halloween source, didn't seem quite the answer for this one. Beyond all that, within a few days it became apparent that this invitation was so much sought after that people were even planning to leave town if they weren't asked. This put a prodigiously large dollop of joy into my already full cup since I knew that this time we had been asked largely on account of *me*. Not only did Truman love *The Sweet Birds of Gorham,* he had told many of his society friends about it, including as she enthusiastically informed me, the former Bubbles Schinasi, aka Mrs. Arthur Hornblow, a name familiar to me for years from gossip columns.

Back to what to wear. I hightailed it over to Shapiro's on Broadway, as usual, and there miraculously found the absolutely perfect ball gown for the occasion in the back of the store, among the clothes rods dedicated to formal wear. Well, maybe not exactly perfect in the sense that the price was a bit more than we could afford, but I would surely be able to wear it again—where, I didn't ask myself. That dream dress on Shapiro's hanger had a form-fitting, square necked, black velvet bodice with tiny buttons down the front, below that a tight black satin cummerbund, and then a billowing, long stiff satin skirt of alternating black and white stripes. Every bit of it was made of heavy silk. Not only were the black and white contrasts perfect for Truman's ball, the style was, aptly, a gown that Cinderella herself might have worn.

There were pre-ball dinner parties all over town. Alfred and I got invited to one given by the *Newsweek* publisher, because we were old friends of Kermit Lansner, the *Newsweek* editor, and his wife, Fay, an artist who had made me a beautiful silver mask. Both of them were also residents of the West Side who had risen in the world. Even Alfred consented to wear a mask, a small black one which did come from Levy Brothers. When we got out of the limo at the Plaza, lights seemed to be flashing all over the place. I was half-blinded by my mask, and then photographers quickly began to take my picture, disappointed when I turned out to be nobody because evidently I was dressed like somebody. They didn't seem to recognize Alfred's name and would certainly never have recognized mine. Nevertheless, judging from their first eagerness to snap away, I knew that Shapiro's had come through for me socially yet again.

Finally, we entered the Plaza and the Grand Ballroom, among the select few allowed to do so. Little Truman, in a tuxedo, and tall Katherine Graham, in white embroidered silk, stood beside each other to receive us, both in masks. Beyond them the scene was dazzling. It seemed that everybody I had ever read or heard about was there in that crowd, seated at small tables or out on the dance floor. It was like leafing through the pages of a full-color illustrated magazine, except that the figures were in motion. There were people from the many different walks of life Truman had wandered through on his way. Show business, Frank Sinatra and Mia Farrow, high finance, Henry Ford, Jr. and the ravishing Christina Ford, politics, some Kennedy sisters (but not Jackie), a smattering of intellectuals, us, the Trillings, high society, William and Pat Buckley. And what gowns, reeking of money and the ateliers of the grand couturiers. Beautiful masks, too, many gilded and fantastic. Christina Ford's was in the shape of a gorgeous butterfly.

It was the party of all parties. On that evening we all felt we were in the exactly right place to be. Peter Duchin and his society orchestra provided the music. I danced and danced—

with whom I can't remember and probably didn't know at the time—except that one of my partners was the sheriff from Kansas who played a leading part in Truman's nonfiction novel, *In Cold Blood*. It didn't seem the time to tell Frank Sinatra that I was Rabbi Birstein's daughter—besides he seemed to have already gone home. But I did look around and think, I'll bet I'm the only one here who knows anything about the niceties of davening *Ne'ilah,* maybe even that it's the final prayer on Yom Kippur. The ball ended with a breakfast of scrambled eggs being served from chafing dishes. I ate them in the company of Douglas Fairbanks, Jr.

No doubt Alfred and I made love when we got home. It had been that kind of night. Hours later the room turned from black to pale gray. But I still wasn't sleepy and I still couldn't stop thinking about the ball. I lay in bed, gazing at all my finery thrown carelessly hither and thither, a delightful sight. Especially my ball gown with its black and white satin stripes, draped over a chair. It was beautiful. I too had been for that evening beautiful, one of those actually called "the beautiful people." And I had been invited because I was a writer Truman Capote admired. It was an incredibly rare and perfect moment.

I was Scarlett O'Hara and the duck who went to the party all rolled into one.

Chapter 8

BUT WHAT HAPPENS when the ball is over? I've often imagined the prince saying to Cinderella, "Okay, now take off those stupid clothes and get to work on *my* hearth." On the other hand, in effect this had already happened many times over. So that was no news.

Still, although I took care of all of it, the garbage, the cooking, child rearing, dirty laundry, entertaining, I got no points for any of it. What rankled Alfred was that these domestic duties, especially his need to have dinner on the table, didn't mean more to me than anything else in my life, which alas included my work. I remember a not atypical day in the late sixties, when I went to teach at CCNY in the morning— I was a writer in residence, though where my residence would be except maybe the IRT I couldn't imagine. It was a scary campus way uptown that I was always relieved to come home from, in addition to which there was the occasional bomb scare. Then I picked up Katey at school to take her on some errand or other, came back home to work on a collection of short novels, and then I took Alfred to a screening as part of my job reviewing movies for *Vogue*, came home again and settled him down to eat stuffed peppers, his favorite, which our part-time cleaning lady had made and left for me to reheat for him. Then I went and did a draft of my movie review, which I had to get down quickly before it fled from my head. When I finally emerged Alfred was furious because I personally hadn't made the stuffed peppers for him. That I was getting paid for the teaching and the reviewing and putting it all in our joint account didn't matter. I still hadn't *cooked* his dinner, only made sure it was there for him. A year or so later, tired of being called a parasite—the influence no doubt of some girlfriend that as usual I knew nothing about—I screwed up my courage and almost sick with anxiety opened my own little bank account. Not until many, many years later did I ask myself why Alfred hadn't cooked for *me* while I worked. Which still seems like a loony idea.

I guess it was inevitable that from psychological abuse came physical abuse as well. Even now when such things are discussed openly, it embarrasses me to admit it. I can hardly bring myself to believe it's true. At what point in our marriage the physical attacks had started I could no longer recall, since in between I went about successfully pretending they never had. This didn't happen to a nice Jewish girl, this didn't happen in the home of two intellectuals dedicated to the life of the mind above all else. What brought on the attacks could be anything at all, though it was always understood they were my fault. An argument about Fidel Castro, for example, who at first was very much in vogue among intellectuals, including Alfred. I had said I thought Castro was a dictator, not a political hero, and this made Alfred so furious he drew his hand back to slap me in the face. When I put up my own hand to protect myself, he hit my finger instead, breaking it. I remember the doctor being suspicious of how it had happened,

and my indignity that he should be so, by now totally viewing the matter as private, something between me and my husband. As the years went on, there were many, many other such
incidents, often in bed. We'd be making love, I'd be happy.
Then Alfred would suddenly say that I didn't know how to do
it, and fly into a rage. During other arguments he would rip
the sleeves out of my bathrobe—I was always having to buy a
new one—or tear at my hair, which the next day I would
comb out in bunches. Always after these episodes, Alfred
would cry, say he had never hit any other woman but me.
There was a strange kind of compliment implied.

Why did I stay, why did I put up with it, why did I never
tell anyone about what was going on? Obvious questions, easier to answer now that the profile of abused women has been
established, though to fit it so well does seem to undermine my
vaunted sense of individuality. But to begin with I had been
brought up and lived most of my life at a time when it was the
best of worlds for men, the worst of worlds for women, and so
to me Alfred really differed only quantitatively, not qualita-
tively from most men. After all, I had spent my young years
sitting up in the balcony while the males sat importantly
below. I had had it drummed into me by my mother that if I
didn't get married I counted for nothing, no matter how much
I achieved elsewhere, and even if I told her she was crazy. If my
sisters didn't have a date on Saturday night, they lied about it,
for fear of being considered social pariahs. (Recently, a graduate student told me she couldn't believe that someone like
Sylvia Plath could also place so much importance on a Saturday night date. I told her to believe it.) College had been a welcome interlude, but after that even Rosie the Riveter came
home from the war, and in the terrible fifties it was back to the

kitchen throughout the whole country. Certainly life among the intellectuals had proved no different.

To whom could I have told my secret, anyway? To the outside world Alfred was a distinguished literary figure, never mind that many of his contemporaries disliked him. But they could afford to. They were distinguished too. (And who knew what really went on in other people's houses?) In terms of family, my father, who might have come to the rescue, was dead. My mother, who wouldn't have, was also dead. My siblings in this connection were hopeless. All my sisters were committed to men who wanted their dinner. Once I did try to confide in my brother Yossie, who had come in after a fearsome quarrel. I showed him the bloody marks from Alfred's fingernails on my arm. My brother shuddered. But when Alfred himself came home, far from saying anything, Yossie was all smiles and servile respect. Celebrity beat family ties every time.

On top of all this I had no place to go, and even if I had, I had no real desire to leave my life. I loved Alfred. He was handsome and brilliant. An extraordinary writer. He had justified my existence. What would justify it without him? Maybe he abused me (*sometimes*, but he didn't mean it), but he also told me how wonderful I was, how beautiful and brilliant too. He was always wanting to make love to me, even if I didn't always do it right. He remembered our wedding anniversary, which I almost always forgot. He often brought me flowers. He gave me jewelry, including a long strand of pearls that Julia was amazed to find out he had bought *retail*. When we quarreled, he was the first to want to make up, which made me guilty for sulking. The first to say, "You know I can't live without you." And so it became the price of admission to the marriage to believe that Alfred, who loved me so much, would never intentionally hurt me. Whatever unpleasant things he said about me had to be true.

Gradually, it was established that I was pretty ignorant about everything. Hannah Arendt's favorite saying to me, "Shut up, little one, what do you know?" was certainly never challenged by my husband, who assumed that Hannah knew *everything*. After a while it was taken for granted that I didn't know anything about music, that I didn't know anything about politics, nothing about sex, certainly not compared to that *"grande amoureuse"* (whom Lionel Abel later identified as a village nymphomaniac with B.O.), that I hadn't read anything—"She's the only one who's written a book without having read one," Alfred said, laughing hugely at his joke—that I didn't like to walk, and later that I couldn't write and couldn't teach. Some of these statements were so patently untrue they made for fierce quarrels at first, which eventually became violent. Often, I futilely hit back. Alfred was hardly athletic, in build or in inclination, but his rage made him very strong, as happens I understand with some mental patients. He could knock me down easily. I would find myself on the floor without knowing how I got there. But then again, and to repeat, it was all my fault. Didn't he say with tears in his eyes that I was the only woman he had ever hit?

Why Alfred abused women, not only me, went out of his way to make their lives miserable, is a matter whose origins I'm not equipped to answer. Maybe Alfred too fit a profile. Whatever the reason, he was determined to turn us all into losers. He truly was someone who couldn't succeed unless others failed. His sister was "poor Pearlie" from the start. His first wife, evidently a lovely woman otherwise, was "dry." His second wife, after their son was born, actually brought home food from her mother's house instead of cooking it herself. (Hannah didn't think much of this wife, either, which crossed *that* T.) And of course he was determined to turn me into the biggest loser of all, even though in my saner moments I would cry out, "You're trying to make a silk purse into a sow's ear, and I won't let you!" Still, I'll never forget a walk we were taking on a lovely day, and his casually beginning a sentence with, "The reason you're a failure, Ann, is—" A sentence I began to nod to until I mercifully snapped out of it.

But most of the time, as I said, I pretended this sort of thing never happened.

In a way, the ball was soon over for everyone. True, Truman Capote's lavish party was reported on and hashed over for weeks and weeks. The Upper West intellectual contingent itself was also featured regularly in such places as *The New York Times Magazine*. A group caricature of local literary celebrities suddenly appeared hanging on the wall in Zabar's, above the smoked lox. Inaccurately as it turned out. Alfred, who had long ago stopped smoking, was pictured with a cigarette in his hand, and Wilfred Sheed, who wore heavy legs braces, was shown casually lolling, his legs crossed. Even the immigrants' grandchildren began to receive publicity. Michael had been accepted by Harvard, a cause of great rejoicing by his mother and father, united for once. And soon there was Michael too, pictured in a spread in *The New York Times Magazine,* this time about the scions of famous men in the Harvard freshman class, which included James Trilling and Andy Schlesinger.

But the place our parents had continued to think of as the *goldene medina*, the golden land, no matter how much hardship being here actually meant, was getting less and less shiny.

After President Kennedy was assassinated, Martin Luther King was assassinated, and then Robert Kennedy was assassinated too. I'd wondered briefly if Arthur Schlesinger would now support Teddy for president, but that hadn't happened. Arthur divorced his short plump wife and married a very tall one, having moved to New York to take up a glamorous life here. Looming larger and larger, above and beyond everything else was the curse of Vietnam. Soon it was hard to persuade kids like Katey that once the United States had fought a *just* war, that the American flag had been something to be proud of. After all, in her own living room she could hear Dick Goodwin, who now worked for LBJ, saying smugly that little wars stopped the big wars.

There was a huge upheaval at Columbia. Alfred and Irving Howe and I walked uptown to see college kids hanging from window ledges, dangling their legs and catcalling. We all automatically thought, particularly Irving, who had a big problem with the New Left, naughty children, why don't they go back inside? That night the police busted them. The next day we went back up again, but the picture had changed for good. The cops were mounted on skittery horses, they had sticks and blue riot helmets and they had been beating our children bloody. It was awful. The fact that Michael was at Harvard took a darker turn too. One day, visiting New York, he told me, as we were walking along Riverside Drive, "We'll get Harvard too." "Don't be crazy, Michael," I said. "They'll see what's happened at Columbia." But, of course, Michael was right. Harvard saw nothing except itself, nothing in the lowly outside world pertained to it. I wasn't happy when Harvard was broken up too, but in some ways I was glad it wasn't just New York and "you people." Michael was a big shot in the

SDS, co-chair, what my father would have called a *macher*. I must confess I was very proud of him. All his life, all *their* lives, these kids had been squeezed like toothpaste through a tube from one goddamn prestigious school to another, and finally they had broken away from these dictated values, which didn't value *them*. I must also confess that Michael looked gorgeous, with a big droopy black mustache, like a combination of Sacco and Vanzetti. Meg Greenfield, covering an SDS meeting at Harvard, laughed like hell because during a contentious meeting she heard words shouted she had never expected to hear, which were: "Shut up, Kazin!" Michael wasn't expelled from Harvard. To his chagrin, he found it was almost impossible to be expelled. So he left with something like two credits to go in his senior year and went off to cut sugarcane in Cuba. This was followed by the obligatory stint in a commune in California. Eventually he cleared up those credits, and much later wound up with a Ph.D. from Stanford.

From the student protests, in which the boy radicals said to the girl radicals, who were bringing them coffee, "Which one of you chicks can type?" arose the women's movement. Which, I am ashamed to say, I first called in its incipient stages—until Katey irritatedly corrected me—"Fem lib." After a while, though, I caught on that this movement was the real thing, that it was saving my life, or at least my sanity. After years of hearing the phrase, "You women," I was now hearing, "We women." Listening to other women's stories, so like my own, though still nobody mentioned *physical* abuse, I finally understood I wasn't crazy after all, that maybe I had never been crazy. The initial breakthrough in my case happened when I appeared on a PBS program called "Women

Writers." That was it, the whole title. There was no distinction made between us—the program might have been called "Dogs Dancing"—though in fact among the writers were Germaine Greer, who had just published *The Female Eunuch*, Adrienne Rich, at that time a young widow with two sons, whose poetry was just becoming more widely known, myself, a novelist, Rosalyn Drexler, also a novelist and a painter and a sometime wrestler, and Susan Brownmiller, who had just published a book on rape. By the end of the program this group of us, though so motley, were also so united in exhilaration and a heady sense of freedom, that we went off to Ninth Avenue and sat talking in a bar until we closed the place and the guy with the mop asked us "girls" to please pick up our feet. At home Alfred met me in frozen silence. But for once, just that one night, I didn't feel I had somehow wronged him.

Soon after, Katey and I went on Women's Rights marches the way we had gone on anti–Vietnam War marches. She was a most dedicated feminist, and once very sweetly called from a meeting downtown to ask if she could "bring a woman home for dinner." I said yes, though I was feeling uneasy about who this woman might be and what she wanted from my kid. Then Katey appeared, alone, and explained that, "The woman called her mother and her mother said to come home." Other funny things and awful things happened along the way. At Town Hall, Norman Mailer sat on the stage preening, among five women, as if one Jewish mama's boy, who longed to be taken for a tough Irishman, not to mention almost wife-murderer, was the equivalent of five females. Who thought this one up, I have no idea. But Diana Trilling seemed to think it was fine, as she sat proudly on the stage too, one of the selected women, she who had never openly exhibited any feminist impulses. Katey had also volunteered to help out Betty Friedan in her campaign to be a delegate for Shirley Chisholm, who was running for President. But one day Katey, who had been sent to bring back leaflets with Betty's picture, brought back leaflets with Shirley Chisholm's picture instead, headquarters having run out of the others. Betty, to Katey's amazement, flew into a great and scary rage. Evidently, sisterhood was not powerful in all circumstances.

Still, sisters kept popping up all over the place, and I made an unexpected new friend, Sue Kaufman, the novelist. In summers, Sue was part of the Hamptons set, which was much more jazzy and commercial than that of Wellfleet, probably because the Hamptons were oriented toward New York rather than good old stodgy Boston or Cambridge. The rest of the year, Hamptonites tended to live on the East Side, not the grungy West Side, and have pots of dough. In these circles, the women writers were allowed a certain celebrity, provided they kept up with their domestic duties both personally and in reference to their work. Sue Kaufman, in fact, had written a bestseller called *Diary of a Mad Housewife*, which was being made into a movie. Among true literati, on a scale of 1 to 10, Sue's work would maybe have rated a 2, though she was herself very literary, much more than I, and had not only heard of Lionel Trilling but read him early on, and was a Vassar honor graduate in the days when that meant female bluestocking.

But Sue not only sold well, which automatically made her a middlebrow, she was also married to a *doctor*. Even in her sophisticated circles this counted as much as it had in my house when Sookie landed Sandy, though Sue was so different. Also, like the rest of us female writers, she had learned to sweep her accomplishments under the rug, pooh-pooh them when the

subject arose, and take her protective coloration from her husband, who, like my husband, was only too willing to dominate
the scene. Sometimes he even managed to dominate Alfred, the
idea being that no writer, not even a well-known critic, certainly not a best-selling (equals frivolous) female novelist could
compare in importance to an eminent physician whom most of
their literary set went to anyhow. Sue and her cigar-smoking
husband were all big bucks. There was the latest thing in land-
scaped swimming pools behind their grand pseudo-colonial
house in the Hamptons, while their large otherwise modern
East Side apartment contained expensive antiques. Physically,
Sue was not only tall and tailored, obviously well-bred, with a
neat brunette page boy, she was naturally skinny—a condition
that would have driven Julia up the wall. English was decidedly
not her second language.

In spite of these differences, social and otherwise, we became great friends, a friendship largely initiated by Sue herself, who laughed whenever I unconsciously sighed, *"Oy vey."*
Yiddish was unknown to her, though it seemed to her possibly that it had been spoken by her grandparents. She thought
it totally amusing that I knew it, incredulous that it had been
my *first* language. "Oh, sweetie," she said. Soon one of us was
phoning the other every morning the minute the husbands
left the house. We talked about everything under the sun,
complained sotto voce, like prisoners, about the endless stupid demands of married domesticity. We also talked about our
work. She admired mine. I certainly admired hers. Political
prisoners though we might be, we were sisters under the skin.

Sue's latest novel was about to be published, and I assumed with a deep sigh that it was sure to hit the best-seller
lists. It was a strange book, though, called *Falling Bodies*,

whose heroine was obsessed with the possibility of being hit by a body falling out of a window. Incredibly, this was a message nobody caught, including all the smiling Hamptons shrinks, since shortly after its publication, Sue threw *herself* out of the window. No, this wasn't possible. We were all stunned. We couldn't get over it. It was unbelievable. It made no sense. But why hadn't *I* suspected? We were best friends. We talked on the phone every day. We told each other everything. Well, almost everything. Real sisters, nothing like Julia and me. Maybe if the last time I'd spoken to Sue—? "Oh, Ma," Katey said, "don't you think that everyone who knew her is asking the same thing?" She was right, of course. Who can ever really tell why someone commits suicide? What I didn't say to Katey (maybe because I was ashamed) was that to me, who had slept head to toe like a sardine until I was twelve, who had been educated for free by the City of New York, whose stomach stuck out, who wasn't famous, Sue Kaufman had seemed to be the woman who had everything. It wasn't just that I really hadn't understood Sue. I didn't understand why everything wasn't enough.

Amid all the upheavals, some situations stayed exactly the same.

Roger Straus had to rush down to where a big ocean liner was docked one day to rescue Edmund Wilson, who had been idly revising his passport while waiting to board. In those days, passport descriptions included complexions, and Edmund found "ruddy" no longer apt in relation to himself. He had no sooner crossed it out than a steamship official accused him of defacing a government document and refused to let him sail. How Roger got it all straightened out I have no idea, but somehow a respect for the niceties of language prevailed over bureaucratic usage. Maybe for the last time. My father, on the other hand, with his respect for his "papers," probably would have been shocked by what Edmund had done, though he would have understood that it took someone who never doubted he was an American.

There was a citywide schoolteachers strike. Most of the teachers involved were Jews, as opposed to much of the student body, which was black, and the New Left and *The New York Review of Books* took a grim view of the strikers. One day I called Jason Epstein and asked him if he had ever met an actual Jewish schoolteacher. And he said no, did I know one, he'd take her to lunch. When I said it was my sister Julia, a Jewish schoolteacher now temporarily at liberty, he sighed deeply and suggested Stage Delicatessen. I changed it to Gloucester House, an expensive fish restaurant around the corner from Random House, where Jason was a big-shot editor. I thought he'd really want to know what the view was like from the other side. Julia had often told me about the difficulties of her job as a math teacher in a Brooklyn junior high. She was a good teacher, and a dedicated one, only she kept saying she had no guidelines, no help for herself in trying to help kids who weren't up to understanding the subject. She told me what it was like to teach her heart out for an hour, think she had gotten through, only to see a hand shoot up, and a young boy say, "Mrs. Glasser, what do dat x mean?"

Jason brought along I. F. Stone to our lunch. For what reason I didn't know, but the effect was like producing a cannon to shoot a mosquito. After her first shock at Jason's patrician bad table manners, which included reaching across to stab at other people's food, Julia, with my encouragement, spoke from the heart, and told the two men the stories she had told me.

Afterward, Izzy Stone wrote a column in his *Newsletter* viciously attacking and deliberately misquoting her. The New Left position, naturally, remained as it was. Equally naturally, Julia thought I set the whole thing up on purpose and announced that she never wanted to speak to me again.

Murray Kempton remained the one genuine gentleman and wit in the lot. When Norman Podhoretz's book *Making It* came out, he said cheerfully, "Ann, you must agree that someone who lives on 106th Street and West End Avenue and thinks he's made it has an interesting mind." He was still one of the few Gentiles on the West Side intellectual scene. The other Gentiles were mostly connected with *The New Yorker*, and lived on the East Side.

Alfred and I took another trip to Israel, which turned out to be almost as much of a disaster as the first. The first week I was introduced as "my wife, Ann Birstein," the second as "my wife, Ann," the third as "my wife." I had a feeling that if we'd stayed another week I would have become a number. But I did manage to see my old high school friend Helen Weisgal, who had transmogrified from Glenn Miller fan into fiery Zionist kibbutznik. Her name was now Chaya Amir, but she had left the kibbutz and was living an ordinary bourgeois life, except that like many Israeli women she was desperately worried about her sons, four of them, having to go into the Israeli army and fight war after war. Then, there was that first sight of the Western Wall, which had only recently been liberated. It was incredible, looming, pale, empty, so much of Jewish history, so much of my own history embodied in it. I burst into tears. Alfred looked around angrily, a weeping wife not exactly what he wanted at that moment. Or ever, I guess. "Stop it," Alfred said. "You're embarrassing me."

For some time I had been writing a long story, maybe a short novel, called *Love in the Dunes*. It wasn't finished yet, and I hadn't shown it to anybody, but one day I came home to find Alfred reading it uninvited. This was absolutely *infra dig*.

Between writers you didn't read anything you weren't asked to, since we often left things around. Even worse, the look on his Alfred's face was like Daddy's when he read my first novel. An expression meaning, "How could you *do* this?" Sorrow compounded with rage. But I had been so proud of that story and thought Alfred would be too. Alfred was supposed to be so different from Daddy. I mean, hadn't he been my passport to intellectual freedom? A fellow writer. A superior, dedicated writer. So dedicated to writing that he couldn't love me if I weren't a writer. He had said so himself. Eventually, though still suffering, he came round. But it didn't matter. Nobody wanted to publish *Love in the Dunes* at that point, anyhow. Still, at Alfred's suggestion I sent it to Philip Rahv at *Partisan Review*. (This was the old pack of cigarettes syndrome.) Rahv read it and asked me to come down and talk it over. During the course of the talking, at a table in adjoining chairs, I felt him groping at my thigh in the region of my garter. I pushed him away and got up. "What are you trying to do?" Rahv said, waving a dismissing hand at my manuscript. "Make fun of the intellectuals?"

Ultimately, *Partisan Review* wound up in New Jersey, published by Rutgers University. But by then, many of the noted radicals and independent thinkers had become associated with colleges too, often granted special professorships and chairs that were essentially sinecures and allowed them to continue to feel vastly superior to mere academics. And some

of them, before Nixon was almost impeached, wound up dining in the *Nixon* White House. It was kind of like a bunch of
heavy thinkers subscribing to the *Reader's Digest*.

Though conditions for women in general might be improv-
ing, the situation of females in our home-grown West Side
shtetl remained more or less static. (And again, who knew
what went on behind closed doors?) Publicly, the women with
the biggest mouths, such as Midge Decter or Diana Trilling
were heard from loudest, though ironically neither of them
was a feminist and Midge Decter became more and more hostile to feminism as time went on and imagined herself to be a
Conservative. (Conserving what, though—traditions that
scorned her both as a woman and as a Jew?) There were also
those with protective coloration, the helpless Southern lady
but with a mind of steel, such as Elizabeth Hardwick. For
similar reasons Emily Dickinson had been Amherst's favorite
poet(ess) because she hid out, wore white, and was never
driven by a desire to be published. It was still best to be not
overtly sexy, not threatening, certainly not make fun of sex,
which was what Erica Jong did in *Fear of Flying*, and caused
an otherwise normal male novelist I knew to say that she
should have a clitorectomy. Reviews of my books still referred
to me in parenthesis as Mrs. Alfred Kazin, as if that were a career in itself. I often imagined a book jacket that would read,
"In private life, Mrs. Kazin is Ann Birstein, the novelist."
    The big winner, of course, in the unpretty female division
was Hannah Arendt. In a hiatus between increasingly fiery
hostilities, we had planned a romantic evening, Alfred and I,
complete with martinis and blazing fireplace in a winter rental
in East Hampton. But when he heard the news of her death,

Alfred wouldn't come near me. (We had gone on making passionate love after we heard over the radio that Stalin had died, but I guess that wasn't the same thing.) "You won, Hannah, you won!" I cried in my drunken rage and disappointment. (I had finished the pitcher of martinis on my own.) Ugly, androgenous, a force of darkness—that was what she was to me. In my life at that point it seemed such things always won.

Looking back, would I modify my feelings about Arendt in any way? No. And I certainly don't understand why her longtime hidden infatuation with Martin Heidegger, Nazi sympathizer, lately revealed, should surprise anyone. The woman was herself a Nazi. Still, I do realize now that all those years I was maneuvered into doing what Alfred couldn't. I was the one who said shit to M-O-T-H-E-R. It did turn out, by the way, that her real name wasn't Hannah any more than mine was. It was Johanna.

On a beautiful summer night, Viking Press was celebrating itself with a boat ride. They had chartered a Circle Line boat (if not a Viking ship), equipped it with two bars and an orchestra, provided box suppers, and were now taking us around Manhattan. It was a vast floating cocktail party, except that you couldn't leave until it was over. Alfred was on an upper deck flirting with Aileen Ward, a beautiful scholar who had written an impressive biography of Keats, and was now working on a life of Blake. This flirtation was unusual for Alfred. His specialty was ugly women, or pathetic failures, or both. And Aileen was certainly neither. On the other hand, she *was* a prodigious and therefore possibly intimidating scholar, which might have been a mitigating factor. On a lower deck I was standing at the railing, talking to Saul Bellow. "Where's

Alfred?" Saul asked. I told him. Saul laughed and said, "Is he at it again?" Alfred had always been very generous in his reviews of Saul's books, but personally they were incompatible. Apples and oranges. I looked down into the dark water— water under the bridge?—and for some reason, maybe the privacy of the night, maybe the thought that I wouldn't ever have another chance to say it, told Saul how crazy about him I once was. I glanced up. Saul was nodding. "You knew?" I didn't need to ask if he had felt the same thing, since he added, "Those things are never unilateral, Annie." "Then why did you never—?" "You were married to my friend." "Your friend? You've never even liked the guy." Saul shook his head. "That doesn't matter. You don't do that to a friend."

I looked down into the murky water again. Literally water under the bridge. The Verrazano Bridge, which was now looming to my right. Saul had gone. After a while the Verrazano Bridge loomed to my left. Then to my right again. I realized that the boat wasn't circling Manhattan anymore. I asked a crew member what had happened and he said that the captain realized that most of the guests didn't know the difference and was simply going back and forth, back and forth.

Chapter 9

*I*T HAD TAKEN over thirty years, but I finally got it through my head that I had married my mother, not my father. Whether Alfred ever discovered he hadn't married *his* mother, I'm not sure. Probably he did, but had to keep denying it. Bad news all around.

At a think tank in Stanford, California, the whole thing blew up for good. This wasn't surprising since Stanford was a kind of California version of Amherst, Massachusetts. Nicer weather, but just as smug and isolating, with the same values. At one point the Institute gave a party for all females involved with it, including—across the board—those distinguished Fellows who happened to be women, plus faculty wives, and female janitorial and secretarial staffs.

In our daily routine, Alfred went off to his prestigious paradise on the hill, while I stayed behind in the lowlands without any reason for being where I was except my husband, a husband who, even by his usual standards was becoming more and more demanding and violently irrational every day. I realize now that as usual he must have been having an affair with someone or other, but again that never dawned on me since he always made it seem that the problem was all about me. Ultimately, Alfred was shouting and carrying on so loudly

229

that complaints from the neighbors caused our landlord to ask him to leave our apartment. But before that, being a child of my time and a still utterly stupid believer in psychotherapy, I had insisted we go together to a marriage counselor. A disaster from the start. I remember her saying to Alfred, "I hear you, I hear you." Which made no sense, because the way Alfred was carrying on, as usual, he could have been heard in the next county. It turned out to be a California expression. Alfred, smitten with our counselor, continued to go to her long after we separated and she encouraged him in ways that weren't exactly helpful to me. But then, I had known that this woman would be trouble from the moment I laid eyes on her. She was fat and homely, a born loser, what I used to call a "pathetic professional"—exactly Alfred's type.

After he moved out, most of Alfred's clothes stayed in the closet until one day they disappeared. What didn't disappear was the manuscript of his latest book, which was still sitting on the closet shelf. We had done some work on the ending, which Alfred's publisher with good reason wanted him to change, and we figured out some kind of uneasy compromise, which was how it went to press. It finally occurred to me that Alfred had left the manuscript behind so that I would read the whole thing, which I never had. It was like when he had brought another manuscript to me in the hospital the day after Katey was born. A touching moment. He wanted to make sure I still loved *him*. Now it wasn't touching, no longer a matter of love but of expecting a literary opinion. I never did read the whole manuscript—I had argued against the title *New York Jew*, which I thought was vulgar and offensive, in addition to which Alfred had staked his literary capital on coming from *Brooklyn* (to my mind a serious difference)—

and then one day the manuscript too disappeared while I was out, like his clothes. A little later on Alfred did come over for some reason while I was home, and on that day we made love, for the last time. (Years later, he claimed angrily that I had seduced him, which when you consider that we were married at the time was an odd accusation.) When Alfred left, some books that were out on the coffee table disappeared also. I guess he could never get over the idea that passion notwithstanding, *all* books belonged to him.

I couldn't hack it alone, and finally after months of trying and failing, I set out for New York. Alfred wrote me later that he watched me as I left our apartment, weeping in his hiding place around the corner. This was very touching and beautiful, but since I was struggling with seven pieces of luggage at the time, it would probably have made more sense for him to stop crying and give me a hand. It was January, cold and bleak back East. I had no place to live. We had given up our big West Side apartment and put our things in storage. Alfred and I were supposed to meet in New York in March when *New York Jew* (still a terrible title) was due out. March came and went, but if Alfred did, I never saw him. He had always had a friend who was a lawyer and now I got a lawyer too, a stranger.

People often asked why we got divorced after thirty years of marriage. The real question, of course, was why we stayed together so long. And the answer was that, with all of it, the storms, the rage, the fury, even the physical abuse, we couldn't bear to give each other up. We were like two dogs hanging on with our teeth to a bone, clinging to that old desperate belief that we were the best and deepest part of each other, that we had banished each other's loneliness, that we justified each other's existence. For all those years Alfred, the Alfred I imagined him to be, was the love of my life, and I, as he imagined me to be, was his. Which, when you think about it, is more than most people ever have—except in the movies.

My own life didn't come to an end, far from it, though for a while it seemed to, and for a longer while I wished it had, and kept having nervous breakdowns and going to sleep and praying never to wake up again. Except I did keep waking up and finally figured that there was no avoiding being a survivor. But for all the sophistication of my previous existence, there was so much I didn't know how to do. I had never lived alone before, never been on my own before. I had never rented an apartment, never applied for a credit card, never bought a TV set (and Daddy wasn't around to get one wholesale), never filed my own income tax return, certainly never hired my own lawyer. I had now entered the world of the divorced woman, where women always wore watches, went Dutch at the movies, paid for their own dinners, came back to empty houses.

I was warned that this world would be an unfriendly place, but in fact though it was certainly frightening that wasn't true. Alfred's world was so hostile that this one seemed amazingly friendly. A rental agent rented me an apartment on the basis of projected income when at that point I had no income at all because she said she knew I'd pay the rent somehow. A banker on the basis of the same spurious income, which he knew to be spurious, got me a credit card. My agent, whom I had no work to give, tried to get me a job and an apartment, and was a clearinghouse for messages. One day, soon after I had come back to New York and in the midst of several temporary addresses, she told me there was a package waiting for me at her office. The two of us unwrapped it, and there was a copy of *New York Jew* by Alfred Kazin, with a card saying "Compliments of the Author." We fell into each other's arms, laughing and crying, it was so awful. Naturally, there were friends I did lose custody of, but I retained custody of an amazing number of others—not only women, but men too, who seemed to have gotten liberated along the way. I guess that politically speaking it was finally a period when it was okay for a woman to go it alone. Or try to.

Still, a death in the family would have been easier. (I have since noticed that widows were always married to saints, divorced women to bastards.) But there I was, good Jewish girl, member of a huge family, rabbi's daughter, former wife of an eminent critic in the center of an eminent literary circle, now outside of any circle at all. The subject of money, formerly Alfred's exclusive obsession on account of his Depression background, he said, increasingly terrified me. Katey tried to persuade me that it was okay to buy theater tickets in the balcony instead of in the orchestra, that you could still see the show. (But I had been brought up on free house seats, courtesy of my father's Broadway connections.) When I went to the bank to get cash, I took a cab back home so no one would rob me on the way. I was down to my last pair of shoes, though how that happened I'm still not sure.

What made it all worse was when I finally got myself to read the "complimentary" copy of *New York Jew* that had been sent in care of my agent. It was certainly an out-of-body experience. In Alfred's "autobiography," my name had been changed, maybe to avoid a lawsuit—-though how many young blond novelists who were also rabbi's daughters could have been married to him? (Also, as a fiction writer I felt the changed name was all wrong—"Beth"—Alfred had no feel for the thing.) On top of this, whole sections of my life had been wrenched away and ascribed to another of his wives, while many other of my experiences, not to say opinions, were appropriated by Alfred as his own. I seemed never to have lived on the Upper West Side at all, much less among the intelligentsia. No, I was just another brief amorous episode in the long series of them that constituted Alfred's flaming (to hear him tell it) love life. Except that he did say with some exasperation that being married to me was like living with Saul Bellow. Nobody would ever have guessed that Alfred and I had in fact been married during all the years that book covered, except for a few in the beginning before we met. Considering what had happened to his sister, Pearl, in his first volume of autobiography, Alfred could have given lessons in how to make people disappear.

My existence in my old family had, if not ceased, certainly transmogrified too. Far from being the golden girl, I had become something of a sad sack, right there with Yossie, who was now known to fail at everything. "Goodness," Sookie said, laughing, "between you and Yossie, I can't keep up with the addresses in my address book." "I'm not like Yossie," I said, a remark that for a while fell on deaf ears, with only me to believe it was true. Yossie, giving up journalism for the law, had failed three bar exams and finally passed the fourth only to become one of the few dead-broke lawyers in New York, though he kept up his assiduous attendance at the Art Students League. My three sisters meanwhile had all become schoolteachers, though I never knew what had brought this on. It was more obvious why two of them, Sookie and Julia, formerly brunette, had turned into blondes. (Millie, characteristically, went gray.) In terms of pedagogy, however, Sookie was forced to remain only a temp. Sandy didn't want her to get a permanent teachers license because this would have interfered with her major role as a *doctor's wife*. They lived in a drab row house in Queens, distinguished by the fact that when you opened the door, there was a sudden and remarkable view of masterpieces of art hanging from the walls—here a Cézanne watercolor, there a Marsden Hartley, a Matisse, et cetera—since Sandy's oldest brother was a noted collector and had helped Sandy start his own collection. The collection varied from time to time, though. It didn't do to become attached to any one masterpiece because it could be sold or traded away before the next time you came.

Millie, now known as Midge, was still lodged in Philadelphia and still sure all the exciting stuff was happening in New York. She taught in a public school near her house, and proudly showed me a photograph of her second-grade class, in which she was remarkable as the only white person, a fact that to her credit, she never thought to mention or maybe didn't even notice. To me Millie was her usual passive aggressive self. "Maybe you're a late bloomer," she said of my own situation, not by way of consolation but merely observation. Julia was happy to live in Brooklyn, teaching math in junior high (to little Chuck Schumer, among others) and above all basking in the reflected glory of her husband, Irv, now a top-level administrator at Kingsborough Community College and politically somewhat to the right of Atilla the Hun, right up there with Irving Kristol—the usual ex-Socialist position. Sookie was right about one thing, though. At that point I still didn't have a permanent place to live, since without a job or a legal separation agreement, and with Alfred unwilling to cosign a lease, no landlord would rent to me. Before I found the only one who would, Julia said she and Irv would cosign for me. A remarkable feat of generosity. "Julia, why are you being so good to me?" I asked. "We always hated each other." "You're my sister," Julia said, astonished at the question.

Still, as time went on and I began to publish regularly again, my old literary cachet began to resurface within the family—especially since their relation to Alfred's was now kind of tricky. Yossie, who had left his job to go to Florida and write a novel, his magnum opus at last, urged me to come and visit him. It was nice of him and, since in the old days we often had fun wandering around town finding cheap places to eat, I went down to St. Petersburg. After a day or two, it became clear why Yossie desired so urgently to see me. He wanted me to read his novel, or that part of it that he had managed to write. I did. I began to talk to him wildly about character development, about the uses of real dialogue rather than a succession of soliloquies, about anything I could think of. But there was no avoiding the plot, which was about a man in a freak car accident, which causes his penis to grow and grow. Luckily I don't remember much more than that— except that the characters did philosophize about it a lot— and mercifully don't think I need to remember. But with this "novel" my brother intended to make his literary fortune, and wanted me to give it forthwith to my agent. I said no politely and left sadly. Good-bye Yossie. This was the prince of my youth to whom we all kowtowed, the intellectual of our family, the one who knew all the big words. After a while Yossie quit on his novel—he told his other sisters I had deliberately discouraged him—came back from Florida and got another job he hated, and returned to the Art Students League.

In terms of other family, my daughter, Katey, now working on her Ph.D. at Cornell, remained the surest, sweetest thing in my life. Michael, also sweet—Alfred was very lucky in his children—had, as I've said, finally made the big time and earned the approbation of his father when he got accepted at Harvard. This approbation had ended and brought his mother and father together for the first and only time when Michael became a big shot in the SDS, left Harvard, and went to cut sugarcane in Cuba. (Alfred had long ago reversed himself on Castro.) I admired Michael mightily at this time, but that carried no weight. Anyhow, in the fullness of time, Michael settled down, earned those two missing credits at Harvard somehow or other, got a Ph.D. at Stanford, found a lovely *Jewish*(!) girl, as opposed to Chinese, Japanese, or anything exotic, and wrote to me that they were getting married. I was moved and sent a letter to Alfred wishing him mazel tov. Alfred, obviously less moved than still rankled by the sugar cane, wrote back saying he hoped they didn't name the first one Fidel.

Another transmogrification, cutting across even more societal strata, was that of Alfred's sister, Pearl. When I first met her she was so habitually referred to by Alfred as "poor Pearlie" that it seemed to be her whole name. "Poor Pearlie." I finally got annoyed. "Why is it always poor Pearlie?" I asked Alfred. "What have I got that she hasn't?" "Me," Alfred said. At that time Pearlie was what was called "interesting" looking. This meant that you had to be intellectual and make references to Virginia Woolf to appreciate her. A new and intriguing concept for me. She wore black velvet over-blouses and had some kind of huge ornate cross hanging down her chest. She had done graduate work at Radcliffe, then became a copy editor at *The New Yorker*—high voltage stuff. Not to mention her stay in Taormina with Truman Capote and his boyfriend. Her own boyfriend was a famous composer's ex, whom she eventually married, going down to Brazil to join him carrying a bag of her mother's cookies. A terrible marriage, which once ended up in night court when they returned to New York. Then came the celebrated affair with Dylan Thomas. When both Dylan and her perpetually aggrieved mother had died, Pearl fell in love with Daniel Bell. Alfred and I were in Northampton, and she was sharing our New York apartment with Saul Bellow's girlfriend. (At that time lovers didn't just move in together.) Saul himself was sharing an apartment with a male writer, David Bazelon, another heavy-duty New York intellectual, with whom he ultimately had such a big falling out that Saul told David to remove himself—at once! David had sox soaking in the bathroom sink at the time, but Saul was adamant. Out! When David told about it later, he was still worrying about his sox left behind in the sink Oh, yes, a time of great passion all around.

In any case, Danny Bell was getting over his second wife. (All the first wives had long since been left in the dust.) Though now a professor at Columbia, Dan remained very much a man about town, as Pearl was a girl about town. (The drift toward academe, like the abandonment of the first wives, was endemic among the once radical intellectuals.) In time, Danny came around to appreciating Pearl's many virtues, and proposed. At my suggestion we went to Bergdorf's for her wedding dress, where in the elegant dove gray fitting room Pearl stripped down to a slip whose broken strap was held together by a huge safety pin. The last vestige of "Poor Pearlie," no doubt, though I imagine that the saleswoman probably thought she was very rich. Pearl and Dan were married in our apartment, over my objections. I kept telling them to elope and I would give them a big party afterward. I didn't really feel much like mother of the bride, especially since I was *younger* than the bride. But the wedding happened, and the guests split up on either side of the room, like opposing firing squads, and poor Katey scratched away at her organdy party dress, and little David Rieff, Susan Sontag's son, who had been brought by her divorced husband, horrifyingly started to gobble up almost all the tiny very expensive hors d'oeuvres, and the rabbi went around asking guests to give free speeches at the Columbia Hillel. (Aside from the required presence of the rabbi no one was claiming much of a Jewish identity yet.) Afterward, there was to be a big *Partisan Review* party and the rest of us were going. Danny wanted to go too, but Pearl pointed out that it would be unseemly since it was their wedding night, so poor disappointed Danny had to stay away, and I'm sure from his point of view miss all the fun.

Within a year the Bells had a baby boy, and Pearl became, as a friend put it, "an island surrounded by baby." The death knell of girl about town and man about town came one New Year's Eve, when they gave a party. Jules Feiffer and I came to it from another party, a festive black tie affair given by Abe Burrows, first dropping off Jules's wife, who was pregnant and tired, and Alfred who was tired without being pregnant. Jules and I came in laughing merrily, but in a minute our laughter faded into thin air. Baleful looks told us we were overdressed and over cheerful, disturbing the funereal atmosphere. Then Pearlie brought out orange juice in a baby bottle, and shortly after *that* we were all asked to leave because we were disturbing the baby. In about two minutes the whole party was out on a snowy sidewalk near Columbia on New Year's Eve and even the Trillings seemed unable to figure out how it had all happened to us so fast.

After Columbia came Harvard, and by now Danny was so much a Harvard Professor, and Pearl so much a faculty wife, that when she went shopping with me in New York, she picked up shoes that would be "perfect for giving dinner parties," and at home in Cambridge cheerfully raced down four flights of stairs to pour Danny another cup of coffee for his breakfast. Did Pearl ever mind being plunged back into a pure shtetl existence, that she had fought against as much as I, fancy Cambridge version though it was? I suppose not. And who am I to say I did any better? Still, I miss the old Pearlie, who was such a pal and who had fabulous lovers and got drunk at parties.

Michael's wedding was scheduled for the summer, at a time when I was at the MacDowell Colony in New Hampshire, trying to work on a new book. The occasion was so fraught and my own emotional state still so precarious that I didn't know whether or not I could go. I finally decided I could. I came back to New York where Katey was waiting for me. I called Sookie, but she was at the beauty parlor being freshly touched up. Why? Because she was going to Michael's wedding. So was Sandy, so were Millie and Milton, so was Yossie. Yes, Alfred had invited them all. And though nobody knew yet whether *I* was coming *they* all happily accepted. Evidently so great was Alfred's eminence that nothing else counted, including the fact that they wouldn't have known Michael if they had stepped on him. The only holdout was Julia, a monument to common sense, as usual, who said she had no connection with Alfred, much less his son, so she would send a check and stay home. And *why* had Alfred invited my only too-willing-accomplice siblings to his son's wedding? Because, as he said to Katey, "I needed a family." For the one occasion only, of course, and so had in effect rented mine. My sisters' and brother's presence certainly seemed peculiar at the ceremony and at the reception. Yossie was red faced and pleased as punch for no apparent reason, Sookie wiggled her ass flirtatiously throughout, Millie was soberly taking mental notes, and Michael had to be introduced to all of them. Some time later, I asked Millie why exactly she had gone to Michael's wedding, and she said pleasantly, "I know why *I* was there. Why were you?" Of the ceremony I remember very little except that Alfred and Carol walked down the aisle on either side of their son in time-honored Jewish tradition, seeming to have been caught in a time warp, and that Michael's mother Carol and her second husband Mario kindly and diplomatically insisted on my being seated at the main table at the reception. But then, Carol and I had always gotten along since I so clearly loved her kid. Alfred's date for the occasion was Lucy Davidowicz, a safe bet. Since I knew nothing about his latest live-in, I guess it was a community decision for her not to come. Pearlie and Danny drove me back home, I crying in the back seat the whole way, and imagining that for the whole rest of my life, I would be in the backseat, crying.

Through it all I was still committed to the prevailing belief that psychotherapy could show the way. This in spite of already overwhelming evidence to the contrary. Anyhow, the whole aim for years had been to keep the marriage together. Now the aim was to keep *me* together. To this end I consulted one shrink after another, and they certainly came in all shapes and sizes. The first one to be approached in my new bachelor girl state was a psychiatric social worker, also presumably a bachelor girl, who spent some time assuring me that it was okay, not immoral, to buy takeout food, thst you didn't *have* to cook your own dinner. This was revolutionary and helpful to some extent, but not altogether since this connection ended in a breakdown Another, a male this time, referred to me blithely as a lovable kook. Another, again male and importantly connected with Payne Whitney, informed me that I was psychotic, and for the rest of my life would have to spend two hundred dollars a week on therapy and three dollars a day on food. Next came a *mittel* European woman of some sophistication who complained that I always made her feel put down. Another gentleman, whom I saw only once, recommended that I forget about writing and go to a doctor's convention to meet men.

Then came the last and worst of all, which was why he turned out to be the last. This genius had a lot of protective coloration. He was small, pale, with thinning hair and eyeglasses, mild mannered, soft spoken. In short, a complete nerd and the opposite of Alfred. Unfortunately, he became so hooked on being the opposite of Alfred, tailoring himself along those lines, that soon nothing else mattered, which kept *me* connected to Alfred too, even though the point of it all was for me to break away. In time, merely being the antithesis gave way to open hatred, and one Thanksgiving the good doctor expressed the hope that Alfred would choke on his turkey. Since all he really knew of Alfred was what I'd told him I felt vaguely guilty and hoped Alfred would survive his Thanksgiving dinner after all. Also, in this case unintentionally the opposite of Alfred (and me), was my shrink's frequently appalling use of the English language, in such sentences as, "What do you guesstimate the enrollment will be?" He also combed his hair across his bald spot out on the street in nervous preparation for his next patient and rushed upstairs letting the door slam in my face, though he knew his next patient happened to be right behind him and that it was me. Oh, well. By then Prozac had been invented.

Dr. Nerd had been opposed to my having lovers since he said I had already done that. Which was something like saying, why read a book when you've already read one? This meant that during his reign I was uneasily and for the most part celibate. But still on the lookout. As much on the lookout, shame to say, as when Peppy and I were hoping to attract the attention of some bar mitzvah boy, though naturally I didn't admit it. I preferred to think that I was merely back in my Cinderella mode. Obviously, the solution to everything was to find, no, to be found by, another *him*. Then all my cares would vanish, loneliness disappear, I would be happy and fulfilled. My whole family said so, among others, though hoping that this time the *him* might be a bit more sensible. But could lightning strike twice? Could love swiftly smite me once again and catch me unawares? Why not? I forgot that the first time I wasn't looking for lightning. It had come looking for me. Also, that in those young days, I hadn't been eager to get married at all—with good reason, it turned out. I forgot that too. I forgot everything but the good parts. I did have standards, of course. Married men were out, for moral and ethical reasons. I had always felt you shouldn't fool around with a married man unless you were married too. Level playing field and all that. Women lovers were out also, on account of personal

predilections. As to the rest, as a friend said to me, "It isn't
that there aren't any men around, it's *who's* around." A who's
who, she meant, of the walking wounded.

In the interests of honesty, I must admit that there were
attractive men, intelligent and very sophisticated men, who
weren't particularly interested in me. I will even admit that
maybe they were the best of the lot. But even of this group,
one became quite amorous toward me once he was stricken
with Alzheimer's, and another, a former great drunk, I understand now goes around peeing in his pants on social occasions. Is this revenge or merely the fate that awaits us all? Anyway, going on down the list, it doesn't get much better.
Among them, a blind date who made running into Bloom-
ingdale's afterward to try on bathing suits a treat. (Any
woman will know what that means without further explica-
tion.) Another potential prospect, mistakenly imagining I was
of childbearing age, told me he wanted more than anything to
be a father—however much he loved a woman he would never
marry her unless she would make him a father. But since
things weren't turning out that way, I suggested maybe he
should get a dog meanwhile, and he shook his head and said
it would be too much of a responsibility. There was also, notably, an extremely depressed psychiatrist who wore space
shoes. Then an elderly woman friend took a great interest in
my singlehood and kept trying to fix me up. Her first try was
a dinner party where my intended love object spilled food and
red wine all down his already soiled white shirt, which had
popped a few buttons, and kept saying to me, "I *like* you."
"Charming, isn't he?" my hostess said to me in the bedroom
where I was hastily finding my coat. Charming? "I thought
you needed an escort." To where? Hell? Soon after, he himself

was escorted by his daughter—to an old age home. My friend's next attempt to fix me up I sidestepped altogether, although the description sounded interesting—a handsome architect recently widowed—until she added cheerfully, "And they've made wonderful advances in the treatment of brain tumors." When I asked about this guy a year later, he was already dead. My friend, as usual, said she'd thought he'd make a nice escort, for a while, anyway. I didn't point out that even in the best case scenario, he wasn't someone you'd want to buy a theater subscription with. This isn't even to mention randy geriatric poets, an aging Communist still heatedly defending the Nazi Soviet Pact, which I admit did make me feel young again for a minute or two, especially since his nose was running in his excitement. This choice list goes on and on. I'm sure every other divorced woman has one to match. Julia, of course, pointed out that it was very flattering to have a man interested in you at all.

Maybe this snapped me out of it. That kind of flattery I could live without. In fact, after a while, it turned out to my surprise that I could live very well on my own. Maybe in marriage one person can cover all the bases—be there for sex, sociability, movies, fine dining, illnesses, letting your hair down. When you're single these functions have to be deployed all over the lot, and then you find you have a lot of friends. Real friends. I am now ready to swear, even have it notarized, that I don't want to live with anybody again, certainly never get married ever again. Naturally, this firm conviction has made me extremely popular with the opposite sex. "I don't get it," Julia said.

Neither do I. What she didn't know, what I don't tell anyone, is that still sometimes at night when I've seen a TV program

on abused wives or read about it, I curl up in bed and tell myself it's okay, I'm safe now.

Ever since college, I had taught on and off, throughout my
marriage too, and now I was teaching steadily. Creative writing,
of course. I wasn't allowed to teach literature because I had
never gotten that Ph.D., and without it I was assumed, as Alfred had originally suggested, merely to have written books, not
to have read them. This was curious, because at Barnard, where
I wound up for many years, and we sat at the big table in the
faculty lunch room, I happily talked away about Dickens with
our Victorianist, King Lear with a Shakepeare professor, Hemingway with the American lit professor. But they never talked
about any of it with each other. They were specialists and did-
n't cross lines. You had to be without an advanced degree, like
me, to be stupid enough to plunge ahead. I suppose it was
something of a leg up from the days when the Columbia English department worried about Lionel Trilling because, being a
Jew, he might be deficient in an understanding of Western literature, but I couldn't help thinking that though it was okay to
teach Keats, the fact was that in the present-day academy, Keats
would never have been allowed to teach Keats.

   More interesting to me than the faculty was the student
body, which at the least was good-looking and full of vitality,
and at best brilliant. There were also the changing demo-
graphics. In time, the smart Jewish girls, whose parents had
been born here, were being replaced by smart Asian girls
whose parents hadn't. It was touching to sit in my office listening to a young female voice saying, "No, I don't really
speak Korean. When my mother speaks Korean I speak English back to her." Or, "No, I'm not allowed to marry anybody

who isn't Chinese. I'm not even allowed to date boys who aren't." Same tune, different words. They might have been me at the same age except that their eyes were a different shape and the language in question wasn't Yiddish.

This long and happy connection came to an end when one day the chairwoman of the English department met me on the way to class and blurted out, "Elizabeth [a friend and colleague] was afraid to tell you, but your ex is teaching a course next term." What a piece of news to be met with in the hall. It was like having your child ask about sex on the checkout line at the supermarket. It turned out that a great deal had been going on behind the scenes. Alfred had told Elizabeth at a party that he wanted to teach a course at Barnard—I think because I was suing him at the time and he was out for revenge. The original idea had been to install him in the religion department, of all places. How far my free thinking Socialist lover had come from his origins and also in persuading people he was an expert where he wasn't! This appointment fell through, maybe because others in the religion department *did* know something about religion. Alfred wound up teaching a small seminar on Emily Dickinson, a subject Barnard College hardly needed to hear more about. But because I was openly sore about Alfred's being hired by Barnard in any capacity without my knowledge—from Columbia, I said, that was understandable, but from Barnard, a *women's* college? Where was sisterhood in all this?—I was doomed, and there soon came a note from the chairwoman saying cheerily that we'd never discussed the limits of my appointment, had we? End of Professor Birstein. I was getting tired of teaching anyway, and was beginning to feel like a windup toy every time I stood up in front of my class.

Meanwhile, I had learned to swim, which I had always wanted to do.

And furthermore, *Love in the Dunes,* scorned by Philip Rahv, popped up in in Woody Allen's *Hannah and Her Sisters.* Mia Farrow was reading it in bed. Of course, I couldn't ask Woody Allen, whom I didn't know, *why,* since this would have suggested that I didn't understand either his movie or my book. But there it was.

Curiously, this was not the first time my writing had pulled me through—in one way or another. Curiously, because all my life the *fact* that I wrote—never mind what I wrote—had always occasioned such hostility from my siblings, my father, my school friends, and to my horror, my husband, that I was still basically convinced that for me to write at all marked me as evil. Yet evil or not, writing was a great source of joy, kind of right up there with sex. Sometimes in a bout of depression I would stare at my computer and think all I have to do to get happy again is turn that thing on—and I wouldn't do it. But sooner or later I always did. I went on writing novels, essays, stories, reviews—all the things that everybody else wrote without, evidently, fear of being punished. The first review of one of my books that referred to me simply as Birstein knocked me for a loop. Women writers didn't need first names anymore? No more Virginia Woolf and Faulkner? *Mein man Pollack,* as Big Sarah used to refer to her husband, was giving way to my wife, Birstein? Well maybe not right away, not in those circles. Gloria Steinam once said we have become the men we wanted to marry. True. But if I had had all my needs taken care of by my spouse as did the man I actually married, I have no doubt that I could have become the President of the United States.

Never mind. This is not a time when being President is something to aspire to. There are other ways of making it, as little Norman Podhoretz called it in his book. Recently, I saw a documentary movie entitled *Arguing the World*, which was certainly about arguing but not about the world. The stars were four guys I'd known for years, now eminent and esteemed commentators on the sociopolitical scene, Daniel Bell, Nathan Glazer, Irving Howe, and Irving Kristol, who were happy to trace their own evolution from their City College days to their present high estate.

The early footage was very touching. Young men on fire in their various college alcoves, radicals in suits, vests, ties, and hats, vehemently debating political positions. Now the same ones, light-years older, were self-satisfied beyond belief, conservative in every sense of the word, with the possible exception of Irving Howe, who doggedly remained a Socialist. They presented themselves as pure thinkers. There was no hint of not so youthful indiscretions, such as being caught by a wife with the baby-sitter and summarily divorced, of multiple other adulteries and entanglements, and lecheries, of first, second, and third marriages, of step-children, of half-brothers and -sisters. In this "world" wives didn't figure at all, neither did any women in terms of being heavy thinkers on their own. Nor, though all these men were Jews, was the Holocaust mentioned as having been any kind of an intellectual influence. They hadn't after all gone through the Holocaust, only various positions vis à vis the Communist party. *That* they knew about and that was all that mattered. I remember once saying to Irving Kristol, "You weren't a radical, you just wanted in." And he with his usual amiability agreed. But how had these street fighters transmogrified into oh such distinguished and revered icons, legends not only in their own minds, but evidently in the minds of others? Was there no one old enough to remember otherwise, was it merely a question of survival?

The worst joke maybe is that on a very small scale I, too, have become something of an *eminence grise*, a historical relic—simply by virtue of having survived. These days, young women and young men, scholars especially, marvel at the plight of women in my day and how we fought to overcome it. I actually kept my own name professionally? How brave. They want to hear more. They shake their heads. They love me for the dangers I have passed and I love them that they do pity them. And so in a way I've become not Desdemona, but Othello.

One of the first things Alfred did after our divorce, even before remarrying, was to buy a country house, Socialist background notwithstanding. He had called me, hoping I'd help finance it, and saying he was the only writer he knew who didn't have one. I still don't, but that never seems to have been relevant. Somewhat truer to his background as a Jew of his generation, Alfred is quoted in a biography of Norman Mailer(!) as saying that "we were the first Jews to get divorced, the first ones to have sex." Talk about self-made men. Literally. Even more unhinging is another quote from him. "By definition, fucking is opposed to having a wife." I wish he had told me that to begin with. Or maybe it was better that he didn't.

Soon after my divorce, Saul wrote me a lovely affectionate letter, in effect wishing me well. I wrote him back saying that in case he didn't know it, Alfred had written that being married to me was like living with Saul Bellow. Saul answered that this was odd since Alfred had never held any sexual attraction for him. Saul had won the Nobel Prize some years before. At which point, Paolo Milano, the Queens College professor who had warned me not to sell out to poor old staid Dodd, Mead and Company, telephoned and said, "Give Saul a call, Ann. Cheer him up. He's depressed."

America.

Isaac Bashevis Singer won the Nobel prize too. On the flight to Sweden Alma Singer sat in tourist, where Isaac said she would be more comfortable, among her friends. Isaac sat up front with Roger Straus in first class. *The Jewish Daily Forward* couldn't afford to send a reporter to the ceremony, but they printed a story about it nevertheless because they said they knew what was going to happen anyway. The *Times*, on the other hand, borrowed a slug from the *Forward* containing some of Isaac's acceptance speech, and for the first time Yiddish appeared in *The New York Times*. On the front page.

Definitely America.

(*Later on, Elie Wiesel won a Nobel Prize too, but it was for peace, not for literature, and in our circles that didn't count.*)

Chapter 10

ALL ALONG, naturally, people had been dying. Even some of the people you wished would drop dead had dropped dead. There had been some very shocking early deaths. Isaac Rosenfeld, Saul Bellow's best and dearest friend, who had given all those parties in the Village, had a heart attack in his thirties, leaving his widow Vassiliki to wander around looking for jobs in a ratty fur coat held together by a diaper pin. This last detail was offered to me by Jason Epstein, who found it funny, but certainly didn't offer her anything at Random House. Years later when I was in the same boat, without the diaper pin, Jason suggested I start a cheese boutique. This was over the phone, so at least he didn't know what state of disrepair I was in. Which was just as well. After all, this same Jason at the beginning of his way up in the world told his banker he was thinking of buying a yacht, and the banker said, "Let's!" On the other hand, or maybe it was the same hand, Jason called his son whose first name was Robert by his middle name, Jacob, also Jakey. "He's going to waste a good name like Robert?" Julia cried, horrified.

Dylan Thomas had also died, despite his protestations going very gently into that good night. And Dick Hofstadter, in his fifties, of leukemia. Dick's leukemia, though, wasn't like

Love Story. It was painful and horrible and turned him gray. He was also in particular agony since a resident had lowered Dick's morphine dose when Dick had about two days to live in order to forestall addiction. Sylvia Plath, that golden girl, made good on her suicide attempt at Smith, and put her head in an oven, becoming a feminist heroine, which I didn't think she was.

Frequently, the funerals had themes. We really didn't know how to handle death. There was no shiva, no weeping, no wailing. We had left all that behind, and so we made up our funerals as we did most of the rest of our lives. Harold Solomon, husband of a novelist friend, had a service at Campbell's that was in effect a tribute to F. O. Matthiesen, the distinguished literary critic with whom Harold had briefly studied at Harvard, the *yichus* of a literary connection prevailing, even though Harold was a lawyer, not a writer. There was Saul Levitas, editor of the *New Leader*, whose funeral was a political gabfest, where an old crony, pointing down directly at the coffin cried, "And then came *Hungary!* And I said to Levitas, here . . ." At Sue Kaufman's funeral her young son compared her life to *Finnegan's Wake* (or was it *Ulysses?*), ending as it did in the middle, in the fashion of the times trying to put a literary spin, poor kid, on his mother's devastating death. Sometimes nobody said anything at all, and a string quartet played away in perfect taste, and you didn't know when to stand up or sit down or whether in fact the funeral was even over. In time many of the funerals ceased altogether and gave way to memorial services, at which there was no body, no coffin, nothing but a lot of people voicing their solemn opinions, interspersed with a little joke here and there to ease the tension.

But whatever the sendoff, the deaths began piling up in earnest. The real stuff, close to home, people who were supposed to always be there. A lot of the Cape friends died. Ed O'Connor had a stroke in his newly acquired huge mansion in Beacon Hill, maybe overcome by a level of high living that really wasn't his style. Edmund Wilson had predetermined what would be said on his tombstone. It was a Hebrew phrase he often repeated to himself in the dead of winter, he had told me. *"Chazak chazak v'yit chazak."* From strength to strength and yet more strength—what Jews say when they finish reading the Torah and start all over again. Edmund's daughter Helen had a boyfriend who was a sculptor, Gentile, however, and when he incised the Hebrew letters he had the words but not the music. The effect, actually, was primitive chic. More in tune with East Hampton, which the Cape was beginning to resemble more and more anyway. Except for "our" part of the beach in Wellfleet, where we all used to congregate. Once I went out there and stood at the top of a dune looking down on it. At that moment, it was empty.

In New York, Jimmy Baldwin had one of the greatest send-offs of all times, from the Cathedral of St. John the Divine, which was packed to overflowing, while drums beat and Odetta sang. A funeral for an African prince, which funny, hard luck Jimmy seemed to have turned into. With Marc Rothko, we were back at Campbell's, but saying kaddish. Afterward I walked over to the Whitney. When I came out of the elevator, there was that beautiful bright orange painting, the same one as that night when the Whitney opened and Rothko, who couldn't get in on account of the crowd, sat in the bar at the Carlyle. Months later I went to the Marlboro to see his last grieving black and gray paintings, and remembered Rothko standing there at another artist's exhibit. The atmosphere this time was very snooty, and some man came sashaying by carrying a big wrapped-up painting. I asked what it was, and though I didn't catch the name of the artist, it was made clear that the painting was worth over a million dollars. In Rothko's honor—he had always liked a good joke—I asked the man to peel a small corner and show me twenty-five bucks' worth.

Also one day, Bernard Malamud's photograph suddenly appeared on the obituary page in the *Times*—a real sweetheart, though a bit lugubrious. When I first met him he had asked me, "How long are you going to be so beautiful?" And I had said, to encourage us both, "I just started." There was a special feeling between Bern and me, a sort of underground affection based on getting around Alfred. Alfred had always said he never wanted to be a novelist and perhaps this was true. But the subtext seemed to be that he didn't want any of his contemporaries to be one, either. (As Saul Bellow could have told him.)

Irving Howe had a memorial service at the 92nd Street Y that people began to walk out of because, as a performance, it was running too long. Maybe the Y setting encouraged this. I saw Alfred there with a nondescript, middle-aged woman I assumed was his current wife. He didn't acknowledge my presence, nor I his. We were too far apart from each other for it to become an issue, anyway. Later, I understood that he had wanted to speak at the memorial but been turned down. Alfred did love any kind of a funeral service and attended them all, except, it turned out later, his own.

Murray Kempton, in his usual witty and gentlemanly fashion, had outfoxed us all, planning his funeral in writing well in advance and down to the last detail. It was a strictly Episcopalian ceremony at a West Side church—none of us had realized that Murray was a practicing Episcopalian, but evidently he was. (In fact some people assumed he was Jewish because we had so many uncles with the same name, not to mention Mr. Klein at Zabar's.) During the service, the Gentile Murray's name was mentioned only once, and then merely as "Our brother Murray." The text was *The Book of Common Prayer,* the music a few of his favorite hymns. Important people from all walks of life were there, and I could feel Murray's presence and knew he was amused by all those big shots slavering away, dying to make speeches and not one allowed to. No, Murray's funeral was totally dignified, with bells tolling out every year of his life, mournful, and private, with a final private joke at the end, because who knew how religious Brother Murray actually was? When it was over, Alfred came up the crowded aisle stooped and leaning heavily on a walker—another joke, this time a grim one. The Walker with a walker. He didn't acknowledge me, either, because he didn't see me, or chose not to. "Alfred?" I said. "Alfred? . . ." (It was the last time I ever saw *him.*)

Murray would have appreciated the postscript too. Everybody shaking off the event and networking and socializing like mad on the sidewalk, including people dashing around who hadn't known Murray at all. It was Alfred, of course, who coopted the event in *The New York Times Book Review* by writing a piece recalling "my friend Murray Kempton," as if in spite of the overwhelming evidence to the contrary, Alfred was the main friend, or at least the only one who counted.

Closer to home, that whole bunch of relatives who had cluttered up my parents' house and our lives when I was a kid were long gone. Aunt Sarah, sexy to her last day, and Uncle Jack, aka Hymie the horseplayer, and Uncle Alex the tiny

Communist capitalist, and Uncle Max the painter, whose
work our set always seemed to know though he mainly
painted subways and housing projects. And Uncle Cathrael
with his fig tree, and even his sons Easy and Oscar. Now five,
more immediate, members of my family died within three
years of each other. We kept meeting at funerals and then each
time another one would be missing, like the Ten Little Indi-
ans. First, Julia's husband, Irv, he of the khaki honeymoon underwear, then Yossie, to the end wearing an artist's beret and
going to the Art Students League, then Yossie's former still
beautiful Viennese wife, with her "B*rrr*ussels sp*rrr*outs." Then
Millie, whom we left buried in a cemetery in Philadelphia, a
final abandonment on our part, I felt. And then, Sookie, who
took her place in the family plot alongside Mama and Daddy
and Yossie, and Yossie's young son, David, who had of all
things, OD'd, something we could never have expected. Now
only Julia and I were left, still locked in our old uneasy al-
liance. We called each other almost every day because we were
sisters, but she still thought I was mean because I was smart.
Then she died, too.

Alfred had been busily anticipating his demise ever since I
first met him. He said he always knew he'd die young and kept
on saying it until one day I encouragingly pointed out that it
was too late. A few years ago, spurred perhaps by Anatole Bro-
yard's article on his impending demise from cancer in *The
New Yorker*, Alfred also wrote a long piece in *The New Yorker*
about his own impending demise from cancer, which from
the sound of it had been recently diagnosed and imminent.
People called to commiserate, but it was an old story. Years and
years before his article, in a note accompanying an alimony

check (which he insisted on calling my "stipend"), Alfred had accused me of knowing he had just been diagnosed with cancer, which I didn't, and containing the memorable words, "I long for the end of life and getting rid of you." Evidently, Alfred regarded his death as a form of estate management, or at least a way of saving money. Not surprising, since money was a major theme in his life too. He informed me of his impending marriage in a flowery card also containing an alimony check. It was like the "compliments of the author" that had come with *New York Jew*. I wrote back wishing him happiness, careful not to wish him the happiness he deserved. To other forms of happiness he adjusted himself in his usual fashion. Michael now had two children, and since neither of them was named Fidel, Alfred was able to say in interviews, "I am a grandfather twice over." No doubt another person would have said, "I have two grandchildren," but Alfred, characteristically, viewed the kids as attributes of himself.

Now, however, all of Alfred's threats about dying were coming true. The man I saw stumbling out of Murray Kempton's funeral clinging to a walker, was a very old, very stooped man. He had been in and out of the hospital, almost died, miraculously clung to life, came out again. But by late spring of 1998 his death really was imminent. Katey came from her new home in Israel, to be with him in his final illness, staying with me, as she always did. Every morning she left the house to be with her father, every night she came home shattered by what she had seen. Sometimes I knelt at her bed to console her, rubbing her back as I had when she was a baby. Except that when I tried to straighten up again I realized I was no baby, either. Katey was a witness to terrible things. Alfred was lying in agony in a hospital bed in the middle of his small living

room, skeletal, his many filing cabinets blocking the air con-
ditioners so that it was stifling. Visitors came and went, young
acolytes, older connections, more importantly Alfred's lawyer
and stockbroker, busily conferring with his soon-to-be widow.
Looking away from all this, Alfred asked Katey how I was.
"She's sad for you, Daddy," Katey said truthfully and Alfred
said, "Send her my love." I would have wanted to see him one
last time, say good-bye, something. But except in Alfred's
mind I seemed to have been eliminated from the configura-
tion. After a week of awful suffering, Alfred died on the
morning of his eighty-third birthday. I was right. He hadn't
died young, after all.

Alfred didn't want a Jewish funeral. He didn't want to be
buried. He had always had a fear of being buried alive. And so
he was cremated and wound up in a little cardboard box that
was mailed back to his apartment. While this was being attended to, some kind of small service was cobbled together at
Riverside Memorial Chapel, to which I wasn't invited. Alfred's
loyal cousins who *had* been invited by Pearlie were subse-
quently disinvited, maybe because it was feared they would
lower the tone, or maybe make the occasion too Jewish. Later
it turned out that Alfred's will had also in effect disinvited his
children. He left them nothing, not in trust, not in any way.
Nothing. It all went to the current wife, and ergo to somebody
else's children—she had three of her own—but not to Alfred's. Even knowing Alfred, I can't imagine a father who
would do such a thing to his own children, who were hardly
estranged from him. I don't want to imagine a woman who
would abet him in doing so.

Months later there was a memorial service at the 92nd
Street Y, where I had seen Alfred at Irving Howe's memorial. I

wasn't invited to this either, but from what I hear it seems to have been a compendium of life's little ironies. Pearlie had now become a chief mourner, grieving away in the front row—for a brother who had totally left her out of his first autobiography, who had let her down and put her down her whole life. (Another triumph of the need to believe over experience?) Her husband, whom Alfred cordially detested, had become one of the chief eulogists. Michael's mother, who detested Alfred, and didn't mind saying so, sat in the front row also, as a courtesy to Michael I imagine, who was now for the first time in his life enjoying most favored nation status. Katey was back in Jerusalem. Among the speakers, Alfred's stockbroker got up to say he had made Alfred a rich man, though Alfred never believed it and was sure he would wind up eating catfood. Alfred's celebrated literary lawyer, defender of the oppressed except when it came to drawing up wills, was also represented, as were a smattering of academics, and a surprising number of people who admitted they had met Alfred only recently.

Where was the old crowd, the writer Barbara Probst Solomon asked me, the poets, the novelists to talk about this famous literary critic who, say what one would, was absolutely devoted to literature? Obviously, I didn't know. Months later the group that had organized the memorial service gathered together to dump Alfred's ashes, box and all, into the already littered New York harbor. Then, full of emotion, they all watched the little box bobbing along, bobbing along. I keep thinking of Alfred in there. Not only was he claustrophobic, he was given to seasickness.

It had always been hard to escape Alfred in person or in print during the forty-eight years I knew him. Now it was just as hard to escape him in death. In fact, for a few days there it was hard to escape my own death through him. What happened was that the Social Security Administration had got it through their heads that I too had died on June 5, or as they put it when I called, "There's been a slight error. You'd better get down to your branch office as soon as possible." As instructed, I went down with two pieces of photo ID, which seems to be how you establish your official presence back among the living. (But what if you don't have two such pieces of ID? What if the pictures have mysteriously faded away to nothing?) I sat down next to a woman whom Social Security judged never to have been born, and waited my turn amid general hilarity. "I can see through you," the guard said. Then I signed a paper that asked you to swear that you were not deceased. I asked if there was another form swearing that you *were* deceased, but nobody answered me. On the bus going back I said cheerfully, "Good try, Alfie, but no cigar." He laughed.

Meanwhile, there were obituaries all over the place. Tributes to Alfred Kazin as a critic. Many quotations from his autobiographies, which gave the impression that all those fabrications and *bubba maynses* were true. I had once written a biography of my father, and now I decided to take on my own life story. Not so easy. In search of a few solid facts, I went down to the Berg Collection of the New York Public Library to which Alfred had sold a batch of his papers some years before. I was treated royally. "You're a walking archive, Ma," Katey said later, only too accurately. Because the first thing shown to me to my horror was a box of *my* letters to Alfred, just about all of them, going back to when we had first met, and spanning over thirty years. Steamy letters, love-smitten letters, angry letters, quiet letters, comfortably domestic letters, some handwritten, some typed, all of them painfully personal. There were also birthday cards, cablegrams, valentines, notes saying that I had gone down for milk and juice, even by mistake a birthday card from Sandy and Sook.

It is very hard to describe the effect of seeing the eviscerated guts of one's love boxed, catalogued, and open to the public. I wanted to run out of there, I wanted to stay and not leave them alone, I wanted to cry, I thought I would be sick. I tried to imagine what had been in Alfred's mind when he packed them up and sold them. Recently, there was a stir about Joyce Maynard selling J. D. Salinger's letters. What if it goes the other way and the great man sells the young woman's letters? And Alfred had sold more than letters, the operative word here being *sold*. (It's amazing how people hearing this story substitute the word *donated*.) Also carefully catalogued were first editions of books of his which he had given and inscribed to me and which I had been looking for for years, finally assuming they'd been lost in the shuffle of moving and separation—you didn't call Alfred and say, by the way I can't find that book of yours. The catalogued books included *A Walker in the City*, inscribed "To my darling." (In the interests of scholarship I was able to give the librarian an exact attribution for that one.)

And finally, there was the typescript of *On Native Grounds*. This typescript had a history. Alfred had impetuously presented it to Columbia, hoping they would hire him. I told him to please get it back—Columbia didn't love him, it loved Lionel Trilling—and that the manuscript was valuable. He did get it back and in gratitude had it formally bound along with a handwritten page inscribing it to me. I had carefully put it away in my own filing cabinet. How had it gotten out of there into the Berg Collection? The answer was only too obvious and chilling. I looked at it, as at a mutilated old friend. The front binding was very loose, the remaining stub of a page that had been torn out still stuck in there, the page with the loving inscription to me. From a practical point of view it must be explained that this whole Kazin archive was sold for a down payment on the famous country house that Alfred had tried to cadge money from me for. So I figure I own a closet in that house, or at least a faucet. From a less practical point of view how had it happened that that little girl in Hell's Kitchen, afraid to go to the local library on Tenth Avenue because it was in such a bad neighborhood, and where she was too long kept in the children's section, had walked into the great Forty-second Street library and been shown her own letters by a respectful and distinguished librarian? America again?

Some people said it was a compliment to me that Alfred had kept every bit of what I'd written to him all these years. But he hadn't kept them. On the other hand what monetary value could my letters and the books inscribed to me possibly have had? For myself, did I even want those books back, because what *sentimental* value could they have once Alfred had sold them? (It was that old swiped cigarette package conundrum again.) And what else of my property might still be waiting in that place where he'd died, packed and waiting to be sold also?

It's all a mess, all such a muddle. And it gets harder after all this to remember what it was like being married to Alfred, which is even more painful than when I do remember. I sit next to him at a concert, feeling his arm through the sleeve of his jacket, I lie next to him in bed curled like a spoon against his back, I wake up and hear him make coffee in the kitchen,

I see him reading the *Times* in his paisley bathrobe, I walk with him across the Brooklyn Bridge, I take off with him on a plane to Europe scared of flying but excited, I sit beside him in the car on the way to the Cape and have him take my hand and put it on his thigh as he drives. My built-in lover, my built-in friend, my built-in enemy.

Get a lawyer, some people said, referring to the property. But lawyers aren't really my best subject, and neither is property. Maybe loss is. Other people said—write about it.

Home

Epilogue

'VE ALWAYS LIKED to think that I was looking for roots before anyone, even Alex Haley. But where others had found them I was still looking (as I had, vainly, in Birstein). I still didn't know where I came from, or where I could possibly go back to. Which didn't seem fair since even people from Iowa could return to Davenport, or some place like that, after they'd lived out their dreams in the Big City. But I had been born and bred in the Big City, albeit on the West Side instead of the East Side, where I now lived. Was I supposed to return to my roots in Hell's Kitchen? Make a pious pilgrimage to Broadway and Forty-second Street?

Finally, I realized that what I needed to do was go back a step before all that, and so in the summer of 1995 I made plans to take my daughter, Katey, with me on a trip to Eastern Europe, where she was willing, if not eager, to go. Unfortunately, my proposed itinerary turned out to be unrealistic, to put it mildly, since I wanted to visit my mother's birthplace in Shpikov, the tiny shtetl in the Ukraine, "six miles from the train that went to Odessa," and also Brest-Litovsk in Byelorus where my father was born, and also Slobodka, the yeshiva town near Kovno in Lithuania where he was educated. These places seemed pretty close on the map, places that blurred together and became one when were they were talked about, but administratively turned out to be light-years apart. The Ukraine, in fact, was said to be extremely dangerous besides, and run by gangsters. Also, the people who ran the tours that I looked into had a few less than honest impulses of their own. Besides not going where *I* wanted to go, they were in the habit of canceling trips to where they had said *they* wanted to go. One day, I reminded myself that Kate and I would in effect only be looking at one big Jewish cemetery, anyhow, and that moreover my parents had wanted to hightail it out of there even when Russia, as they called it, had a living Jewish community.

Then I had another thought. If we were looking for existing Jews, why not go to Israel? After all, it was not only the first chapter of the Jewish saga, it was also the latest and most triumphant one. Besides which, didn't I have my own ancient history with the area, having been brought up as I was on all that olive wood and filigreed silver work, with Israel and Jerusalem in practically every line of every prayer I had ever read or spoken? I also had a running set of subsequent memories. Daddy hurrying Mama off to meet Prime Minister Ben-Gurion before she had to pee yet again. The disapproving specter of Hannah Arendt, sneering at the visa in my first passport to what she saw as a contemptible country of "little Jews." My own two trips with Alfred, as the insignificant wife of the great big guest of the government. Kate, though, was even leerier of going to Israel with me than she had been of going to Eastern Europe. She herself was longing to go to Israel. But she was only too familiar with my past vociferously voiced opinions of the country. Pure claustrophobia. No place for the mind to move around. I explained that there had been extenuating circumstances, which she correctly understood to be her father. I promised to behave, which she doubted.

But, oddly, there was no need to "behave," or even to make or break promises. The trip to Israel with Kate was a completely new experience for both of us. Had Israel changed so much over the years, or was it me? Both, actually, but then again, I had never been in Israel as myself. Also, I was now the guide, showing my daughter around, the two of us seeing a country that was a miracle, manmade and otherwise. A country amazing in its physical beauties, its antiquities, its startling modernity. Jerusalem the golden was actually golden. Tel Aviv a real city, with a melange of great new architecture, awful new architecture, a bustling populace, a long Mediterranean coastline. The Sea of Galilee, actually a lake in the shape of a harp, a shimmering body of water it was not so hard to imagine walking on. The Red Sea wasn't red and didn't part, at least not for us, but it was there and it was real and from the tip of it you could see Egypt, Jordan, and Saudi Arabia. Every mountain looked as if Moses could have come walking down it. Most astonishing, everyone spoke Hebrew and almost everybody you met was a Jew—old people, young people, policemen, busdrivers, shopkeepers, and whores too, I suppose.

Also a miracle, we could be citizens of this place right now, if we wanted to. In fact, we already were, give or take a few papers.

When we got back to the United States, Kate took this miraculous circumstance quite literally. She decided that she wanted to go and live in Israel. Not take a leave, not spend six months or a year there. Officially emigrate. Make *aliyah*. Become an Israeli citizen. Was she nuts? How could she be an Israeli, my Ivy League, beautifully spoken American daughter, whose mother *can* speak English? My daughter who had a Ph.D. *and* a J.D. My daughter, the poet, my daughter who had been a professor of English at the University of Iowa before she decided to become a lawyer. My daughter who was ready now to give up a prestigious job working directly with the Secretary of Labor in Washington, writing speeches, position papers, testimony for Congressional committees. My friends and relatives were worried too, if not downright appalled. Had Katey suddenly become religious? (God forbid.) While he was still alive, Alfred, who in one of his many 90 degree turnabouts had become violently anti-Zionist, (through whose new influence I didn't know) was enraged, taking it all as a personal insult, as usual. But Katey calmly explained that she felt that Israel was her birthright, a place that belonged to her and where she belonged.

What about her American citizenship? She would keep that, even have two passports. I finally asked myself, what's wrong with this picture, why are we all *that* concerned? If I had said she was going to work in France for the next five years, nobody would bat an eyelash, it would be regarded as an interesting adventure. No, it was that Katey was going to be an *immigrant*, a word and condition we thought we had long ago left behind. She would be a newcomer in a strange land, struggling to make herself understood in a foreign language. She, who had once laughingly said to me, "Words R us, Ma."

The next summer, I was back in Israel and Kate was meeting me at the Ben Gurion Airport. We took a taxi to my hotel in Tel

Aviv—there was no room in her absorption center (horrible phrase) for her to put me up, since it was teeming with other new immigrants. I was thrilled to see my daughter but not so thrilled to be back in Israel. Everything looked the same but different. It was so familiar, it felt strange. Jerusalem was golden but full of sour-looking men in black hats. The shimmering lakefront of ancient Tiberias in the Galilee was lined with fish restaurants offering bargains, some now clearly dubious, while tacky disco music echoed along the shore. Mediterranean Tel Aviv was not only modern and crowded and ugly in many areas, but unbearably humid. Israelis shoved and pushed, ignored lines or orderly progressions of any kind, and stuck their noses into your business even at an ATM, where you would look up and find an inquiring face an inch away from yours. Last year the plethora of children was adorable. This year they were all over the place and seemingly always underfoot.

Kate too was the same, but different. Impatient, irritable, not at all like her ecstatic self last year. Even the mildest criticism of Israel annoyed her. I put it down to the terrible heat. But the heat had been terrible last summer when we were larking about as tourists. Gradually, the source of Kate's irritation became clear to me, especially when she began to wonder aloud why I couldn't manage even to ask for simple directions in Hebrew, why when I bought something I held out my hand for the Israeli money in it to be counted. Yes, I was a greenhorn, an ignorant newcomer. I *embarrassed* her, the way my mother had embarrassed me.

After a while, the strange familiarity eased up. Israel started being beautiful and exciting again. I finally understood that I was not in a Judaized version of something I knew but in another place entirely, a foreign country, very much

Middle Eastern, in fact. Once more I began to appreciate the ravishing antiquities, the wonderful contrasts between old and new, the breathtaking vistas. Even the ubiquitous nosiness became endearing. Sort of. Above all, the sheer existence of all those Jewish children became a tremendous, stunning triumph.

In time, Kate got less embarrassed and more affectionate. She started talking about my emigrating too one day. *My* emigrating? Was she nuts again? Bad enough that she herself had emigrated. No, a crazy idea, I started to tell her. . . . Or was it? . . . I looked around dubiously. . . . And then I thought— this place that, as usual, I know next to nothing about, where I really don't even *want* to live—could this be home?